EVALUATION IN TRANSLATION

Critical points of translator decision-making

Jeremy Munday

The research for this book
has been part funded by the

Routledge
Taylor & Francis Group

LONDON AND NEW YORK

Arts & Humanities
Research Council

First published 2012
by Routledge
2 Park Square, Milton Park, Abingdon, Oxon OX14 4RN

Simultaneously published in the USA and Canada
by Routledge
711 Third Avenue, New York, NY 10017

Routledge is an imprint of the Taylor & Francis Group, an informa business

British Library Cataloguing in Publication Data
A catalogue record for this book is available from the British Library

Library of Congress Cataloging in Publication Data
  Munday, Jeremy.
  Evaluation in translation : critical points of translator decision-making / Jeremy Munday.
    p. cm.
  1. Translating and interpreting.   I. Title.
  P306.M864 2012
  418'.02–dc23

                                                            2011047891

ISBN: 978-0-415-57769-4 (hbk)
ISBN: 978-0-415-57770-0 (pbk)
ISBN: 978-0-203-11774-3 (ebk)

Typeset in Bembo
by RefineCatch Limited, Bungay, Suffolk

MIX
Paper from
responsible sources
FSC
www.fsc.org   FSC® C004839

Printed and bound in Great Britain by the MPG Books Group

To my mother and in memory of my father
with love and thanks

CONTENTS

FIGURES AND TABLES

Figures

Tables

ACKNOWLEDGEMENTS

There are many people I would like to thank for generously enabling me to work on and write up this research. First of all, my sponsors: the University of Leeds, for granting me research leave during 2009–2010; the Arts and Humanities Research Council for funding a Research Fellowship in 2010–11; the British Academy and the University of Leeds for funding my conference paper at the Third IATIS conference, Melbourne, July 2009; to the Friends of Princeton University Library for funding my archive visit.

At various stages of conception and drafting, versions of Chapters 1, 2, 3 and 5 were delivered in seminars or conferences in Bergen, Copenhagen, Lodz, Macau, Manchester, Melbourne, Norwich and London. My thanks to all those who offered comments and suggestions for improvement.

I would like to acknowledge the generous assistance of Falih Al-Emara, Kiyoshi Kawahara, Li Defeng, Robert Lee, Idris Mansor, Yukie Ono, Gracie Peng, Serge Sharoff, Martin Thomas, Wang Binhua, and Zhang Meifang, who helped with the analysis of examples from various translations and Inti Aedo Orozco for work on the bibliography. I am grateful to those translators who gave their time to be interviewed for Chapter 3, particularly to Jan Arriens for recommending the SENSE forum and to SENSE secretary Brigid de Wals for permitting me some access to the archive. And to my colleague at Leeds, Jo Drugan, for putting me in touch with some of the translators. For Chapter 4, special thanks are due to the librarians of the Translation archive at the University of East Anglia (where the Bellos papers are held), the Harry Ransom Center (University of Texas at Austin), the Penguin archive (University of Bristol), the Manuscripts Division Department of Rare Books and Special Collections and Princeton University library (for the Carlos Fuentes and Mario Vargas Llosa papers), as well as to librarians at the University of Leeds and the British Library, London. To the above and to David Bellos and Joanna Prior (Penguin) for permission to quote from these works. Also to James

Rives at Chapel Hill, for agreeing to interviews about their translations. For Chapter 5, I am grateful to the MA students in Translation Studies who participated as volunteers in the study.

My thanks to colleagues at the University of Leeds School of Modern Languages and Cultures for their support over the past years. To all at Routledge, especially Louisa Semlyen and Sophie Jaques. To the anonymous reviewers of the original book proposal and to Nikky Twyman for copy-editing and Ron Macfarlane for correcting the proofs. Most of all, though, my thanks go to my family, for their support and patience and love. To Cristina, Nuria and Marina, without whom this would not have been possible.

Jeremy Munday
London, October 2011

INTRODUCTION

In Los Angeles in the early summer of 1966, literary translator Sam Hileman sums up the condition under which he is working in a letter to his friend Carlos Fuentes, the young Mexican novelist. Hileman is battling against time to complete a translation of Fuentes' new novel, *Cambio de piel*, with a young family and in severe financial straits, lacking even the money to post the finished manuscript to the publisher. He is struggling to come to terms with a task that is overwhelming him:

> You would never know it, but I hate translation more than I hate anything in this world. I am constantly afraid while doing it, afraid that I won't get it good enough ... either not close enough or not strong enough. Or either too close. It is a miserable business, at best always a failure, at worst a disaster.[1]

This haunting fear, deriving from uncertainty and lack of confidence, almost paralyses Hileman, as he anguishes over the choices he must make in the text. Hileman, a highly creative translator, agonizes over 'closeness' and 'strength', which are conflicting, or at least distinct, objectives. The question revolves around what a 'strong' translation is meant to be and how much a translator may intervene in order to achieve it. Six months earlier, in a letter written before embarking on the project and in which he gives a very detailed and sensitive critique of the Spanish text, Hileman seems to perceive strength at least in part to be related to higher-level order features of structure and language in what is a complex and adventurous novel: 'It seems to me that this book takes some big chances, that is one of the sources of its strength, but ... you and I must be very sure that the English takes no chances you don't want to risk.'[2]

Narrative and textual strength, the degree of intervention in decision-making and the risk entailed are interlinked concerns for Hileman. They are also starting points for this book, which seeks to investigate those places in a text, written or spoken, where the translator or interpreter's intervention and subjectivity are potentially most telling. A translator/interpreter as an active participant in the communication process, one who 'intervenes' not as a transparent conduit of meaning but as an interested representer of the source words of others and in a communicative situation constrained and directed by extratextual factors including commissioner, brief, purpose, audience expectation and target text function. In addition, the translator or interpreter brings his/her own sociocultural and educational background, ideological, phraseological and idiosyncratic stylistic preferences to the task of rendering a source text in the target language.

This book is an attempt to investigate the linguistic signs of a translator's intervention and subjective evaluation. To add objectivity to the analysis, the main theoretical model adopted is drawn from what is known as appraisal theory (Martin and White 2005). This is designed to describe the different components of a speaker's **attitude**, the strength of that attitude (**graduation**) and the ways that the speaker aligns him/herself with the sources of attitude and with the receiver (**engagement**). This theory is itself embedded within Systemic Functional Grammar (Halliday 1994, Halliday and Matthiessen 2004), which locates lexicogrammatical choices within a framework that examines the function of different choices. Appraisal theory particularly relates to what is known as the **interpersonal function** of language that deals with the relationship between the writer and the reader. It has been called the 'intruder function' (Halliday 1978: 117).

Appraisal theory has been used in recent years in the analysis of original writings in English, particularly in genres of academic and newspaper discourse, but has rarely been used for the analysis of translation. This book seeks to test out the validity of the theory as a model for translational analysis. Rather than a wholesale imposition of an English-oriented theory on to a translational context, the aim is to discover those features of the model that, in practice, are 'critical' for a translator. These may be elements which are essential to retain in the TT (target text), but particularly they are those points in a text which require interpretation and in some cases substantive intervention from the translator. They potentially alter the orientation of the text in the target locale. Critical points share some of the properties of what the anthropologist Michael Agar (1991, 1994) calls 'rich points', defined as 'locations in discourse where major cultural differences are signalled' (Agar 1994: 232). Agar (ibid.: 227) recounts his work for a US company in Mexico which sold *rebuilt* engine parts. This caused a problem in translation, where the literal equivalent *usado* ('used') connoted 'old' and of inferior quality because the concept of reused parts was unknown in the target culture.

In some instances, the critical points may be located at a high textual or cultural level. Standard Thai, for instance, has a special sacred range of language used of royalty and Buddhist monks, distinguished by lexical differences (kinship terms, animals, parts of the body, some actions) and by the special prefixed or compound forms of all verbs (Smalley 1994: 58). It is a strong social marker of difference, and more or less impossible to translate into languages that do not have a similar range. Thai speakers themselves may be extremely sensitive to this. Thus, in 1960,

Prince Chula wrote that members of the ruling dynasty often preferred to write to each other in English precisely 'to avoid the elaborate language required for the different ranks amongst relatives' (Chakrabongse 1960: 271, in Smalley 1994: 55). In its most dramatic form, it may be the erroneous selection of a whole language which may have devastating effects. So, in predominantly Pashto-speaking Southern Afghanistan, it was found that Dari speakers were being recruited to interpret for the Canadian military. Dangerous breakdowns in communication resulted that allegedly led to the arrests of innocent bystanders and the flawed translation of sensitive documents (Brewster 2009).

In other cases, it is an individual keyword that may be so sensitive it becomes a critical ideological point of translation. Mona Baker (2006) gives various examples, including the phenomenon of naming: *Derry* vs *Londonderry* in Northern Ireland, *Judea and Samaria* vs *the West Bank* and *Jerusalem* vs *al-Quds* in the Middle East, for instance. The most sensitive term of all is the name for deities, as is illustrated by the proselytizing missions of the Jesuits in the sixteenth and seventeenth centuries. In Japan, Francis Xavier (Francisco de Jasso, 1506–1552), realized that the early Japanese translation *Dainichi* had in fact rendered the Christian *Deus* as the Vairocana Buddha and he ordered that it no longer be used. It was replaced with the loanword *Daiusu* (Kim 2004: 81). In Peru, the Jesuits under José de Acosta (1540–1600) imposed the lexical and semantic borrowing of the Spanish *Dios* on an indigenous tradition that already had its own monotheistic divine names *Viracocha* and *Pachacamac*; the latter was deliberately distorted by early missionaries, who construed it as 'the devil' (Kim ibid.: 97). By contrast, the Italian priest Matteo Ricci (1552–1610), who spent half his life in China, decided to use the ancient Chinese term and Confucian concept *Shangti* rather than coin a phonetic loanword. In modern times this attempt at establishing a point of contact with the local religion has been described as 'a risk-taking "identification" of the Christian God (*Deus*) with the Confucian Most-High (*Shangti*)' (Kim ibid.: 1, 166–71).

The very real controversy caused by such sensitive terms is not only of historical relevance. For example, in 1986 the Malay government banned the use of the word *Allah* to refer to the God of religions other than Islam, claiming that it was potentially confusing but with the implicit fear that it could be used for proselytization. *Allah* had been used in translations of the Bible into Malay since 1629, when the Dutch merchant Albert Cornelius Ruyl's translation of the Gospel of Matthew was published. Indeed, in preparation for the most recent translation, the *Revised Malay Bible*,[3] a conscious decision was even taken by the Language Committee to retain the term *Allah* (Soesilo n.d.).[4] However, distinguished critics of such decisions have included the President of the Universitat Sains Malaysia, Tan Sri Professor Dzulkifli Abdul Razak. He attacked 'insensitive, inconsistent' translations of proper names in the *Behasa Indonesia Bible*,[5] more than 20,000 imported copies of which were confiscated by the Malay government.[6] In Razak's view, the translation casts doubt on the Quranic Tauhidic concept of the oneness of Allah and, in the expression *Son of God*, may be regarded as blasphemous by Muslims (Razak 2009).[7] In December 2009, the Malay government's ban was successfully challenged in the courts by the Catholic paper *The Herald*, which led to the backlash burning of a number of churches.[8] The government appealed the verdict, which was suspended pending the appeal. Elsewhere, and more prominently, President George W. Bush's use of the term *crusade on terror* in the aftermath of the 11 September 2001 attacks generated understandable alarm in the Muslim world, where *crusade* is a hugely negative term associated with the violent Christian military expeditions to Jerusalem in the Middle Ages. Counterbalancing this is the debate (see Hatim 2005: 54) over the meaning and translation of the Arabic *jihad*, represented either as 'holy war' (to construct an anti-Muslim message) or as 'a struggle to do right' (by more favourable or nuanced observers). The way in which these critical points are resolved produces a specific representation of the foreign that reflects an ideological point of view and evaluative reading and seeks to guide the response to international events.

It is the translation of such lexical evaluation, and how such evaluation operates and varies in real, contemporary settings, that is a focus of this book. The following is a striking example from a prominent stage. During a European Parliament debate on 24 February 2010 on the follow-up of the informal EU 20–20 European council, the right-wing United Kingdom Independence Party MEP Nigel Farage launched a string of insults at the newly appointed President of the European Council, Herman Van Rompuy, and his State, Belgium:

> We were told that, when we had a President, we would see a giant global political figure: the man that would be the political leader for five hundred million people; the man that would represent all of us on the world stage; the man whose job was so important that of course you're paid more than President Obama. Well, I am afraid what we got ... was you. And I am sorry, but after that performance earlier that you gave ... and I do not want to be rude ... but, but ... you know, really, **you have the charisma of a damp rag and the appearance of a low-grade bank clerk.** The question that I want to ask and that we are all going to ask is: who ARE YOU? I'd never heard of you; nobody in Europe had ever heard of you. I would like to ask you, Mr President: who ... voted for you? And what mechanism – *[he addresses other members protesting at his comments]* oh, I know democracy is not popular with you lot – what mechanism do the peoples of Europe have to remove you? Is this European democracy? Well, I ... I sense, though, that you are competent and capable and dangerous, and I have no doubt that it's your intention to be the quiet assassin of European democracy and of the European nation states. You appear to have a loathing ... for the very concept of the existence of nation states; perhaps that it's because you come from Belgium, which of course is pretty much a non-country.[9]

The headline sound-bite is indicated in bold in the transcription: *you have the charisma of a damp rag and the appearance of a low-grade bank clerk*.[10] These are evident, and very hefty, instances of subjective evaluation from Farage. He uses parallel syntactic structures (*the charisma of a damp rag; the appearance of a low-grade bank clerk*) and analogies designed to be mocking and hurtful. The strong negative evaluation of adjectives *damp* and *low-grade*, collocated with the nouns *rag* and *bank clerk*, here merely exaggerates the overall ideational negativity of the speech. It would seem obvious that such intensity of evaluation would be a critical consideration for the interpreters working on the spot in the interpreting booths. In this respect, analysis of the simultaneous interpreting on the day is indeed revealing, but also rather surprising. It is true that most of the interpreters hesitate at this point in the text, doubtlessly taken aback at the virulence and the directness of the attack on the President. A hesitation (or 'disfluency', Pöchhacker 2004: 109) is likely to be one indication that a translator or interpreter is faced with a 'problem nexus' (Angelone 2010) and possibly that he/she considers a point to be especially sensitive. As far as the lexical realizations of the evaluation are concerned, the French interpreter gives *vous avez le charisme d'une serpillière* ['you have the charisma of a floor-cloth'] and the German *das Karisma eines nassen Lappens* ['the charisma of a damp flannel']. Both omit any reference to the bank clerk, while the Italian explicates and downplays the first part as *Lei ha un charisma di una persona incapace* ['you have a charisma of an incompetent person']. Perhaps this reduction in the strength of the evaluation, by omission or explicitation in the target text (TT), has something to do with the severe face-threatening act and the interpreters' concern to avoid the risk of exaggerating it. Since the interpreters are using the first person, they place themselves in the position of representing the speech act of Farage. They thus incur the risk that the words they utter may be taken to be their own subjective interpretations of the ST (source text).

Some of the interpreters used the technique of compensation (Klaudy 2008), inserting evaluation elsewhere in the text. This was clear in the inflection of their voice and in the addition of expressions and particles designed to heighten the intensity or graduation of the pejorative evaluation at other points. Hence, the German stresses *Wer SIND Sie denn eigentlich?* [lit. 'Who ARE you then actually?'] for *Who ARE YOU?*, adding the modal particles *denn* ['then'] and *eigentlich* ['actually']. The Spanish interpreter, who translates both parts of the major sound-bite more or less literally,[11] adds evaluative interpersonal markers: *¿quién demonios es usted?* ['who **the devil** are you?'] ... *usted no tiene ni pajolera idea* ['you don't have the **foggiest** idea']. The overall 'evaluative prosody' (Bednarek 2006: 8) of a text influences other points too. Towards the end of the extract, Farage makes the rhetorical move from scathing attack on Van Rompuy's standing and legitimacy to a grudging acknowledgement of his ability (*I sense, though, that you are competent*). In Farage's opinion this is all the more 'dangerous', since Van Rompuy's competence may enable him to fashion a more centralized Europe. At this point, the negative evaluative prosody of the rest of the passage seems to colour the attention of the French and the Spanish interpreters, who render this with the opposite meaning – *you are **incompetent*** ... This error does not appear to have been picked up in the media, which shows that the receiver, too, listens selectively.

Differences in interpretation of evaluation may be subtle, but that does not mean they are only of academic interest or always go unnoticed amongst the audience. Indeed, the role of modal expressions and reporting verbs were crucial in the rewriting of the notorious dossier prepared by UK Prime Minister Tony Blair's inner circle of advisers in the run-up to the invasion of Iraq in 2003. The 'WMD dossier', based on intelligence at the time, was published on 24 September 2002 and purported to show that Iraqi President Saddam Hussein was developing weapons of mass destruction.[12] It has subsequently been the source of much controversy, as the government of the time was accused of 'sexing up' the report, rewriting the intelligence to exaggerate the threat and thus to garner support for war.[13] In the drafting, the most noted insertion was of the claim that Iraq might be able to launch chemical and biological weapons within 45 minutes. Here, crucial evaluative features are those that deal with the language of certainty and truth.[14] The above claim, along with others in the Executive Summary, is presented as a series of fourteen bullet points, commencing as follows:

As a result of the intelligence we judge that Iraq has:
- continued to produce chemical and biological agents;
- military plans for the use of chemical and biological weapons, including against its own Shia population. Some of these weapons are deployable within 45 minutes of an order to use them.[15]

The bullet points mask the modal expression *we judge that* ... and therefore suggest a factual list rather than opinion. Even more stark is the certainty value in the document afforded by the choice of reporting verbs (cf. Thompson and Ye Yiyun 1991). Revisions in the drafting consistently reduce hedging (Hyland 1998) and instead move towards the certainty pole, as shown by the highlights in the following example:

Within the last month intelligence has **suggested** that the Iraqi military **would be** able to use their chemical and biological weapons within 45 minutes of an order to do so.

(draft dossier 10.9.2002)

The Iraqi military **may be** able to deploy chemical or biological weapons ...

(draft dossier 16.9.2002)

Intelligence **indicates** that the Iraqi military **are** able to deploy ...

(draft dossier 19.9.2002 and published dossier 24.09.2002)

Intelligence has suggested becomes the more certain *indicates*, while the conditional *would be able to use* shifts to *may be* and finally to the simple indicative statement *are*. This presents the speaker as being sure of the truth value of the proposition. That these shifts have a real effect on the reader and are a site of contestation of evaluation is underlined by the attention given to them in two UK investigations: the Hutton Inquiry of 2003 into the death of consultant Dr David Kelly[16] and the Butler Inquiry of 2004 into pre-invasion intelligence.[17] In the Hutton Inquiry, testimony by Martin Howard, Deputy Chief of Defence Intelligence at the Ministry of Defence, reported the discussion of alternative wordings at the time of the preparation of the dossier. These wordings were related to different interpretations of the information available, as Howard makes clear:

> At the time the dossier was produced there was a very wide variety of views on different parts of the dossier and the language that was used in it. They were not differences of view about whether intelligence should be included or not, it was more about how the intelligence was described or how it should be interpreted. It was, for example, the difference between saying 'intelligence suggests', 'intelligence shows', 'intelligence indicates'. These meanings have quite a lot of – you know, to intelligence analysts they are quite important distinctions.[18]

An example of this was provided by another witness, Dr Brian Jones, former branch head in the Scientific and Technical Directorate of the Defence Intelligence Analysis Staff. He relayed his concerns at the excessively categorical statements in the dossier which use the reporting verb *show*. It is used four times in the Executive Summary, as follows:

> It [Information] **shows** that Iraq has refurbished sites formerly associated with the production of chemical and biological agents ... It [Intelligence] **shows** that Saddam attaches great importance to possessing weapons of mass destruction ... It **shows** that he does not regard them only as weapons of last resort ... Intelligence also **shows** that Iraq is preparing plans to conceal evidence of these weapons ...[19]

Jones' own comments attest to the certainty value attached to *shows*, which was well understood by those in the intelligence services who needed to express subtleties of judgement:

> JONES: I think we felt that it was reasonable to say that the intelligence indicated that this was the case [i.e. that Iraq possessed and was prepared to use chemical and biological weapons]; and I think I felt it was a reasonable conclusion to draw; but we did not think – we did not think the intelligence showed it absolutely beyond any shadow of doubt.
> Q: And there is a difference, I take it, from your answer between 'indicates' and 'shows'?
> JONES: Yes.[20]

In other words, to say *Information shows that Iraq has refurbished sites* demonstrates the text producer's commitment to the truth-value of the statement. For Jones, the use of *shows* is equivalent to implicitly stating that it is 'absolutely beyond any shadow of doubt'. By contrast, less conviction is connoted by *indicates*, as in:

> [Information] **indicates** that Iraq remains able to manufacture these agents, and to use bombs, shells, artillery rockets and ballistic missiles to deliver them.[21]

An even greater degree of hedging is conveyed by *suggested*:

> The ... report also **suggested** that Iraq could assemble nuclear weapons within months of obtaining fissile material.[22]

Such nuances, particularly the use of *shows*, which creates the impression of the certainty of the information and the conclusions drawn, constrain the responses from the reader. They were extremely influential and devastatingly consequential, promoting the stance of the authors of the dossier and helping to enlist public and parliamentary support for war. In the event, of course, they were erroneous and misleading because no chemical and biological weapons were to be found in Iraq.

The practical insights of the intelligence analysts are supported by the theoretical and applied frameworks of discourse analysis. In appraisal theory, the shades of meaning expressed in reporting verbs are discussed under the heading of 'engagement'. They are seen to be central to the expression of the writer/speaker's attitude and stance and to the negotiation of alignment between the writer/speaker and addressee:

> [W]hen speakers/writers announce their own attitudinal positions they not only self-expressively 'speak their own mind', but simultaneously invite others to endorse and to share with them the feelings, tastes or normative assessments they are announcing. Thus declarations of attitude are dialogically directed towards aligning the addressee into a community of shared value and belief.
>
> *(Martin and White 2005: 95)*

For Martin and White (ibid.: 98), *shows* is an example of 'proclaiming' attitude where the textual voice does not permit alternative positions to be adopted by the reader. *Indicates* or *suggests* would reveal more subjectivity ('entertaining' more voices) and a verb such as *claims* would represent a subjective external voice that would provoke challenge. We might represent these differences as a cline between poles of positioning that are, to use Bakhtin's seminal terms, at the one extreme monoglossic (univocal, not permitting of other voices or responses) and at the other heteroglossic (openly engaging with other voices and permitting a wide response from the addressee), as in Figure 0.1.

Monoglossic   **Heteroglossic**

| categorical statement | demonstrate, show | *indicate* | *suggest* | *claim* |

FIGURE 0.1 Engagement positioning of reporting verbs

The translation of these linguistic signals poses significant problems. First, languages may differ in the range of resources used in reporting – English conventions point to a wider range than in Arabic and Persian, for example (Ardekani 2002). Second, translators may not always be finely attuned to the positioning that is conveyed, which may cause shifts along the cline. Thus, in the Arabic translation of the Iraq dossier posted online by the UK government *indicates* is rendered as the more monoglossic دكّؤي (*yuakid*, 'asserts/confirms') and *suggested that Iraq could . . . is* the more explicit and direct أشار (*ashara*, 'pointed to/indicated . . .'). In some instances this may have a significant impact on the reception of the text.

The structure of the book

Critical points can therefore range considerably in their form and subtlety. This book seeks to uncover their range and to identify the trends in their translation. It looks at the translator's mediation, or intervention, through an analysis of evaluation based on the model of appraisal theory, a development of the interpersonal function described in Hallidayan linguistics. The structure of the book is as follows:

• Chapter 1 is an introduction to the main ideas of appraisal theory and how these may relate to translation. The theory is then tested on a range of translation[23] scenarios in order to begin to reveal the critical subjective points of translation and the decision-making processes that are associated with them. These scenarios are:

• Chapter 2: the simultaneous interpreting of President Barack Obama's inaugural address in January 2009. Three different interpretings into Spanish are studied, together with written translations of the same speech and interpretings in other languages (French, Italian, Chinese, Japanese, and American Sign Language).

• Chapter 3: the views of professional technical translators as to what are critical points in a text. These are investigated through direct telephone and email interviews and through the analysis of discussions on the online forums KudoZ™ and SENSE.

• Chapter 4: the literary translator and reviser. Translator archives are used to research decision-making through the revisions made at different points of drafts. Analysis of related correspondence between the authors, translators and editors helps to explain some of these decisions and to monitor problem areas in their texts.

• Chapter 5: an experiment into translation variation involving the study of multiple translator trainee student versions of the same extract from the Jorge Luis Borges short story 'Emma Zunz'. The aim behind the study is to see what remains invariant (which would suggest readings and encodings that are not contested) and what is subject to most variation (which may indicate key critical points). The experiment is explored further by the comparison of some of the same students' works in a different genre – technical translation.

Together, these scenarios constitute a study of critical points in different modes (simultaneous interpreting and written translation), different genres (literary and technical translation) in a range of languages (European and non-European) and with different levels of experience (professional translators and trainees). They also encompass different forms of research (detailed analysis of individual texts and a corpus of translations, interviews with professionals, the study of online forums and of translator archives and correspondence). In sum, therefore, they are selected to offer a multiple perspective on the concept of critical points. The study is innovative both for its subject of study and also for the form of analysis. It does not take for granted that the form of analysis based on appraisal theory is necessarily going to be applicable or revealing in its entirety. The results are not predetermined, the examples not picked to order. Indeed, the study specifically seeks to test out appraisal theory in order to determine to what extent it fits the purpose of analysing and better understanding the translator's work. The avoidance of the indiscriminate importation of a linguistic model developed for English means that the current book is truly an experiment.

1

EVALUATION AND TRANSLATION

1.0 Introduction

The starting point of this chapter, indeed of this book, is that evaluation is central to communication and central to translation. In the words of the Soviet Bakhtin-circle linguist Volosinov:

> No utterance can be put together without value judgement. Every utterance is above all an *evaluative orientation*. Therefore, each element in a living utterance not only has a meaning but also has a value.
>
> *(Volosinov [1929] 1973: 105, emphasis in original)*

Volosinov (ibid.) supports this with the claim that evaluation cannot be limited to the connotation of a word, nor even to a comment on the propositional content. Evaluation (or an 'evaluative accent'; ibid.: 103) is present in every aspect of communication – in the choice of word and in the intonation that accompanies it in speech, in the syntax, in the arrangement of an argument, in the choice of genre, and form of language or dialect. Volosinov's Marxist philosophy sees language as the site of a struggle for expansion, a never-ending process of 're-evaluation' (ibid.: 105) as meaning changes over time with the production of new and more powerful utterances. Within this struggle, value choices constantly propel one form or another to a more salient position in the system of what Bakhtin (1981) terms 'heteroglossia', the co-existence of the different varieties of a language. Bakhtin gives the example of slogans, slang, swear words and laudatory terms that are constantly coined and reinvented by different social groups. The values are negotiated by the writer/speaker and reader/listener in tandem, in a 'dialogic' process where each utterance is oriented towards an expected response and at the same time draws on the vast intertextual freight of words from previous utterances (Bakhtin 1981: 283, Volosinov [1929] 1973: 80).

Such dialogic negotiation of meaning through evaluative language located in socially and culturally located norms of expression forms the basis of the study of evaluation in applied linguistics that has developed over the first decade of the new millennium. Before then, Malrieu (1999: 114, quoted in White 2002) was still lamenting that 'very little attention has been paid to evaluation in language'. It is also true to say that the phenomenon has been neglected in translation studies, despite the growing interest in the role of the translation/interpreting as 'intervention' (Munday 2007) and in translation and ideology (e.g. Lefevere 1992, Álvarez and Vidal Claramonte 1996, Tymoczko and Gentzler 2002, Calzada Pérez 2003, Cunico and Munday 2007, Munday 2008). This is surprising, since evaluative language is in many ways the bridge between the central concepts of ideology and axiology.

1.1 Ideology and axiology

For Volosinov ([1929] 1973: 105), evaluation goes beyond simply 'the expression of a speaker's individual attitude toward the subject matter of his discourse'. He rejects such a limited conceptualization, unnecessarily separating meaning from form. Considered as a dynamic process within a system of language that enacts social exchange and is semiotically motivated, evaluation actually performs various additional roles, constructing the 'ideological space of a discourse' into which it positions both writer and reader in a dialogic movement.

Bakhtin and Volosinov's work has been highly influential in work on evaluation from a systemic functional and discourse analytic tradition. Thus, Lemke (1995, 1998) draws on Bakhtin's concepts of heteroglossia and the dialogic principle to discuss how the various voices in discourse may differ **ideologically** (in their ideas and beliefs) and **axiologically** (in their values). Even apparently monologic texts (e.g. a formal written novel) set up a dialogue and anticipate a response from the reader (Bakhtin [1953] 1986: 76, see also Macken-Horarik 2003a: 287, and this chapter, Section 1.6). From a communication studies perspective, Grant (2007) draws on Bakhtin's idea of the inherent 'axiological accentuation' of language as social discourse, together with Habermas' *Theory of Communicative Action* (1984) and Luhmann's *Social Systems* (1996), to develop an argument around the central notion of the uncertainty of communication. 'Axiological accentuation' is here understood as 'subjective evaluation ... a belief system which is peculiar to a world view of a language ... located amidst tensions of centripetal and centrifugal forces of discourse' (Grant 2007: 53). There are three key elements: the *subjectivity* of the speaker who evaluates through *language*, itself underpinned by a system of beliefs and values in a wider *discourse* environment that is pulling in two directions ('centripetally' towards unification and 'centrifugally' towards stratification). This brings together the individual (subjective/axiological) and societal (discourse/ideological) dimensions through the medium of language that is both an expression of individuality and loaded with the ideological weight of its uses in other contexts. Grant points to the instability and imbalances in the communicative act:

> Social communications are a complex tension between dominant cultures and ideologies and the uniqueness of selves. This uniqueness and the asymmetries between self and others are factors of contingency which generate uncertainty.
>
> *(Grant 2007: 54)*

Grant (ibid.), still following Bakhtin, challenges the assumption that the speakers share the same social and ideological perspective and attitude. Instead, he sees an unresolved tension between the individuals' subjective evaluations and the values of the wider social and ideological context in which the communication takes place. A speaker uses words to evaluate an object but this evaluation is subjective, is open to interpretation and negotiation and will not be shared by all (see also Beaton 2007: 274). Grant's interest lies in the 'interstices' of intersubjectivity, the 'spaces between utterances ... the elastic environment of other, alien words about the same subject, the same theme' (Bakhtin 1981: 276). These spaces or gaps in communication concern the negotiation of meaning where the speaker chooses one of many possible linguistic formulations with no certainty that the same meaning will be shared by the interlocutor. So, the most interesting area of research is actually those words and utterances that are not selected by the speaker since they are always there, lurking behind the actual selections and, if we look, telling us much about the values underlying those words.[1] In Grant's concluding words (ibid.: 183–4), 'The uncertainty of communication actually means that, even when we think we choose a clear, stable form, the *penumbra of unselected information* remains' (author's highlight). That is, an individual choice of word or expression does not exist in isolation but in relation to the other possible choices that the writer or speaker has discarded or otherwise did not use. As we shall see in the case studies described in this book, translation, especially multiple translations, is a particularly promising scenario for the investigation of the relation between selected and unselected forms and for the analysis of the value orientations that underlie these selections. These become perceptible, for example, in the comparison of one translator's choice against another's or in the study of the forms which are revised at different stages in the translation process.

1.2 Systemic functional linguistics and the value orientation of language

The question of how to analyse selected and unselected forms is complex, but it relates quite closely to the concept of 'meaning potential' in systemic functional linguistics (SFL), which is also attuned to the fine-grained analysis required of these choices. SFL was primarily developed by Michael Halliday, drawing on the work of the Prague School[2] and of J.R. Firth (e.g. Firth 1957). It considers language as 'social semiotic' (Halliday 1978: 108–9) and as 'a resource for the construction of . . . multiple social realities' (Lemke 1992: 82). These realities are both 'enacted' by the performance of socio-semiotic practice and 'construed' by practice and description. That is, language enables us to perform a social interaction (whether it be virtual or face-to-face chatting to a friend, writing a blog or an essay for a university professor, or delivering a presidential inauguration speech) but at the same time it also modifies, constructs and makes sense of the reality in which it takes place. This can be seen in the analysis of the Obama inaugural in Chapter 2, where Obama describes the crisis and attempts to construct a 'new era of responsibility'. The social realities are described as 'multiple' because of the heterogeneity of social communities, their different semiotic codes and interpretations, 'heteropraxia' in Lemke's terms (1992: 83), a broader and more dynamic understanding of Halliday's 'context of culture'. Given the complexity and potential instability of communication in a world of varying viewpoints and possible interpretations, one important consequence is that some linguistic 'orientation' is necessary from the speaker (Lemke 1992: 85). This is part of the interpersonal function of language and includes the construction of a value orientation that is a crucial element in the text's projection of reality.

At different functional levels throughout the text (discourse, genre, Register, semantics, lexicogrammar), the writer or speaker chooses from the options available to create a text that has meaning in a communicative context. In technical terms, the system of a language is 'instantiated' in the form of text (Halliday and Matthiessen 2004: 26). In his *Language as Social Semiotic*, Halliday explains it as follows:

> The *text* is the linguistic form of social interaction. It is a continuous progression of meanings ... The meanings are the selections made by the speaker from the options that constitute the meaning potential: text is the actualization of this meaning potential, the process of semantic choice.
>
> *(Halliday 1978: 122)*

The crucial concepts of meaning potential, of choice and the relation to social structure represent fundamental building blocks of the model. Meaning potential is 'the range of options that is characteristic of a specific situation type' (therefore genre-specific) and the text itself is 'actualized meaning potential' (ibid.: 109) – that is, the choices that are made in a particular context from the range of lexical and grammatical ('lexicogrammatical')[3] choices open to the writer at each point. These perform the meaning potential in each clause according to three discourse semantic functions (Halliday 1994, Halliday and Matthiessen 2004):

1. the **ideational**/experiential, which constructs a representation (of an external reality) through subject-specific lexis and transitivity patterns including nominalizations;
2. the **interpersonal**, which facilitates an exchange between participants (and comments on its truth value) through mood, modality, forms of address, pronoun choice and 'evaluative epithets' (adjectives); and
3. the **textual**, which sees the clause as a message that contextually organizes information through thematic structure, cohesive devices and logical coherence.

TABLE 1.1 Intrinsic and extrinsic functionality of metafunctions

Metafunction	Intrinsic function	Register variable and reality
Ideational	Scaffolds action	Field, 'naturalized reality'
Interpersonal	Scaffolds affiliation	Tenor, 'social reality'
Textual	Distributes information	Mode, 'semiotic reality'

Martin (2004a: 323) differentiates these three interlinked metafunctions according to their specific functionality' (see Table 1.1). The metafunctions operate simultaneously, but it is the interpersonal that serves to construct or negotiate solidarity, and value judgements, between participants. In his description of this function, Halliday focuses on the speech acts of exchanging (giving and receiving) information and services and its realization through the mood and modality systems of language (Halliday and Hasan 1989: 31–3, Halliday 1994: 68, Halliday and Matthiessen 2004: 107, 150). **Mood** is conveyed through the selection of declarative, interrogative, imperative mood forms (see the discussion in Section 1.3.3 below). There are four types of **modality**, with a wide range of possible realizations:

1. probability (*could, might, perhaps, certainly* . . .)
2. usuality (*usually, never, tends to* . . .)[4]
3. obligation (*should, must, ought* . . .)
4. inclination (*will, wish, want, determined* . . .)[5]

There is also the 'continuous progression or unfolding of meanings' noted above, as each choice builds on previous selections in the text and contributes to future selections. This is known technically as **logogenesis** (Martin 1999, Halliday and Matthiessen 2004: 43). Thus, in a political speech, the decision to address the public using an inclusive first person plural form (*we are faced with a difficult challenge* . . .) rather than a first person singular and a second person (*I am speaking to you today*) or a more distancing formula (*The White House is seeking to allay concerns*), would define the positioning of the speaker and the audience as it unfolds.[6] Importantly, lexicogrammatical choices of interpersonal meaning represent an 'intrusion' by the speaker/writer into the communicative situation (Halliday 1978: 17) and can be linked to his/her ideological orientation. For example, the inclusive first person *we* form 'can be used to induce interpreters [i.e. receivers of a text] to conceptualise group identity, coalitions, parties, and the like, either as insiders or as outsiders' (Chilton 2004: 56). The consistent selection of the *we* form would align the audience with the speaker as 'insiders' and would help the speaker to manipulate the audience towards a possible shared solution based on common values and beliefs (see Section 1.3.3 below).

Martin (2004a, 2004b) shows how the ideological relates to Halliday's ideational metafunction of language, and the axiological to the interpersonal metafunction.

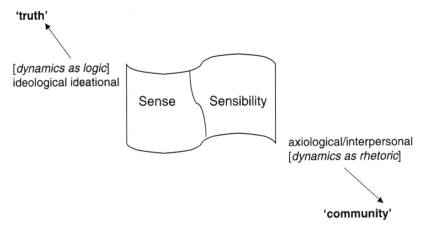

FIGURE 1.1   Sense and sensibility (adapted from Martin [2004a: 327, 2004b: 299])

The ideological/ideational function is directed at seeking or representing truth (or at least reality from the speaker's perspective), while the axiological/interpersonal builds or negotiates community or solidarity and gives the text its 'value orientation' (Martin and White 2005: 215). This mixture of 'sense and sensibility', as Martin terms it, is graphically illustrated in Figure 1.1.

Although those studying evaluation focus primarily on the axiological/ interpersonal, it is important to reiterate that this works co-terminously and dynamically with the ideological/ideational and also depends on the textual metafunction of language. So, cohesion as instantiated through connectors such as *and, but* ... signals expectancy relations (Thompson and Zhou 2000, Miller 2004a, 2004b) and the interpersonal and textual may combine to create texture (Thompson 2005, Forey and Thompson 2009). In sum, representations of truth and negotiations of value and solidarity are realized through texts and discourses in a social system (Martin 2004a: 341).

1.2.1 Ideology and axiology in translation

As well as providing a vital link between language, social practice and value orientation, the usefulness of SFL in translation has to do with the significance allotted to choice. The reader (and translator or interpreter) approaches the ST in the belief that the writer's choice is meaningful, asking questions such as: Why this wording rather than another? What choices did the writer have at each point? What is the function of the writer's choice? And what form of communication is produced by this choice? The translator needs to uncover the ST writer choice and to re-encode that choice as appropriate in the target language. Thus, the translator's choices are also meaningful and represent conscious or unconscious decisions at the lexical level that, together, represent the translator's interpretation of the ST.

Hallidayan linguistics has formed the basis of some prominent work on text and discourse analysis in translation theory, among which are House (1981, 1997), Hatim and Mason (1990, 1997), Bell (1991), Baker [1992] (2011), Teich (2003), Steiner and Yallop (2001), Munday (2002, 2007, 2008, 2009a) and Calzada Pérez (2007). Basil Hatim and Ian Mason's *Discourse and the Translator* starts from a Register analysis perspective, analysing Field, Tenor and Mode through the realizations of ideational, interpersonal and textual functions in STs and TTs. Their aim was 'to relate an integrated account of discourse processes to the practical concerns of the translator' (Hatim and Mason 1990: xi). In their later *The Translator as Communicator*, the authors proceed to emphasize the role of translation as a form of 'mediation ... the process of incorporating into the processing of utterances and texts one's own assumptions, beliefs, etc.' (Hatim and Mason 1997: 220). Here, they are openly speaking about the potential for translation to create ideological distortion of a ST discourse.[7]

Hatim and Mason (ibid.: 153–9) discuss the now well-known example of an English translation of a history text about the indigenous peoples of Mexico by the Mexican historian Miguel León Portilla (b. 1926), published in the *Unesco Courier* and earlier studied by Mason himself (Mason 1994 [2010]). They analyse the ideological shifts which occur in the translation according to 'lexical choice', 'cohesion' and 'transitivity' and which lead to the erasure of some important elements of the indigenous culture. Thus, for example, under 'cohesion' they note that the key concept of oral *memoria*, which occurs five times in the source, is diluted and re-perspectivized through a European lens into *history, knowledge of the past* and in one case omitted altogether; the term *memory* is only used twice. The semantic field of 'effort' is similarly distorted: *esfuerzos* ('efforts') becomes *obstinate determination*, while *épocas de gran creatividad* ('epochs of great creativity') is downplayed to *bursts of creativity*, and so on. But it is the general category of 'lexical choices' where the most obvious distortions are to be found: the Mexicans' *sabios* ('wise men') are translated into the less rational *diviners*, and the *hombre indígena* ('indigenous man') himself becomes *pre-Columbian civilization*. In this way, translators exert 'maximal mediation' (Hatim and Mason, 1997: 153), 'interven[ing] in the transfer process, feeding their own knowledge and beliefs into their processing of a text' (ibid.: 147).

Mason's later work has included important studies on the effects of translator mediation as expressed in shifts in deixis in literary texts rendered into Romanian (Mason and Serban 2003) and shifts in the transitivity selections in institutional settings (Mason 2004). In the latter, Mason examines a corpus of articles from the *Unesco Courier* and from European Parliament speeches, making the important and commonsense point that, while 'individual shifts may be individually significant and provide some clues to translators' approaches to their task', it is what he calls the 'concatenation' of shifts which may establish a trend and cause a shift in discourse. One example is the English and French translations of a Spanish MEP's speech criticizing the United Kingdom for its response to Bovine Spongiform Encephalopathy ('Mad Cow disease') in 2001. Mason (2004: 478–81) suggests that there is a mitigation of the discourse of blame in the English translation but an intensification in the French translation, for example:

> **ST** La supeditación de las decisiones políticas a las presiones económicas en el Reino Unido está en el origen de la problemática inherente a la EEB.
> [The subordination of political decisions to economic pressures in the UK is at the root of the inherent problem of BSE.]
> **English TT** The underlying problem with BSE is that political decisions have been subordinated to economic pressures in the United Kingdom.

> **ST** La enfermedad se originó con la introducción de harinas de carne.
> [The disease began with the introduction of bone meal.]
> **French TT** Cette maladie est due à l'introduction de farines de viande ...
> [The disease is due to the introduction of bone meal.]

Mason analyses these examples according to a framework of transitivity (who does what; who is responsible for actions) and the speech act performed. Thus, through nominalization, the Spanish ST presupposes the subordination of political decisions to economic pressures, while the English TT presents it in a passive verbal construction as a claim about a problem; the French TT makes the illocutionary act of accusation more explicit, through the causal statement *est due à* ('is due to'). Such analysis is certainly convincing, and shows the importance of what might seem to be modest changes in transitivity structures. It is taken further by the more detailed study in Calzada Pérez (2007).

The concentration on *patterns* of shifts, rather than individual instances, reduces the obstacle of the crucial question of interpretation. While, for example, ideational choices of language (e.g. transitivity choices or nominalizations) may generally construct a perspective on experience, they do not absolutely determine them and do not fully constrict the possible interpretations the reader might bring to the text (cf. Fairclough 1992: 75, Widdowson 2004: 96). Indeed, from a very early point Hatim and Mason (e.g. 1990: 11) emphasize the importance for the translator of maintaining as far as is possible in the TT the range of interpretations in the ST, of not constraining the reader by imposing a reading. Here they are considering what they term the 'static–dynamic' continuum of language, where they relate it to reader expectations and norms (Hatim and Mason 1997: 28). 'Static' texts are described as 'expectation-fulfilling' and 'norm-confirming', while 'dynamic' texts are 'expectation-defying' and 'norm-flouting'. This is clearly and explicitly related to the concept of markedness, a linguistic feature that occurs in a text with greater than expected frequency or significance.[8] Thus, for example, in the textual function VS order in modern English is generally 'marked' (that is, infrequent and hence potentially more informative). A marked term is more 'dynamic' since it defies reader expectations, which may be genre-linked. For instance, the use of the English conjunction *and* in a first position in a sentence is generally discouraged by teachers, yet it is likely to be less marked as a feature of traditional fairy tales, some older translations of the Bible (e.g. King James Version) and in transcriptions of oral language.

Of equal importance in translation theory has been Juliane House's influential model of translation quality assessment (House 1981, 1997), designed to identify 'mismatches' (shifts), categorized mainly at the level of Register. The development of the model is summarized in House (2001), where, in the case study of a children's book, House uses the Register variable of Tenor, linked to the interpersonal function of language, to describe the author's 'emotional and intellectual stance' and how the social role relationships of author–readers, protagonist–readers and protagonists–protagonists are altered in the German translation. The textual and lexical 'mismatches' include the reversal of the title, from ST *Peace at Last* to TT *Keine Ruh für Vater Bär* ('No quiet for Father Bear'), shifts in naming, from *Mr Bear, Mrs Bear*, etc. to *Vater Bär* ('Father Bear') and *Mutter Bär* ('Mother Bear') and other, generally negative, renderings in the German. House perceives a shift from humorous neutrality in the English to an authoritarian and negative parent–child relationship in the German.

Writer–reader relations, specifically contrastive subjectivity between English and German, has been central to the work of House's team in Hamburg. In House (2008, 2011), she notes language-specific dimensions: English tends to be geared more towards the interpersonal orientation, implicitness and indirectness while German prefers a content orientation, explicitness and directness (House 2011: 189). However, she argues that there has been a shift over the twenty-five years of her study: speaker–hearer deixis (direct address using the first and second persons) has increased in German popular science texts and in translations from English. The frequency of German modal particles (such as *auch, doch, eben, einmal, ja, schon*, see Introduction and Chapter 3.1) has also risen, possibly as a result of the influence of the English interpersonal rhetorical style.[9]

The terminology for the study of such phenomena has shifted. Whereas Hatim and Mason saw the translator/interpreter as 'communicator' and translation as 'mediation', more recent work has preferred the more assertive and evaluative term 'intervention' (e.g. Munday 2007). So, Maier (2007) discusses the role of the translator as 'intervenient being' and Kang (2007) analyses intervention through the 'recontextualization' of discourse (cf. Fairclough 2003: 139–41) in translations of news stories on North Korea. Analysing a selection of English ST articles and their editing and revision in translations in South Korea, she concludes that 'the choices made by translators and editors may be the result of a complex interplay of the subjectivities of institutional translators and editors based on situated and interpretative readings of the ST, institutional goals, routines, and a set of institutionally-defined discursive resources' (Kang 2007: 240).

Intervention is defined by House (2008: 16) as 'a manipulation of the source text beyond what is linguistically necessary'. She continues:

> Manipulation or 'intervention' for ideological, socio-political or ethical reasons, however well-meant they may be in any individual case, are generally

risky undertakings. Who is to judge that the interventions are really desirable and that addressees of a translation would not rather be confronted with an equivalent source text? How can we justify well-meant changes to a text made under the auspices of say feminist or post-colonialist thinking from chauvinistic imperialist interventions? We cannot. Personally, I have always pleaded for separating linguistic, textual considerations from social ones. In other words: as a translator (and a translation critic) one must be aware of one's responsibility to the original author and his or her text, and one must use the power one has been given to re-textualise and re-contextualise a given text with discretion. In many – if not most – cases it might be wiser to not intervene at all.

(House 2008: 16)

While I would not argue with House's argument, she is here talking about conscious intervention and manipulation, which certainly have serious consequences in translation. But I would again stress that we crucially need to remember that all intervention is evaluative and to take account of both conscious and unconscious choices made by the translator. In a study of ideology and axiology in interpreting of European Parliament speeches, Beaton (2007) analyses patterns of cohesion expressed by lexical repetition. In her sample, she shows that there is a tendency for the interpreter to reinforce the hegemonic discourse of the institution through, for example, an increase in the use of the superordinate *European Union*, the institutionalization of individual rhetorical phrases and a shift in metaphorical strings. Beaton's work focuses on the textual metafunction. Potentially, though, any word in any text indicates an axiological as well as ideological orientation and we need to have a model to analyse evaluation. In SFL this is done through the detailed system of 'appraisal' that expands the interpersonal function of language.

1.3 Appraisal theory and the concept of evaluation

It should be emphasized that there are various theoretical terms in use for the concept of evaluation. These are, notably:

- stance (Biber and Finegan 1998, 1989, Conrad and Biber 2000, STANCE 2006, Englebretson 2007, Jaffe 2009);
- evaluation (Hunston and Thompson 2000, Bednarek 2006, 2008);
- appraisal (Martin 2000, Martin and White 2005); and also
- metadiscourse (Crismore 1989, Hyland and Tse 2004, Hyland 2005);
- evidentiality (Chafe and Nichols 1986, Aikhenveld 2004); and
- subjectivity (Stein and Wright 1995, Finegan 1995).

Interest in the phenomenon is traced by Finegan (1995), Bednarek (2006: 20) and Englebretson (2007: 15–16) back to the work on subjectivity by Benveniste (1971 [1958]) and Lyons (1977: 739, 1982). Benveniste (ibid.: 226–7) suggests that a coherent subjectivity is achieved through the use of first person pronoun *I* (designating the speaker), and of deixis and temporality (to locate the subject in space and time). Lyons, criticizing semantics for its over-concentration on propositional meaning, proposes a definition of subjectivity as 'self-expression in the use of language' (Lyons 1995: 337, 340) and as 'the locutionary agent's expression of himself and of his attitudes and beliefs' (Lyons 1982: 103). This is echoed by Finegan in an introduction to a volume on subjectivity and subjectivization (the linguistic structures that encode subjectivity). He adds the notion of the speaker's 'perspective or point of view in discourse', the expression of affect and epistemic status as a means to 'convey and assess feelings, moods, dispositions and attitudes' (Finegan 1995: 1, 4). Subjectivity sometimes may encompass the sense of subjecthood (the speaker's construal of self); evaluation or stance is generally understood to have a more reduced scope ('subjectivity with a focus'; Englebretson 2007: 16) or to be better treated as an overlapping but distinct phenomenon (Bednarek 2006: 20–1).

In the introduction to their seminal volume *Evaluation in Text: Authorial stance and the construction of discourse*, Thompson and Hunston (2000: 5) exit the terminological conundrum by opting for the general term 'evaluation' and the subordinate term 'stance', since for them 'evaluation is a broad cover term for the expression of the speaker or writer's stance towards, viewpoint on, or feelings about the entities or propositions that he or she is talking about'.[10] For the same reasons, we shall also adopt 'evaluation'.

Skating over any underlying theoretical tensions, Thompson and Hunston make some generally important points regarding evaluation, outlining its three main functions as follows:

1. To express the speaker's or writer's opinion, and in doing so to reflect the value system of that person and their community. With its emphasis on shared value systems, this is clearly linked to 'ideology' (see note 7). Yet the inclusion of the person's value system allows for the individual input of the text produce – in our case, the axiology of the translator/interpreter.
2. To construct and maintain relations between the writer and reader (or speaker and hearer). This may have a goal of persuading or manipulating, where evaluation makes the author's point less easily challenged (Thompson and Hunston 2000: 8) or directly or indirectly evaluates the truth or certainty of a statement (Fairclough 2003: 171).
3. To organize the discourse (Thompson and Hunston 2000: 6). This relates to those conceptualizations of evaluation, such as Labov's famous sociolinguistic study of the narrative structure of natural storytelling among Blacks in New York (Labov 1972b) or Hoey's problem–solution pattern (Hoey 1983), which explicitly comment on and signal the important points in the discourse, a role that Sinclair termed 'monitoring', i.e. giving feedback to a speaker with expressions such as *That's right, Sure*, etc. or with summarizing nominalizations such as *The misunderstanding* that inherently evaluate the truth element of an argument (Thompson and Hunston 2000: 11–12).

Lemke (1998) emphasizes that significant interpretive skill is required in the analysis and assessment of evaluation. Rather than giving the usual prominence to the ideational function of language, Lemke underlines the 'value orientation' of a text that positions the receiver according to the values of the writer and, by so doing, modifies the perspective and serves to (re-)construe social reality (1992: 88). In a framework in which the text is a site for competing textual voices in a communicative context of socially constructed individuals, Lemke sees value orientations along the axes of the value of 'goodness' (desirability, morality, appropriateness, efficiency), modulation/mood and modality (certainty, truth, etc.). In addition, he underlines the importance of the axis of predictability/expectability, which he understands to be related more to social value (i.e. conformity with social expectations) than with an affective element of surprise. It is interesting to note how far this coincides with Hatim and Mason's concern with the static–dynamic continuum (see Section 1.2.1 above). The latter speak of expectations and norms mainly in terms of texture (cohesion, etc.), whereas Lemke introduces a distinctive value orientation. Bednarek (2006: 81), too, sees expectedness as a signal of evaluation in her study of media discourse.

However, the question remains, and is posed by Thompson and Hunston (2000: 13), as to how evaluation is to be recognized in a text. The system of 'appraisal', developed by Martin and White (2005) within a Hallidayan framework of interpersonal meaning, offers a very detailed model.[11]

1.3.1 The system of appraisal

White (2002)[12] describes the origins of appraisal theory from the late 1980s, developed by functional linguists in Australia who were investigating:

1. forms of narration, such as the anecdote, where the speaker prompted a reaction from the listener (Martin and Plum 1997);
2. essay-writing among secondary school pupils, where the students tended to give personal rather than analytical responses (Rothery and Stenglin 1997, 2000);
3. variation in style in journalistic discourse, which was mapped according to different voices and evaluative phenomena (Iedema et al. 1994);
4. from these evolved the study of the role of patterns of evaluation in the construction of writer/speaker personae and of 'ideal' or 'intended' audiences (Fuller 1998, White 2000).

White (2002, 2005) stresses the two principal questions explored in this work on appraisal: one is the nature of attitude (how positive or negative evaluations are activated) and the other the adoption of stance (the negotiation of evaluative meanings and positioning of subjects).[13]

Appraisal is considered to be one of three constituent 'discourse-semantic' resources for the expression of interpersonal meaning in the Register variable of Tenor. The others are the resources of 'negotiation' and 'involvement' (Figure 1.2).[14]

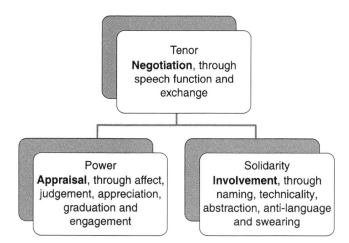

FIGURE 1.2   Discourse-semantic resources for the expression of interpersonal meaning (following Martin and White 2005: 35)

Tenor is to be considered as a superordinate category, with the subcategories of 'power' relating primarily to appraisal and 'solidarity' to involvement. As an aside, we should note (with Martin and White 2005: 34) that solidarity through involvement is partly created through the technical and specialized lexis of the group. While for sociolinguists this could mean the non-standard anti-language of a social gang or the group-specific argot of the like-minded engaged in, for example, tweeting, texting or whatever other activity, for translation theorists it clearly also relates to the use of subject-specific technical language, the language for specific purposes that is central to most translators' business (see Chapter 3). Such technical language is also, of course, part of the ideational metafunction, so there is an overlap between the ideational and interpersonal. Technical lexis is a primary constructive element of the ideational or experiential world (the activity that is occurring) as well as helping to form an interpersonal bond of solidarity between its participants. Similarly, other features of involvement, such as taboo language, have already been problems noted in audiovisual translation, dialogue interpreting, etc. (see, for example, Chiaro 2009).

Although negotiation and involvement will be incorporated into the analysis, the main focus in this book is on appraisal, which is predominantly concerned with the resources for the lexicalization of evaluation. Table 1.2 sets out its main features.

Attitude is the most basic form of evaluation, most archetypally realized through attitudinally loaded adjectives, known in SFL as 'evaluative epithets' (Halliday 1994: 184) or 'interpersonal epithets' (Halliday and Matthiessen 2004: 318). As can be seen in Table 1.2, Martin and White describe three types of attitude – affect, judgement and appreciation. The lexicogrammatical resources for the realization of attitude are vast and diverse. Examples of prototypical realizations are as follows:

TABLE 1.2 Appraisal resources (adapted from Martin and White 2005: 38)

Domain of appraisal	Parameter	Value	Illustrative realization
Attitude	Affect	Through feelings and emotional reactions	*Happy, sad*
	Judgement	Of ethics, behaviour, capacity	*Wrong, brave*
	Appreciation	Of things, phenomena, reactions	*Beautiful, authentic*
Graduation	Force	Raise	**Extremely** *unwise*
		Lower	**Slightly** *corrupt*
	Focus	Sharpen	*A* **true** *father*
		Soften	*An apology* **of sorts**
Engagement	Monogloss	Contraction	*Demonstrate, show*
	Heterogloss	Expansion	*Claim, nearly, possibly*

1. **Affect**, related to feelings and emotional reactions: *happy, sad, horrified*, etc.
2. **Judgement**, of behaviour, ethics, capacity, tenacity: *wrong, right, stingy, skilful, cautious, brave, insightful*, etc.
3. **Appreciation**, the evaluation of phenomena and processes, including aesthetics, taste, worth: *beautiful, pleasant, brilliant, tedious, creative, authentic,* etc.

Importantly, the basis for affect is essentially personal and the response it envisages is mental and emotional; we are happy to hear some news, horrified at a disaster, etc. This is a result of its affinity with the tradition of work on affect and the language of emotion (Ochs 1989, Ochs and Schieffelin 1989). By contrast, judgement and appreciation, though they will vary somewhat according to the individual, presuppose a basis of shared community values which may even be institutionalized (Martin and White 2005: 57). Our evaluations are strongly linked to the values instilled in us by the educational, legal, cultural and other institutions in which we are formed. However, some (e.g. Coffin 2002: 511–12) have questioned how far value judgements really are shared. Cross-culturally, education and legal frameworks and values certainly differ. Likewise, variation is to be expected in the criteria for aesthetic and other evaluation. Whether it concern a modern style of building in an historic setting, a style of fiction or a clothing fashion, it is to a large extent socially instilled but still depends on the individual.

1.3.1.1 Direct, or 'inscribed', attitude

The most obvious expression of attitude is by 'direct inscription' (Martin and White 2005: 61), through openly evaluative epithets. Typical are promotional texts of various types (conventional advertising, tourist brochures, product brochures . . .), such as the following:

TimeOut/HSBC Miniguide to London, Spring 2009
London is cosmopolitan, trendy and exciting: a truly wonderful place to visit. The city combines old-fashioned charm and cutting-edge fashion. Quiet courtesy and a great deal of fun.

Positive inscribed affect and appreciation is explicit and intense: *cosmopolitan, trendy, exciting, wonderful, cutting-edge, quiet*; the nouns *charm, fashion, courtesy* and *fun* are similarly positive. The categorical declaration *London is . . .* also seems to preclude challenge. The very point is to communicate positive appreciation to as many readers as possible, to convey that London, with its huge variety and contrasts, offers something that appeals to everyone. For a translator approaching this text, and given a similar communicative purpose to that of the ST (e.g. a TT available to tourists at ports of entry to London), the goal almost certainly would be to reproduce the positive appreciation in the TT. In the case of the above, we may hypothesize that reproducing this inscribed appreciation should not be an overly problematic task, unless there is some value that would not be positively appreciated by the target culture audience.

This communicative, 'something for everyone' purpose is made more explicit in the continuation of the text:

All of these characteristics will be revealed as you wander from museum to gallery, down Victorian arcades and busy streets, across vast parks and along cobbled streets. The contrasts are endless: next to every historical sight, there's a skyscraper gleaming with the wealth of modern life. Discovering these contrasts is one of the city's great pleasures.

Space prohibits detailed discussion here, but it is easy to see the continued inscribed appreciation of *vast, gleaming, wealth, modern* and *great pleasures.* Positive attitude is conveyed very strongly by verbal processes (*gleaming* and, to a lesser extent, *wander,* which encompasses the sense of relaxed leisure, showing that attitude may be transmitted by various parts of speech, something which we shall return to in Chapter 5). Collocation also plays an important role: *vast* has a positive value here because of its collocation with *park* in the genre of a tourist text. Numerous examples of this collocation can be found in similar texts, such as the following description of a Paris *quartier,* taken from the online English particulars of a property company:

The Apartment Service Worldwide[15]
An authentic, unspoilt district, with open-air markets, streets full of shops, traditional restaurants and boulevards lined with magnificent, early 20th century buildings. And, what's more, it's surrounded by **vast parks**, where you can forget all about the city and stroll for hours listening to the birds.

Not only is the attitude of the whole hugely positive. The second sentence, and especially the final clause (*where . . . birds*), explicitly presents the reason for the positive value accorded to *vast parks* and makes it very difficult for the reader to disagree.

Although inscribed attitude claims to attach itself on values that are 'largely fixed and stable across a wide range of contexts' (White and Thomson 2008: 11), there is nevertheless a cultural and institutional basis to this attitude. The lexical items above are read as positive because the audience envisaged is one that tends to be attracted to London precisely because of some or all of these qualities, and the predominant cultural frame of the city prides itself on them. Some individuals, of course, and some other cultures, may react with a more negative appreciation to some of these qualities. For example, *trendy* and *cutting-edge fashion* are not appealing to the author of this book. However, the point made by Martin and White[16] is that there is a general infusion of inscriptions of attitude which have a wider effect on evaluation throughout a text:

> [T]he prosodic nature of the realisation of interpersonal meanings such as attitude means that inscriptions tend to colour more of a text than their local grammatical environment circumscribes. The inscriptions act as sign-posts, in other words, telling us how to read the ideational selections that surround them.
>
> *(Martin and White 2005: 63)*

This is also attested by Bednarek's study of evaluation in media discourse, where she stresses how the local or global evaluative prosody of a text may influence the evaluation of otherwise neutral or contested terms (Bednarek 2006: 209–11, Hood 2006).[17] One example she briefly alludes to (Bednarek 2006: 211) is former US Secretary of Defence Donald Rumsfeld's phrase *old Europe* in January 2003 to refer to France and Germany, who opposed US plans to invade Iraq. In this context, *old* was inscribed by Rumsfeld with negative appreciation and judgement (equivalent to tired, old-fashioned, out-of-touch compared with the newly integrated countries of central and southern Europe). However, this was subverted by the French Minister for Foreign Affairs, Dominique de Villepin, and also in Germany, where the term *das alte Europa* ('old Europe') was *Wort des Jahres* ('word of the year') for 2003.[18] It is illuminating to take a closer look at Villepin's proud use of the terms *vieux pays* ('old country') and *vieux continent* ('old continent') in his crucial speech at the UN Security Council on 14 February 2003:

French ST

Et c'est un **vieux** pays, La France, un **vieux** continent comme le mien, l'Europe, qui vous le dit aujourd'hui, qui a connu les guerres, l'Occupation, la barbarie. Un **vieux** pays qui n'oublie pas et qui sait tout ce qu'il doit aux combattants de la liberté venus d'Amérique et d'ailleurs. Et qui pourtant n'a cessé de se tenir debout face à l'Histoire et devant les hommes. Il veut agir résolument avec tous les membres de la communauté internationale. Fidèle à ses valeurs, il croit en notre capacité à construire ensemble un monde meilleur.[19]

English TT

This message comes to you today from an **old** country, France; from a continent like mine, Europe, that has known war, occupation, barbarity. It is an **old** country that does not forget and is very aware of all it owes to freedom fighters who came from America and elsewhere. And yet France has always stood upright in the face of History before mankind. Faithful to its values, it wants resolutely to act together with all members of the international community. France believes in our ability to build together a better world.[20]

Interestingly, Villepin's evaluation comes not from any directly positive inscription. *Vieux* ('old') is key because it is repeated three times in the ST, collocating with both *continent* and *pays* ('country') in a form of appreciation. But that on its own is not enough. Its value comes from the prosodic association that sweeps this culmination of his speech. Here, *vieux* becomes positively associated with experience, even of terrible events (*war, occupation, barbarity*), wise with the enduring memory both of the horrors of war (hence the need to avoid repeating those errors) and of France's debt to those who freed it. The intertext points to the Allied campaigns to defend and liberate France in the two world wars, thus gratefully acknowledging that there are times that war is 'necessary'. These are expressions of judgement. Villepin concludes with a series of appeals based on further positive judgement, an ethical assessment of France's behaviour and capacity:

France n'a cessé de **se tenir debout** – has always **stood upright** ...
fidèle à ses **valeurs** – **faithful** to its **values** ...
veut agir **résolument** avec tous les membres – wants **resolutely** to act together ...
croit en notre **capacité** à construire ensemble un monde **meilleur** – believes in our **ability** to build together a **better** world.

Such a combination of positive semantic association and use of intense positive judgement strongly colours the interpretation of the term *vieux*.

1.3.1.2 Indirect, or invoked, attitude

Often, however, evaluation is more indirectly expressed and much more difficult to analyse. It is indirect, 'implied' (Martin 2003: 172) or 'invoked' (White 2002, Martin and White 2005) using attitudinal 'tokens' (White 2006, White and Thomson 2008). There are two kinds of expressions of such indirect attitude: 'evoked' and 'provoked' (White and Thomson 2008: 11).

1.3.1.3 Evoked attitude

Evoked attitude may cause a positive reaction not because of any inherently positive attitudinal qualities of the word but because it foregrounds a piece of ideational (factual) material (Martin 2004b: 288). White (2006) gives the following as an example of foregrounded ideational information that evokes a negative evaluation:

> George W. Bush delivered his inaugural speech as the United States President who collected 537,000 fewer votes than his opponent.

There is no direct inscription of attitude, but the mere fact that Bush was the *President who collected 537,000 fewer votes than his opponent* is sufficient to evoke a response in the reader assuming that the reader shares knowledge of the norms of the electoral process (that there is a free vote and the candidate who receives most votes is normally elected, but occasionally, as in these 2000 US presidential elections, this does not happen) and of the ethics of this context (the controversy over the voting in Florida, where the Republicans were accused of manipulating the vote). Evokedness is a particularly potent form of evaluation since it insinuates itself into the text (Macken-Horarik 2003a: 299) and, by masquerading as a factual and 'commonsense' representation of the world, is often more effective at manipulating the reader by seeming to be incontestable (White 2004: 238, 244). In many English-speaking contexts, newspaper editorials ('op-eds'), for example, present the writer's opinion through categorical statements of fact.

However, such a reading is based on the recipient's sharing the author's assumption, which might not be the case for a Republican supporter reading the above example. Some 'discourse relative evaluative statements' (Bednarek 2006: 212) may even be the site for significant ideological contestation. Fairclough (2003: 172) notes the oft-quoted contested term *Communist*, evaluation of which varies crucially according to the reader's political and historical viewpoint.[21] Other examples in a multilingual context would be naming that indexes cultural, political or national affiliation: in an English text the choice of *Bombay/Mumbai* or *Montreal/Montréal*, for instance, potentially indicates a (post)colonial or political orientation (Mossop 2007). In such a way, ideational configurations become 'evaluatively "saturated" ' with interpersonal meaning (Coffin 2002: 512).

A more subtle form of evoked attitude involves the triggering of a latent contextual association by otherwise neutral content tokens (White 2004: 234, Coffin 2006: 147). In the London *Miniguide* example, positive appreciation is evoked by *Victorian arcades* and *cobbled streets*, not because the epithets *Victorian* and *cobbled* are in themselves positive nor even evaluative, but because in their collocations and in this communicative context they have a semiotic role in representing what institutionally are perceived to be positive traditional values dating from the nineteenth century. This creates a coherence projected by the use of the similarly invoked *old-fashioned charm* of the first London example, the specific connotation of which will vary according to the reader; possibilities are 'authenticity' and 'quality of life', the 'quality of traditional products', seemingly a world away from the frenzy of the modern capital represented by the gleaming skyscraper but in fact co-existing with and complementing it.

That such evokedness lies beneath the surface, and is subjective and perspectivized, is a serious problem for the translator, who needs both to identify the intended evaluation and transfer it appropriately into the TT in a new context of culture which may not apply the same value to the entities – for example, where *Victorian* may negatively connote outdated, restricted or an oppressive empire and where *cobbled streets* relate to dirty factories or the revolutionary stones of Mai '68. A translator would therefore need to recognize the trigger and recreate it appropriately in the TT in the choice of positive (or at least neutral) words. However, it is important to bear in mind the potential difference in the linguistic realization of culturally expected norms of evaluation. Kaltenbacher (2006), analysing a small corpus of tourist websites in the US, Scotland and Austria, suggests that appraisal may be realized differently according to linguistic culture: Scottish websites highlighting national identity (*Scottish, Royal, Lothian*, etc.), Austrian websites using affect (*enjoy a winter stroll/beauty*, etc.) and US websites employing exaggerated words of appreciation (*beautiful, breathtaking*). Interestingly, in view of the findings in the Villepin example above, Kaltenbacher finds the terms *historic, historical* and *old* used, quite frequently and generally positively, in the texts he analyses (ibid.: 287).

Another important question, raised by Hunston (2007: 28, see also 2004), is how far evaluation (Hunston uses the term 'stance') can be retrieved by examining the immediate co-text of the supposedly evaluative words. She points to the deeper discourse role of evaluation, drawing on John Sinclair's corpus-based work (e.g. Sinclair 1991) to suggest that evaluation occurs as a result of phraseology along the lines of semantic prosodies (see Section 1.3.1.4 below), and is sometimes so subconscious that it is best analysed using corpus-based methods. One illustrative example is *Our situation is dramatic almost to the point of tragedy*. On its own, the evaluation contained in the word *dramatic* could be positive or negative. This context, however, has a strong negative colouring from the noun *tragedy* and also from the phrase *to the point of* which, as Hunston discusses with the help of corpus analysis, tends towards a negative prosody (*to the point of exhaustion, to the point of no return*, etc.). A 'rhetoric' of evaluation is created that is cumulative and to some extent intertextual, drawing on the values absorbed and radiated by lexical items and phrases (see also Bolívar 2001).

1.3.1.4 Provoked attitude

Whereas evokedness or evocation focuses on informational content, provocation 'trigger[s] positive/negative responses by means of formulations which are in other ways evaluative' (White 2006: 40). 'Provoked attitude' therefore lies between inscribed and evoked attitude, the latter termed 'invite' and sub-divided into 'flag' and 'afford' by Martin and White (2005: 67). The illustrative examples in Figure 1.3 are taken from texts about the Europeans' destruction of the world of the indigenous Australian peoples whom they encountered. In their original analysis,

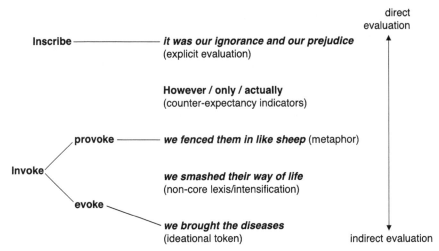

FIGURE 1.3 Strategies for inscribing and invoking attitude (adapted from Martin and White 2005: 67, and Martin and Thomson 2008)

Martin and White focus the attention of 'provoke' on lexical metaphor, such as *we fenced them in like sheep*. Lexical metaphor is said to 'provoke an attitudinal response in readers' (Martin and White 2005: 64). This category of evaluation is later extended (White and Thomson 2008: 11) to encompass counter-expectancy indicators and intensification through non-ncore lexis.[22]

Counter-expectancy indicators such as *however*, *actually* and *only two or three weeks* 'act to alert the reader that attitudinal values … are at stake' (Martin and White 2005: 67). The receiver still has to read off the values, but they are heavily guided by the choice of indicator – so, *only* clearly shows that the text producer views the period of time as short or shorter than expected and *however* counters an earlier argument. Counter-expectation is also a feature of engagement (see Section 1.3.3 below) since it is 'dialogically constrictive' (ibid.: 118) – while a position is stated and acknowledged, an indicator such as *however* then denies or rejects it.

Non-core lexis is described as 'somewhat less provocative, but still indicating that an evaluation is being invoked … [it] has in some sense lexicalised a circumstance of manner by infusing it into the core meaning of a word' (ibid.: 65). Thus, *break* would be a core term, while non-core words such as *crack, smash* and *demolish* indicate a variation in strength and, possibly, provoke an attitudinal response. This is likely in Figure 1.3 with the example *we smashed their way of life*, which would provoke indignation in the reader at the injustice of the treatment. In some cases, there may be a strong association between a non-core term and an attitudinal response: White (2006: 53) uses corpus evidence to suggest that this is generally the case with the verb *disrupt* and with negative judgements. Such analysis is closely linked to the phenomenon of semantic prosody (Louw 1993, Stewart 2009), also known as 'semantic association' (Hoey 2005).[23] This refers to how an otherwise neutral word may be evaluatively coloured by its habitual collocates. Stubbs (1996), for example, shows how the lemma *CAUSE* tends to take on negative connotations from collocates such as *cancer*. Intensification is also part of graduation (see Section 1.3.3. below). Such non-core **intensification** can be seen in the gradation of strength.

The broader presentation of provoke in Figure 1.3 has three advantages:

(i)   it slightly simplifies the taxonomy (by omitting the classificatory and termi-nological distinction between Martin and White's 'afford' and 'flag');

(ii)   it incorporates intensification and counter-expectancy into the overall scheme; and

(iii) it serves to emphasize the core point that there is a cline of evaluation running from the most direct/explicit (overt inscription) to the most indirect/implicit (factual token) (White 2006; see also Bednarek 2006: 46).

The demands placed on the reader vary accordingly. Overt inscription, being the most direct, requires less processing effort from the reader. Indirect evaluation through evocation theoretically demands most effort. Importantly, of course, this difference is also reflected in the demands placed on the translator as reader, and interpreter, of evaluation in the ST.

1.3.2 Studies of attitude in translation

While the general terms 'attitude' and 'intervention' are both areas of inquiry in translation studies (see Maher 2010), the technical resources of appraisal theory have been applied on very few occasions and almost always restricted to the analysis of attitude. Abbamonte and Cavaliere (2006) present an interesting appraisal-inspired analysis of the Italian translation of a UNICEF report, *The State of the World's Children – 2004*. Their close textual analysis claims a loss of intensity of affect and a move to implicitation of attitude through paraphrase, generalization and omission, almost all of which are affect-related. These include two metaphors: *the fruits of economic growth* > *la crescita economica* ('economic growth') and *the price of losing* > *perdere* ('to lose'). The English ST is described as more committed and passionate, the Italian TT more formal, neutral. A degree of distancing is noted, in what Martin and White would term 'engagement' (see Section 1.3.3). These are interesting initial findings, but some of the analysis is limited in its use of the appraisal model. Thus, an example given is *ensuring that all girls are educated*, translated as *il problema dell'istruzione femminile* ('the problem of female education') and *poverty's role* as *il problema della povertà* ('the problem of poverty'). The use of the noun *problema* ('problem') intensifies what is a challenge for the international community and there is even a suggestion in the TT that tackling it is a waste of money: *it is **not enough** to allocate financial resources* is translated as *può essere **inutile** destinare risorse finanziarie* ('it may be **useless** to dedicate financial resources'). The authors suggest a possible political bias in the TT but acknowledge 'an alternative hypothesis could be that the translator opted for a reader-oriented interpretative path, negotiating with his potential recipients a "refracted" text, nearer to what he might have imagined to be their expectations'.

While Abbamonte and Cavaliere start from the terms of appraisal theory but really employ a more general descriptive translation studies model, the work of Zhang ([2002] 2011) and Zhang and Qian (2009) conforms much more closely to the framework of attitude. Zhang ([2002] 2011) analyses attitude in isolated examples of English > Chinese translation. A fascinating example she provides is from W.M. Thackeray's novel *Vanity Fair* (originally published 1848) and its 1957 translation by Yang Bi:

> **ST** . . . yet, as it sometimes happens that a person departs his life, who is really deserving of the praises the stone-cutter carves over his bones; who is a *good* Christian, a *good* parent, child, wife or husband; who actually does have a disconsolate family to mourn his loss;
>
> **TT** 不过偶尔也有几个死人当得起石匠刻在他们朽骨上的好话。真的是**虔诚的**教，**慈爱**的父母，**孝顺的**儿女，**贤良的**妻子，**尽职的**丈夫，他们家里的人也的确哀思绵绵的追悼他们
>
> (Literal translation '. . . yet, as it sometimes happens that a person departs his life, who is really deserving of the praises the stone-cutter carves over his bones; who is a **devout** Christian, a **loving** parent, an **obedient** child, a **virtuous** wife or a **responsible** husband; who actually does have a disconsolate family to mourn his loss')

In the ST the word *good* shows an ethical value of judgement. In the Chinese TT, this is explicated and reveals the subjectivity of the translator, perhaps working to the expectations of the target culture: *good Christian* becomes 'devout', *a good parent* is 'loving', the child is 'obedient', the wife 'virtuous' and the husband 'responsible'. This adaptation of values to meet cultural expectations can also be clearly seen in Zhang and Qian (2009), who analyse the translation of six advertisements according to attitude. One striking example is for Boss perfume:

> Boss for man
>
> Launched in 1986, Boss is a distinctly **masculine** fragrance that combines citrus and tangy apple with woody tones of sandalwood.
>
> 这款香水的设计灵感源自于1986年同名的男装品牌。Boss成功表达男人的自信与品味，前味由香柠檬、柑橘、蜂蜜组成，中味含有胡荽、琥珀及苔藓，后味由檀香、皮革与雪松组合而成。气味清新而充满男人的简洁与自信。
>
> ('The design inspiration of this perfume originates from the 1986 man suit of the same brand. Boss's success lies in its expression of man's confidence and taste. The top note comprises bergamot, orange and honey; the middle note consists of coriander, amber and moss and the base note includes sandalwood, further and cedar. The smell is fresh and full of man's uncomplicated style and confidence.')

Here, the quality of appreciation expressed in the word *masculine* in the English is highly culture-specific. The Chinese adapts the ad with a large degree of explicitation focused on many different qualities. Four of these are forms of judgement, specifically of capacity or tenacity: 成功 ('success'), 品味 ('taste'), 自信 ('confidence', which occurs twice); and two of appreciation: 清新 ('fresh' – of the fragrance) and 简洁 ('uncomplicated' – of the man). The result is a cultural rewriting of attitude in the ad to create a new interpretation in the Chinese.

Such preliminary work on appraisal theory in translation studies has therefore centred on very specific examples of attitude from quite narrowly defined Registers and genres. These are notably taken from literature and advertising. A further example of the the latter includes Qian's analysis of bilingual public notices in Macau, which shows that Chinese sometimes uses declarative sentences to reflect the authority of the text producer instead of an English or Portuguese imperative (Qian 2007).

1.3.3 Graduation and engagement

Although so far the focus has been very much on what Martin and White call 'attitude', it is important to be aware that the whole discourse semantic system of appraisal integrates the other domains of graduation and engagement (see Introduction and Table 1.2 above).

Graduation (described in Martin and White 2005: 135–54) can vary in '**force**', based on intensity (e.g. ***extremely*** *unwise*, ***great*** *pleasure*, ***increasingly*** *distant*) or '**focus**', based on prototypicality (e.g. *a **true** gentleman, an apology **of sorts***). These 'soften' or 'sharpen' the amount of evaluation, decreasing or increasing the intensity (see also Labov 1984). As discussed in the previous section, the use of **non-core lexis** is also a form of **intensification** and is a significant component of evoked attitude. Fairclough (2003: 172) also makes the important point that the intensity of evaluation may tend to strengthen through the clustering in semantic sets of evaluative adjectives, adverbs and mental process verbs. For example, *I love this book*; *this book is fantastic*; *it is beautifully written*.

Engagement (Martin 1992, Martin and White 2005) is 'a cover-all term for resources of intersubjective positioning' (White 2003b: 260); that is, the stance adopted by the text producer to a phenomenon or object and the relative position the producer allows to the text receiver. As we saw in the Introduction, engagement draws on the Bakhtinian concept of 'dialogism' (Martin 2004b: 276), as expounded by Volosinov (1929 [1973], see White 2002, 2003b). It is important to note that dialogism is not restricted to face-to-face communication between speaker and receiver. Any verbal text, spoken or written, is a communicative 'performance' that can 'expand' or 'constrict'. '**Monogloss**' constricts response, for example, with categorical assertions (which assume shared values; White 2003b: 263) or reporting verbs (e.g. *demonstrate, show*; see Introduction) that do not allow for easy disagreement. '**Heterogloss**' is 'dialogically expansive' by acknowledging the possibility of alternative viewpoints, responses and/or truth values (e.g. the reporting verb *claim*, modal particles such as *almost, nearly*, and modal adjuncts and auxiliaries – *possibly, should*) (Martin

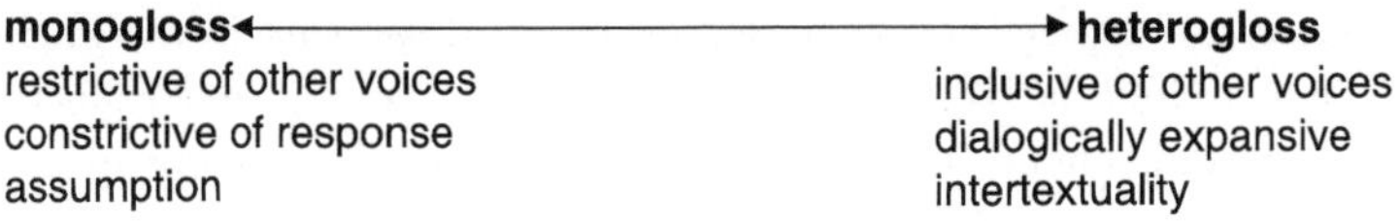

monogloss ←————————————————————————→ **heterogloss**
restrictive of other voices   inclusive of other voices
constrictive of response   dialogically expansive
assumption   intertextuality

FIGURE 1.4 Cline of dialogism

and White 2005: 97–104). These are resources for establishing the relationship and alignment of solidarity between writer and reader (ibid.: 95) and they link to work on 'deictic positioning' (Chilton 2004), which we shall discuss in Chapter 2.3.

The importance of writer–reader alignment is closely related to central questions of status and power in discourse (White 2003b, see Figure 1.2 above). These include the location of the power wielded in communicative processes and what markers are used by the author to manipulate the argument/representation of the world. White goes beyond modality (see Section 1.2 above) to examine a panoply of lexical and discoursal features such as quotation, rhetorical questions, reporting verbs, adverbials and conjunctions, and counter-expectancy indicators. He argues that the crucial function of such devices is rhetorical, in expanding or contracting the room for response.[24] In this, a kind of 'scale of dialogicality' is performed where the most dialogical option is to include other voices through direct quotation (intertextuality) and the least dialogical option is assumption and categorical statement (Fairclough 2003: 61). This may be expressed as in Figure 1.4.

Two important additional points need to be made. One is the relation to and dependence on reader response. The writer may try to position the reader but the response cannot be totally controlled (see Section 1.6 below). The second is the question as to what happens in a communication where an additional agent (such as a translator or interpreter) enters the process. This is the crux of the current investigation.

1.4 Evaluation as an integrated complex

It is important to remember that these various elements of the appraisal system (attitude, graduation and engagement) are said to operate not individually but in conjunction, 'as elements in integrated complexes of meaning' (Martin and White 2005: 159) with an overall rhetorical purpose (Hunston 2007). So, for example, a very evaluative text that seeks to convince the reader of what is the writer's opinion, such as the *Miniguide to London* discussed in Section 1.3.1.1, may adopt a monoglossic, categorical style with 'upscaled' attitudinal evaluation (the obvious inscribed evaluative epithets) together with intensification through force, insisting lexicogrammatically in a fashion that resembles shouting in phonological terms (ibid.: 227). In political texts, this kind of rhetoric may be particularly significant. Take the following example, from Barack Obama's inaugural speech of 2009:

> Obama inaugural speech (see Appendix 2.1, p. 80, lines 34–9)
> In reaffirming . . . the greatness of our nation . . . we understand that great-ness is never a given . . . It must be earned. Our journey has never been one of

short-cuts or settling for less . . . It has not been the path for the faint-hearted . . . for those that prefer leisure over work, or seek only the pleasures of riches and fame. Rather, it has been the risk-takers, the doers, the makers of things – some celebrated, but more often men and women obscure in their labor – who have carried us . . . up the long rugged path towards prosperity and freedom.

Evaluation is inscribed in the nouns *greatness* and *the faint-hearted* and in the epithet *celebrated*, invoked in the positive value of *obscure*. The modality of obligation of **must be earned** is an explicit statement of judgement. Modal adjuncts (**never** *a given;* **never** *. . . one of short-cuts; seek* **only** *the pleasures of riches and fame*) increase graduation. The many categorical assertions and the two counter-expectancy indicators (*rather . . .; but more often . . .*) restrict the reader's response. The rhythm of the triplet *the risk-takers, the doers, the makers of things* phonetically reinforces the positive evaluation of judgement and appreciation at a key point. Attitude is provoked by the metaphor of the JOURNEY extended through *short-cuts* and *the long rugged path towards prosperity and freedom*. Throughout, solidarity is produced by the repeated use of the pronouns *our* and *we*, combining attitude and engagement in an evaluative combination to convey ideological assumptions (see White 2002, Bednarek 2006: 58, 2008: 21).

Evaluation is thus multilayered. It also creates a prosody, with positive or negative values resonating in the surrounding text. Indeed, such resonance occurs over a whole text in a logogenetic process of 'cumulative repetition and reinforcement; it is not the individual choices which are important but the relationship of the choices to each other as they appear through the unfolding text' (Thompson 1998: 44). It may also include the status of a whole text (Hunston 2008: 71). Obama's inaugural speech (Chapter 2) is clearly of extremely high status. The religious texts discussed in the Introduction are perhaps some of the highest status, and most sensitive, texts of all. In such scenarios, evaluation of any type is potentially critical.

1.5 Evaluation, textual voice and evidentiality

In Section 1.3.2 we discussed the few studies that have begun to use appraisal theory for the analysis of translation, noting that there may be significant differences in the projection of attitude between Chinese and English cultures. Forms of interpersonal realization and interaction can vary enormously between languages. Maynard (1993: 4, in Finegan 1995: 7), discusses discourse modality in Japanese interactions and claims that 'when speaking Japanese, one simply cannot avoid expressing one's personal attitude toward the context of information and toward the addressee . . . [I]t is subtextual emotion-sharing that forms the heart of communication.' Genre and cultural differences also appear. McCabe (2004), analysing history textbooks in Spain and the US, notes the different functions of modality – in Spanish, modality tends to be used as a 'booster' (intensification) and as a means of negotiating the imparting of knowledge in a more formal, 'lecture-type' setting.

When appraisal theory has been applied to writing in non-English cultures, this has predominantly taken place in the study of the make-up of various journalistic genres. The volume *Communicating Conflict* (Thomson and White 2008), for example, includes chapters on news discourse in Argentina, Finland, France, Greece, Indonesia, Japan, Spain, Taiwan and Thailand. However, the main focus is not on translation or even the lexical variation of appraisal resources but on the overall textual 'voice'. Textual voice[25] means 'a particular pattern in the use and co-occurrence of evaluative meanings' (White and Thomson 2008: 13).[26] Research on English-language broadsheet newspapers has identified three journalistic voices (see Table 1.3).

It is important to note that this scheme of voices denotes an attitudinal value position but says nothing directly about the truth value of a proposition (White 2003b: 280). For instance, a journalist in writer-commentator voice may indicate an evaluation as to the competence or ethics of a politician based on a biased interpretation of reality. However, the translator and interpreter have to negotiate meaning from the ST based on their interpretation of 'communicative cues' (Gutt 2000), in engagement terms repositioning the ST author in relation to the new TT audience. In that context, the evaluation of the veracity of an argument is very important, since the translated or interpreted TT will stand for the ST and perform a communicative function in the target culture. In the Introduction we saw the crucial role played by monoglossic or heteroglossic reporting verbs (*show, indicate, suggest* . . .) in the Iraq dossier. To the experts, they projected an evaluation of Iraq's state of readiness for launching chemical and biological weapons; the translator/interpreter would need to be able to recognize those indicators and use that knowledge for disambiguation or for the selection from competing translation equivalents in order to avoid unintentionally distorting the message. Not for nothing did Newmark (in Schäffner 1999: 82) call translation 'a truth-seeking activity'.

Such analysis relates to the appraisal resource of engagement, but it also overlaps with the better-known concept of evidentiality (see Thompson and Hunston 2000: 3). Evidentiality is a linguistic category that concerns above all the source of information of a statement and this varies considerably across languages (Aikhenveld 2004).[27] In the seminal volume *Evidentiality: The linguistic coding of epistemology* (Chafe and Nichols 1986), Chafe (1986) reports on evidentiality in

TABLE 1.3 Journalistic voices in English-language broadsheet reporting (following Martin and White 2005: 164) and White and Thomson (2008: 13–14).

Reporter voice	*Writer-correspondent voice*	*Writer-commentator voice*
• little inscribed attitude except for some appreciation • use of direct quotation • preferred for reporting on major events	• some direct evaluation of judgement (capacity, tenacity, normality but not ethics) • some direct appreciation • preferred for general local and international news	• considerable use of inscribed authorial judgement, affect and appreciation • preferred for subjective genres, such as opinion pieces, commentaries and editorials

English, noting that what we would call the unmarked form is what users consider to be 'factual knowledge' (e.g. 'water is liquid'). Chafe describes how evidential marking may indicate a 'scale of reliability' (through the use of modals such as *maybe, might, may, probably, certainly*), belief/opinion (e.g. *I think*), hearsay (*they say*) and expectation (*in fact, of course*), amongst others. He also notes genre distinctions in use, contrasting academic writing with informal conversation. Other chapters in the same volume demonstrate cross-linguistic variation: for example, the Jaqi languages (Jaqaru, Kawki and Aymara), spoken by some three million people in the Bolivian and Peruvian Andes, marks according to whether a statement is made from personal knowledge, from knowledge through language or from non-personal knowledge. Martha Hardman's study of evidentiality in these languages concludes that 'data-source marking is so extensive in the Jaqi languages that it is difficult to utter ANY sentence without indicating the source of one's information' (Hardman 1986: 114). Hardman even suggests that the absence of such marking in Spanish disturbs communication with speakers of Jaqi languages. Non-Jaqi speakers may be unaware that their own categorical statements in Spanish may be distrusted because the source is not explicitly expressed. And the Jaqi are not isolated examples. Back in the 1960s, Eugene Nida was already noting how this caused difficulties for his Bible translation project: translation into languages which mark whether a person or alive or dead are confronted with the resurrected Jesus and with Lazarus, brought back from the dead. In most cases, according to Nida and Taber (1969: 117), translators chose the 'dead' affix for Jesus and the 'live' affix for Lazarus. Makihara and Schieffelin (2007: chapter 7) note similar questions in translations of biblical parables in Papua New Guinea.

1.6 Evaluation and reading positions

The interrelatedness of the various evaluative elements attests to the complexity of communication. In such a model, the role of the reader/receiver is vital. A text may project ideational and interpersonal meanings, but how are these received and responded to by the audience? Lemke (1989: 39), again following Bakhtin, sees that 'texts construct putative models of their addressees and of the discourse world of competing voices in which they are to be heard'. The readers are 'positioned' by the text (and, of course, by the text producer), but their reading position cannot be completely predetermined.[28] Readers may not be passive at all (Hyland 2005: 175, Bednarek 2006: 184). Macken-Horarik (2003a: 286) sees that narrative prose makes various demands on the reader and produces 'active responsive understanding' that may take value-laden forms at different levels. For instance, she perceives two fundamental elements of axiology demanded of a reader: (i) an intersubjective 'empathy' or understanding of a character; and (ii) a more external 'discernment' and evaluation of the character's moral values.

Attitude functions through the triggering of reactions in the reader. Martin and White (2005: 206) make the important point that invoked evaluation, by its implicitness or lack of specificity, plays a key role in 'facilitat[ing] if not encourag[ing]' a variety of reader response. It is a locus of negotiation of meaning, the reader having freedom of action. We saw in Sections 1.3.1.3 and 1.3.1.4 that invokedness relies on the reader's recognizing and reacting to signals that are sometimes very context-dependent. As White and Thomson put it:

> It is a feature of attitudinal invocations/tokens that they are typically conditioned by the co-text and will often be subject to the beliefs, attitudes and expectations the reader brings to their interpretation of the text (i.e. their reading position).
>
> *(White and Thomson 2008: 11)*

In other words, the attitudinal values read from the text depend to some extent on the reader's ideological and axiological orientation ('beliefs, attitudes and expectations'). For the reader, implicit evaluation may actually be more convincing than direct inscription because it allows opinion to masquerade as reporting, at least in scientific discourse (Hunston 1994: 193; see also Coffin 2002: 506). But then questions arise, such as how deep a reading needs to be located to be 'invoked' (Sarangi 2003: 168) and how shallow it needs to be to trigger a reaction. Not all readers will pick up on the evaluative triggers, even if the author has constructed a model reader with shared views (White 2003b: 75, following Eco 1984).

This phenomenon of reading and interpretation is what Martin and White (2005: 206) refer to as 'reaction'. It is obviously of special import for translation since the reading supplied by the translator will decide the formulation of the TT and thus strongly condition the reaction of the TT reader. Martin and White (ibid.) describe three overall types of reading, which are 'tactical', 'resistant' and 'compliant':[29]

> By a **tactical reading** we refer to a typically partial and interested reading which aims to deploy a text for social purposes other than those it has naturalized; **resistant readings** oppose the reading position naturalized by the co-selection of meanings in a text, while **compliant readings** subscribe to it.[30]

These readings may have little to do with the original purpose of the text. Thus, a tactical reading could be provided by a language theorist like myself who selects a text to analyze for a new purpose, and a resistant reading rejects the argumentation of the writer. Translation is clearly an example of a text that is produced for a new communicative purpose, or at least that is normally directed at an audience different from that envisaged by the source. It will therefore be at least partly tactical, since the translator's reading, and interpretation, will underpin the preparation and production of the target text. It will be predominantly 'resistant' if it seeks to overturn the ideology of the source, as with Ralph Mannheim's translations of Hitler's *Mein Kampf*, where footnotes were added to point out the illogicality of the ideas (see Hermans 2007) or the Fitzgerald adaptation of the Persian *Rubaiyat* (see below). It will most likely seek to be compliant if the translator's view of the task is to reproduce the source 'faithfully' no matter whether he/she is in agreement with the source or not.

This classification of reading types quite closely matches the well-known interpretive categories proposed by Stuart Hall in his theory of mass communication (e.g. Hall [1980] 1999). This theory was originally conceived for the understanding of television and its reception by its audiences, but has had important influence on other forms of cultural transfer and is pertinent for translation. Hall incorporates four 'relatively autonomous' stages (production, circulation, use and reproduction) in which the 'moments' of 'encoding' and 'decoding' of the message are 'determinate' for the cultural life of the discursive message.[31] For Hall ([1980] 1999: 510–11), encoding and decoding are dynamic and are conditioned by the sociocultural context and relative power of the participants. Following Eco and Barthes, within this scheme it is the referential meaning and denotative level that tend to be more stable, while the less fixed associative meaning and connotative level are more open to ideological interpretation, between individuals and cross-culturally. This matches White and Thomson's observations about invokedness and will be a crucial area to investigate in the context of translation.

In Hall's conception of the semiotic system, there are 'dominant' orders and codings that are supported by institutions (cultural, political, legal, educational, workplace . . .). These institutions, through their position of power and the force of habituation, cultivate 'preferred readings' of the codes. This is particularly visible in political commentary and news. Nevertheless, the receiver (Hall's television audience or our translation reader and interpreting listener) has an active, 'transformative' role to play in interpreting the code, and Hall (ibid.: 515–17) posits three possible positions:

1. The **dominant-hegemonic position**, where the receiver adopts the denotative and connotative reading and the ideology presented by the dominant encoder and where discourse seems to operate 'transparently', 'naturally' and 'legitimately'. Here, the receiver is said to be operating 'within the dominant code'.
2. The **negotiated position**, where the receiver may accept the reasoning behind the dominant position and the codes it signifies, but where he/she is also aware of its contradictions and may not follow that dominant reading. Hall gives the example of a worker who accepts the dominant, governmental message of wage freezes but still goes on strike for better pay.
3. The **oppositional position**, where the receiver deliberately reads the message contrary to the dominant position or otherwise resists it. Hall gives the example of a viewer who reads the politician's statement of 'national interest' as really meaning 'class interest' (i.e. the viewer deconstructs the underlying ideology that attempts to naturalize a politically biased dominant position).

The dominant-hegemonic position corresponds to Martin and White's compliant reading, the negotiated to tactical reading, and the oppositional to resistant reading.

The ST author may have in mind an 'idealized reader' (Eco 1984) or 'preferred reading' (Morley 1980, 1992), but, in the context of translation, where at the micro-level of individual lexical choice the translator or interpreter interposes between author and reader and is constantly to-ing and fro-ing between languages, the three reading categories are unlikely to remain fixed. Even if a general translation strategy is consciously adopted, perhaps prompted by an macro-level narrative representation of an event (see Baker 2006), there persists constant heteroglossia within the translator, who is faced with micro-level linguistic challenges at every juncture and who projects a new reading position on to the TT audience. How exactly this is operationalized in translation is itself a critical point.

1.7 Evaluation and 'critical points' in translator and interpreter decision-making

As Lemke (1998) says, evaluation is the critical function of language. It positions the writer and the reader, interfacing between ideology and axiology, the 'factual' world and the inner world of subjective and individual value. It represents and helps to constitute both the view of that world and the self-identity of the writer (Lemke 1998, Fairclough 2003: 164). When a new version of a text is produced for a new cultural context, when a translator or interpreter intervenes, the basis of evaluation also shifts. In extreme cases, when the cross-linguistic or cross-cultural differences are major, or where the purpose or function of the translation is very different from the ST, this may affect many points in a text. Modification of the ideational, 'factual' information in a text, or the story level in narrative, could take us into the realm of adaptation, which may be more frequent and even acceptable for target-oriented versions of fairy tales but it may also occur in contexts of heavy cultural manipulation or political censorship (Billiani 2007). Some of the classic examples quoted in translation studies refer to these: in the British Victorian era, for example, where target culture values were deemed to be superior, Edward Fitzgerald's enormously influential translation of *The Rubaiyat of Omar Khayyām* (1859) completely reworked and rearranged the Persian ST; similarly, Richard Burton's ten-volume *A Plain and Literal Translation of the Arabian Nights' Entertainments* (1886–88)[32] contained large numbers of idiosyncratic footnotes with linguistic and cultural perspectives, as well as a defence of his translation, a lengthy 'Terminal essay', index and bibliography.

The study of such works makes for fascinating insights into the culture of translation. However, such translation strategies would likely cause the modern-day translator immediate trouble if applied to other genres and situations, such as the translation of a product manual, if the goal is for the information to allow the user to work the product successfully, or the interpreting of a political speech. What seems to me a more pervasive question, more pressing for the understanding of the micro-level process of translation or interpreting, is the uncovering of values inserted into the text by the translator, perhaps surreptitiously and not consciously. Appraisal theory provides a possible model for the recognition and analysis of the lexical signals and realizations of value insertion. In parallel, my interest is in the identification of those points and lexical features in a text that in translation are most susceptible to value manipulation; those points that most frequently show a shift in translation, and those that generate the most interpretative and evaluative potential; those that may be most revealing of the translator's values. I term these points 'value-rich' and, where there exists the possibility that they will affect the reception of the text, 'sensitive' or 'critical'. So, as we saw in the Introduction and in Section 1.3.1.3, ideationally the phenomenon of naming is critical: to choose *Derry* or *Londonderry* (see Baker 2006), *America* or *United States* (see Gentzler 2006), *Montreal* or *Montréal* (see Mossop 2007) or, in religious texts, the very name of a deity, is likely to be strongly indicative of the writer's (and translator's) ideological positioning in relation to the political and historical identity that is projected. The US action towards Cuba from 1960 onwards is a good example: the trade ban is called *embargo* by the US and its supporters and *bloqueo* ('blockade') by Cuba and those opposed to it. In a different political context, Sánchez (2007) has shown how ideologically sensitive categories of gender terms are discursively reworked between French and Spanish. Critical points would also include more subtle and potentially less conscious choices, involving the recognition and reproduction of invoked attitude that may be culturally located (e.g. *Victorian arcades, cobbled streets* in the London text in Section 1.3.1.1 above). The following chapters present case studies of different forms of translation in an attempt to shed further light on such critical points.

2

THE INTERPRETATION OF POLITICAL SPEECH

2.0 Introduction

In this chapter the model of analysis drawn from appraisal theory will be applied to a key political event, US President Barack Obama's inauguration speech given on 20 January 2009 in Washington, DC. The inaugural was broadcast live across the world, with live interpreting into the local languages, and reproduced verbatim and in translation in the print and online media.[1] The high profile of the English original of the speech is in stark contrast to the common practice of the 'invisibility' of the translator of political texts (Bielsa and Bassnett 2008, Schäffner 2008). Indeed, the wealth of interpretings and translations in so many different languages provides an unusual opportunity to analyse the strategies adopted in the construction of the TTs. The speech furthermore lends itself well to exemplify appraisal analysis specifically because of the inherently evaluative and ethical tone.

2.1 The broadcast context

Because of the huge interest in the new president, many countries broadcast the speech live on TV, cable, satellite and/or the internet, followed by detailed reporting in the print and online media. Nevertheless, some countries restricted the speech by censorship, in various forms. In some cases censorship meant that it was not broadcast at all, as apparently happened in North Korea, except for the briefest of mentions on the news agency KCNA (BBC Monitoring 2009). Or it meant broadcasting edited excerpts, allowing controlled reframing and 'recontextualization' (Fairclough 2003: 139–41, Kang 2007, also Chapter 1, Section 1.2.1) in studio discussion with domestic commentators. This seems to have occurred in Iran, Afghanistan and Russia, amongst others. In addition to the intrusive editing process, the relative weighting of the story compared to other events is itself an indication of the perceived importance of Obama's speech. Thus, in Afghanistan more prominence was given to the opening of the Afghan parliament, while in Russia focus was on President Medvedev's visit to Ingushetia, suggesting Russia's lack of interest in Obama (BBC Monitoring 2009). Of course, lack of interest may be feigned or such moves may be designed to hide the story – in Burma it was claimed that the government ordered the Rangoon weekly *The Voice* to shift coverage of the speech from the front page to the inside pages (Lwin 2009). By contrast, in South Korea the Obama story shared front page with news of a fatal fire in Seoul.

China was a complex, and polemical, case. The speech was broadcast live on state-controlled Chinese Central Television with simultaneous interpreting, but the live broadcast was ended immediately after Obama uttered the phrase 'Recall that earlier generations faced down communism and fascism . . .' (Bristow 2009). The programme cut to the studio where the presenter, caught off guard, had to hastily engage another journalist with a question about how Obama would tackle the economic crisis.[2] The *People's Daily* and the Xinhua, Sina, Sohu and Netease websites also omitted the word *communism* from the translations they posted. In addition, the following passage was omitted from the associated written transcripts:

> *To those who cling to power through corruption and deceit and the silencing of dissent, know that you are on the wrong side of history; but that we will extend a hand if you are willing to unclench your fist* (ST 118).[3]

Even though the section of the speech was specifically directed at 'Muslim countries', it seemed to strike at the Chinese state's sensitivity to perceived criticisms of corruption and 'silencing of dissent'.[4] Very few[5] actually noted that this is in fact an intertextual reference to a speech by US President Clinton on the visit of Chinese premier Jiang Zemin to Washington on 11 June 1998.[6] The allusion is therefore much more specific than might at first seem to be the case, and directed at China. The dialogic 'voices' (see Chapter 1, Sections 1.0 and 1.3.3) that are thus triggered by the reference may only be retrievable by a small number of listeners, but amongst those were the main target audience – the Chinese authorities. This is part of the appraisal resource of engagement, discussed in Section 2.2.8 below.

The reporting across Chinese media was varied. In Hong Kong, the whole speech was broadcast on Hong Kong-based Phoenix TV. The full transcript of the speech in English was included in the *China Daily*, the largest circulation English-language newspaper in China, which targets a foreign audience that will also have been able to understand the original speech. The complete transcript remains on the *China Daily* website at the time of writing.[7] The timing of the speech (12.00 EST) meant that the broadcast went out in the middle of the night in China with an inevitably reduced audience. However, in the era of the internet China's rather clumsy attempts to elude Obama's critical comments only served to highlight the censorship process. Thus, the clip from CCTV was posted by the monitoring organization Danwei[8] and on YouTube[9] and the story was reported prominently worldwide, reinforcing the image of the Chinese state as being overly controlling of their media.[10]

These forms of attempted censorship are fascinating in themselves, particularly as the internet and social media now have the power to permeate previously hermetic societies and potentially destabilize the political landscape (Dahlgren 2005). For some states, the answer is to attempt to control the availability of the new technology, either by restricting home use or by censoring access to what are deemed to be undesirable websites, as has also happened in China, for instance, where the Google search engine was famously restricted.[11]

2.2 The expression of appraisal

A more subtle and central interest for the book is where translation is permitted but where there may be a shift in the value systems expressed in the TT because of cross-cultural differences, deliberate textual manipulation, degree of competence or some other form of translator preference. Such value shifts are complex because of their axiological underpinnings and because they may be expressed by subtle linguistic markers. In order to better understand how value is constructed and translated, the rest of this chapter will analyse in detail the linguistic indication of value through the realization of appraisal in Obama's inauguration speech[12] and in examples of simultaneous media interpretation and print translation of that inaugural. The analysis will take advantage of the rare circumstance that there exist multiple simultaneous interpretings of the speech in the same language. In particular, I shall look closely at those broadcast live in Spanish on major US-based networks CNN en Español (TT1) and Telemundo (TT2) and on the Peruvian Canal N (TT3).[13]

Obama's speech followed his swearing of the presidential oath. It consciously conformed to the conventions of the genre; Obama made known to Jon Favreau, his 27-year-old main speechwriter, that his favourite inaugurals were Lincoln's Second ('With malice toward none') and Kennedy's ('Ask not what your country can do for you . . .') (Alter 2010: 106). The process of planning, and writing, the speech is described as follows:

> Obama's approach to speechwriting was to begin the process by speaking aloud at length, while Favreau or others took notes.[14] He told Favreau that he thought the best Inaugurals describe clearly for Americans 'the moment we're in, how we got there, and the best way out. [They] anchor themselves in that moment' . . .
>
> Favreau worked on a couple of drafts on his laptop at Starbucks, with help from Ben Rhodes and, for the big George Washington ending, Adam Frankel and Sarah Hurwitz . . . Over the weekend of January 10–11 Obama holed up in the Hay-Adams hotel, where he rewrote more than half of the text. The speech was intended to be sober and restrained, not a barn burner.
>
> *(Alter 2010: 106)*

Importantly, also, it should be noted that the speech was released to some media outlets in advance of delivery (Dougherty 2009). This not only facilitated media coverage of the event, including the broadcast of closed caption intralingual subtitling, but in addition opens up the distinct possibility that some of the simultaneous interpreters were working from a written copy of the speech. On the day itself, Obama used a teleprompter (Alter 2010: 271).

When it comes to the overall patterns of attitude, the most striking features are the high level of direct inscription, the large number of abstract nouns and the extreme propensity towards positive realizations of capacity and tenacity (both part of social esteem) and propriety (social sanction). The evaluative profile may in some ways be unusual for the language as a whole, though possibly not for the specific genre, since it varies from the stereotypical realization of attitude is through epithets (Martin and White 2005: 58). I shall first describe the general picture of realizations in the ST before moving on to discuss the ways these were interpreted into Spanish on the day.

2.2.1 Affect

Table 2.1 displays expressions of affect in the ST. Invoked/provoked attitude is indicated by shading. Numbers are line numbers in the transcript in Appendix 2.1.

TABLE 2.1 The realization of affect in the Obama inaugural

Affect

+security

the trust you have bestowed (03), *prosperity* (07), *peace* (07), *hope over fear* (26), *unity of purpose* (26), *surest route to our common good* (81), *our common defense* (82), *our safety* (82), *friend of each nation* (89), *peace* (89), *our security emanates* (94), *forge a hard-earned peace* (99), *lessen the nuclear threat* (100), *our confidence* (147), *hope* (159), *hope* (163), *delivered it safely* (167)

−security

gathering clouds (08), *raging storms* (08), *crisis* (13), *at war* (13), *violence and hatred* (14), *jobs shed* (16), *businesses shuttered* (17), *threaten our planet* (19), *sapping of confidence* (21), *nagging fear* (21), *perils* (83), *new threats* (97), *specter of a warming planet* (100), *terror* (102), *slaughtering innocents* (102), *sow conflict* (113), *uncertain destiny* (148), *when our revolution was most in doubt* (157), *alarmed [city]* (160), *one common danger* (160), *common dangers* (162)

+happiness

full measure of happiness (33), *duties we seize gladly* (144–5)

−happiness

petty grievances (27)

+inclination

we intend to move forward (70), *willing heart* (80), *we are ready to lead* (90), *willing to unclench your fist* (118), *willingness to find meaning* (129), *willingness to nurture a child* (137), *not grudgingly* (144), *seize gladly* (145)

(continued)

TABLE 2.1 The realization of affect in the Obama inaugural *(continued)*

–inclination
indifference to suffering (121)

+satisfaction
grateful (02), *not grudgingly* (144), *satisfying to the spirit* (145)

–satisfaction
starved bodies . . . hungry minds (120)

At the very beginning, speaking in the first person singular, Obama reveals his personal feelings: *I stand here today . . .* **humbled** *by the task before us . . .* **grateful** *for the trust . . .* (02). Both epithets, *humbled* and *grateful*, index judgement (+propriety), but they are also examples of so-called 'hybrids' in that they also inscribe affect. Such hybrids 'construe an emotional reaction to behaviour we approve or disapprove of' (Martin and White 2005: 60) and are 'affectual inscriptions invoking judgement' (ibid.: 68). Other such examples given by Martin and White are *guilty, embarrassed, proud, envious, ashamed, resentful, contemptuous.*

There are surprisingly few instances of happiness or satisfaction in the speech, perhaps because of the deliberately 'sober and restrained' tone and the absence of 'feel-good sentiment' in a time of crisis (Alter 2010: 273). It is security that is a key theme of the speech and which dominates the affect category. This is especially so in the early section (lines 08 and 13–22) where the cluster of items inscribing negative security (*crisis, war, violence and hatred . . .*) sets out the rhetorical 'problem', the *challenges we face* (23). Later clusters relate to threats from terrorists and foreign states (101–15) and to the dangers overcome in the War of Independence by the patriots under the command of George Washington. Their example is used to spur on the American people (154–61). Positive affect centres on the increased security (*peace, hope, safety*) resulting from the removal of threats and the positive intentions of government (*we intend to move forward*), nation (*we are ready to lead again*), people (*duties that we . . . seize gladly*), the military (*willingness to find meaning in something greater than themselves*) and even of previous enemies (*willing to unclench your fist*).

The Spanish simultaneous interpreting of affect shows that generally these are maintained, with the notable exception of TT3, where the journalist-interpreter's struggle with the task leads her to omit many of the references: in +security alone these omissions amount to *trust you have bestowed* (03), *purpose* (26), *surest route to our common good* (81), *our common defense* (82), *our security emanates* (94), *lessen the nuclear threat* (100), *hope* (159). The other two interpreters are not immune to omission, but it occurs only sporadically in their work. Thus, TT2 also omits mention of the nuclear threat in a repair strategy that allows the interpreter to catch up with the speaker.

For some terms of negative security, there is no variation at all and each is translated by the most obvious translation equivalent: thus, *crisis* (13), *war* (13) and *violence* (14) are in all cases translated by *crisis, guerra* and *violencia*. At this stage, we might hypothesize that such basic words form an evaluative core that is most likely to be realized uniformly.[15]

Surprisingly, two references that might be thought of as critical (the address to *those who seek to advance their aims by inducing* **terror** *and* **slaughtering innocents** [101–2]) are actually omitted by TT1 and partly omitted by TT3. This is perhaps because of the speed of delivery at that point, when the interpreters were reaching a limit of their processing capacity. Even TT2 tones down *slaughtering* to *matando* ('killing'). By comparison, the written translation in the Madrid daily *El País*, which was also posted on the White House blog,[16] uses *asesinando*, a slightly stronger verb.

Variation in intensity of evaluation (graduation) is indeed important. This trend occurs in two phenomena. The first is the omission of epithets that index or modify negative security: **raging** *storms* (08), **nagging** *fear* (21), **new** *threats* (97) and *when . . . our revolution was* **most** *in doubt* (156–7) are omitted by all three interpreters; **uncertain** *destiny* (148) and **alarmed** *[city]* (160) are omitted by TT1; **common** *dangers* (162) is rendered as 'shared' (*compartidos*, TT1), 'common' (*comunes*, TT2) and 'same' (*mismos*, TT3). The second is a toning down of affect evoked in the ST through non-core lexis and metaphor (see Chapter 1, Figure 1.3). In this regard, the triplet *homes have been <u>lost</u>, jobs <u>shed</u>, businesses <u>shuttered</u>* (16–17) poses a problem for the interpreter/translator. The three verbs function in a similar fashion (to indicate loss or closure), with *shed* and *shuttered* being non-core items that provide intensification through their semantic strength and alliteration. The various interpretings are shown in Table 2.2, together with the *El País*/White House blog written translation (TT4).

TT1 uses a single, pronominal instance of the verb *perder* ('to lose') for all three verbs; TT2 does the same for the first two, but interestingly uses an alternative non-core TL item *tambalearse* ('to wobble') for the businesses; TT3 omits *jobs* and uses the basic verb *cerrar* ('close') for the businesses. With the extra time at her disposal, the translator of written TT4 manages to find three different verbs but nevertheless still tones down the translation of *shuttered* (*cerrado*, 'closed') and loses the aural impact of the alliteration. The standardization of non-core lexis seems

TABLE 2.2 Translation of non-core lexical items *shed* and *shuttered* in Spanish TTs

	homes have been lost	*jobs shed*	*businesses shuttered*
TT1	*se han perdido hogares* [have been lost homes]	*empleos* [jobs]	*negocios* [businesses]
TT2	*se han perdido hogares* [have been lost homes]	*empleos* [jobs]	*los negocios se han tambaleado* [businesses have wobbled]
TT3	*hogares se han perdido* [have been lost homes]		*empresas se han cerrado* [businesses have closed]
TT4 (written)	*se han perdido casas* [have been lost houses]	*se han eliminado empleos* [jobs have been eliminated]	*se han cerrado empresas* [businesses have closed]

to be a general trend in the interpreting texts. To give just one further example, when the ST speaks of a *sapping of confidence . . . across our land* (21), the TTs render this with *falta de confianza* ('lack of confidence', TT1, TT2) and *pérdida de confianza* ('loss of confidence', TT3). TT4 again projects an alternative, the much stronger *destrucción de la confianza* ('destruction of confidence').

2.2.2 Judgement

The amount of judgement evaluation is much higher than for either affect or appreciation. This may well be genre-specific to this kind of presidential address but also to the expression of political vision in general (Charteris-Black 2007: 219). The detailed classification of lexical indicators below shows clearly that positive values again dominate and that capacity, tenacity (values of social esteem) and propriety (social sanction) are central. This links to the key message of the speech, of the need for individuals and the American people as a whole to fulfil their duty to work together to help the nation emerge from the crisis. Reports indeed indicate that this theme was consciously constructed by Jon Favreau and the speechwriting team (Pilkington 2009, Alter 2010: 107). Table 2.3 presents the examples of the social esteem element of judgement.

The text oozes positive capacity and tenacity, indicators of institutionally recognized social esteem. The message, in its most explicit form, is that *our capacity remains undiminished* (50) and that tenacity, or *our enduring spirit* (30), has and always will be the quality that sees America through.[17] It is on these values that the American nation has been built or, as Obama puts it in the most attitudinally saturated moment:

> *those values upon which our success depends – honesty . . . and hard work, courage and fair play, tolerance and curiosity, loyalty and patriotism – . . .* (139–41).

TABLE 2.3 Judgement – social esteem indicators in the Obama inaugural

Social esteem

+normality
celebrated (38), *new* (11 instances)

−normality
inevitable . . . decline (22), *obscure in their labor* (37–8)

+capacity
skill (09), *vision* (09), *the risk-takers, the doers, the makers of things* (37–8), *bigger . . . greater [America]* (45–6), *most . . . prosperous, powerful nation on Earth* (47–8), *no less productive* (48), *no less inventive* (48–9), *our capacity remains undiminished* (50), *swift [action]* (55), *wield technology's wonders* (57–8), *harness [sun, winds, soil]* (58–9), *transform our schools . . .* (59–60), *the scale of our ambitions* (62), *imagination* (65), *power to generate wealth and expand freedom* (75–6), *success [of our economy]* (78), *reach [of prosperity]* (79), *ability [to extend*

opportunity] (80), *faced down [fascism and communism]* (91), *our power [alone/grows]* (93–4), *force [of our example]* (95), *roll back [the specter]* (100), *our spirit is stronger and cannot be broken* (103), *stronger and more united* (108–9), *farms flourish* (119), *curiosity* (140), *quiet force of progress* (141)

−capacity

far-reaching network . . . of violence and hatred (13–14), *our collective failure* (15), *our schools fail too many* (17), *strengthen our adversaries* (18), *America's decline* (21–2), *worn-out dogmas* (28), *have strangled our politics* (28–9), *standing pat* (50), *society's ills* (114), *small band of patriots* (154), *dying campfires* (155)

+tenacity

sacrifices (03), *faithful to the ideas of our forebears* (10), *true to our founding documents* (10–11), *enduring spirit* (30), *long, rugged path* (39), *few worldly possessions* (40), *toiled in sweatshops* (41), *endured the lash of the whip* (41–2), *plowed the hard earth* (42), *fought and died* (42), *struggled and sacrificed and worked till their hands were raw* (44–5), *bold [action]* (55), *common purpose, necessity, courage* (65), *[the market is] a force* (75), *blood of generations* (85), *a friend of each nation* (89), *sturdy alliances* (92), *enduring convictions* (92), *greater effort* (97), *forge a hard-earned peace* (99), *work tirelessly* (99–100), *brave Americans* (125), *heroes* (126), *determination* (133), *courage* (136), *hard work, courage* (139–40), *giving our all* (146), *difficult task* (146), *coldest of months* (154), *small band of patriots* (154), *dying campfires . . . icy river* (155), *brave . . . the icy currents* (163–4), *endure . . . storms* (164), *tested* (165), *refused to let this journey end* (165), *did not turn back nor . . . falter* (165–6), *eyes fixed on the horizon* (166)

−tenacity

the faint-hearted . . . those who prefer leisure over work . . . seek only the pleasures of riches and fame (36–7), *without a watchful eye* (77), *[market] spin out of control* (77)

There are also several examples of invoked evaluation, ranging from the graphic *expanded by the blood of generations* to the subtler, non-core verbs that invoke capacity (*wield, harness, faced down*) and to the depiction of harsh circumstances that demanded a tenacious response (*long rugged path, difficult task, coldest of months, dying campfires, icy river*). By contrast, the small number of examples of negative values are associated with foreign enemies (*far-reaching network . . .*), those working against the national interest (*the faint-hearted . . .*) or institutions that have failed (*our schools fail too many*; *worn-out dogmas that . . . have strangled our politics*).

Table 2.4 lists the indicators of social sanction, ordered according to the values of veracity and propriety. Positive veracity and propriety, which dominate, are clearly values that politicians wish to highlight, since they project an ethical vision of truthfulness, responsibility and morality. Obama does this throughout and links the vision to *old* and *true* values that have been passed down by the patriots and founders of the nation and which bind the American people together (128–41). Negative values are again attributed to the foreign enemy (*a far-reaching network . . . of violence and hatred*; *those who cling to power through corruption and deceit and the silencing of dissent*) and to attitudes that have corrupted or distorted at home. These are realized by abstract nouns which avoid naming of the specific actors (*greed and*

TABLE 2.4 Judgement – social sanction indicators in the Obama inaugural

---

Social sanction

+veracity

faithful to the ideals of our forebears (10), *true to our founding documents* (10–11), *rightful place* (57), *enduring convictions* (92), *pledge* (119), *honesty* (139), *loyalty and patriotism* (140), *true [things/ values]* (140–1), *return . . . to these truths* (142), *most sacred oath* (152), *timeless words* (163)

−veracity

false promises (28), *false [choice]* (82), *deceit* (116)

+propriety

humbled (02), *grateful* (02), *service* (04), *generosity* (04), *cooperation* (05), *hard choices* (16), *noble idea* (31), *God-given promise* (32), *struggled and sacrificed and worked till their hands were raw* (44–5), *decent wage* (69), *dignified [retirement]* (70), *spend wisely* (72), *vital trust* (73), *force . . . for good* (75), *our ideals* (82–3), *dignity* (90), *prudent use [of power]* (94), *justness [of our cause]* (94–5), *tempering qualities . . . of humility and restraint* (95), *principles* (96), *understanding* (98), *responsibly leave Iraq* (98), *pledge* (119), *humble gratitude* (124), *heroes* (126), *we honor* (128), *spirit of service* (129), *faith* (133), *kindness* (134), *selflessness* (134), *fair play, tolerance* (139–40), *old [values/things]* (140), *new era of responsibility* (142–3), *duties* (143), *virtue* (160), *virtue* (163)

−propriety

far-reaching network . . . of violence and hatred (13–14), *greed and irresponsibility* (15), *sweatshops* (41), *endured the lash of the whip* (41–2), *protecting narrow interests* (51), *bad habits* (72), *force . . . for good or ill* (75), *society's ills* (114), *corruption* (116), *silencing of dissent* (116), *wrong side of history* (117), *indifference to the suffering* (121–2), *without regard to effect* (122–3)

---

irresponsibility on the part of some) or by a generally subsumed first person plural that implicates indirectly previous customs (*our time . . . of protecting narrow interests*).

Examination of the interpreting of judgement shows that the most obvious lexical inscriptions are almost always retained. Thus, a close translation is given of key statements such as *What is required of us now is a new era of responsibility* (142–3), though the fact that each interpreter renders this as *una nueva era de responsabilidad* may be partly because of the ease of literal translation from Spanish. In some cases the inscription is retained even if the realization varies: *our capacity remains undiminished* (50), for example, is rendered as 'our capacity is maintained' (TT1), 'our capacity has not been diminished' (TT2) and 'our capacity retains its strength' (TT3).[18] It is true that there are omissions, particularly from TT3, part of the coping strategy employed by the interpreter, and also to a lesser extent by TT1 and very occasionally TT2. It might be surmised that omissions are most likely to occur in realizations that are deemed peripheral by the interpreter, except in extreme circumstances when constraints of time and speed (a particular consideration for TT3) may lead to the omission of more central examples. Three instances are omitted by all the interpreters, and each is of an epithet: *swift [action]* (55), *hard-earned [peace]* (99) and *dying [campfires]* (155). Other examples omitted by TT1 include *quiet [force of progress]* (141) and by TT2 *enduring [convictions]* (92) and *hard [work]* (139), the major attitudinal load being borne by the noun. Omission of nouns does occasionally occur, for example *greed* (15) by TT2. But this is less common and normally only as part of the omission of a whole chunk or when they occur in a group or list where the remaining noun can cover the required grammatical function (e.g. *greed and irresponsibility on the part of some*). What happens more often is the reduction of the force of the attitude by the use of a more general noun, a form of standardization (Toury 1995): *society's ills* (114) > 'their problems' (TT1);[19] *endured the lash of the whip* (41–2) > 'endured difficulties' (TT1);[20] *kindness . . . selflessness* (134) > 'generosity . . . generosity' (TT1, TT2)[21] and 'spirit' (TT3),[22] and so on. That such a standardization strategy seems to be a feature of interpreting is underlined by comparison with published written translations of the same text which, benefiting from more processing time, all manage to avoid repetition and generalization: for example, translations of *kindness . . . selflessness* include 'goodness . . . generosity' (TT4), 'kindness . . . altruism',[23] 'kindness . . . disinterest'[24] and 'goodness . . . abnegation'.[25]

Although it may be that a relatively small number of shifts will not seriously affect the overwhelming evaluative prosody of the text, omission and standardization are not limited to marginal examples. For instance, the important commitment that *we will begin to responsibly leave Iraq to its people* (98) is translated less clearly by TT1 as 'we will begin in a responsible way, leaving Iraq in the hands of its people'[26] and mistranslated by TT2 as 'we are going to begin to leave the responsibility of its management to Iraq and to its people'.[27] TT3 omits the statement altogether. What seems to be happening here is that TT1 and TT2 process the attitudinal realization *responsibly* as being semantically (and/or axiologically) of high importance. Hence they retain the core lexical item (*responsible/responsibility*) but alter its function and end up creating erroneous or dubious syntactic links.

Just as was the case with affect, what is evident in the lists above is the number of instances of judgement that are invoked by non-core lexis. For judgement, these are especially, but not exclusively, verb forms. The English ST seems especially rich in such resources, and this poses a problem for the interpreters. A few examples may suffice:

*Earlier generations **faced down** fascism and communism* (91).

As we saw in Section 2.1, this part of the speech was polemical in China because of the mention of political ideologies, even though the implied reference is to World War II and the Cold War. The evaluative thrust is located in the phrasal verb *faced down*, whose ideational meaning embodies the value of positive tenacity and security.[28] TT1 translates this as the weaker *enfrentaron* ('faced') and TT2 as the stronger *derribaron* ('overthrew'), more common verbs that vary in intensity. The written translations show a similar tendency, also preferring *enfrentaron* ('faced'), the slightly stronger *se enfrentaron con* ('faced up to') or the very strong *derrotaron* ('defeated'). The trend therefore seems to be for intensity to vary. A similar phenomenon can also be noted in other languages, such as the Bahasa Indonesia translation that adopts a different metaphor, 'bowed down the head of fascism and communism'.[29] The verb *menundukkan* is, however, commonly used to mean 'to defeat'.

The following example is an excellent case of how the ST uses strong, non-core verb forms (*wield . . . harness*) to reinforce the positive prosody of capacity in a passage where Obama is describing the future development of the economy:

> We will restore science to its rightful place, and **wield** technology's wonders to raise health care's quality and lower its cost. We will **harness** the sun and the winds and the soil . . . we will transform our schools . . . (57–60).

In this sequence, the more common and transparent verbs (*restore, raise, lower, transform*) are generally interpreted by common equivalents (e.g. *restablecer, mejorar, disminuir, transformar* – 're-establish', 'improve', 'reduce', 'transform'). Nevertheless, once again there are some exceptions: TT1 omits a translation of *restore* and translates *lower* with the less common *aminorar* ['diminish']. The verbs *wield* and *harness* are non-core, metaphorical uses that invoke evaluation (+capacity) through their strength and purpose. This is partly achieved through the influence of a semantic prosody/association (see Chapter 1, Section 1.3.1.4). Thus, examination of corpus evidence for *harness* shows that it often collocates with and is coloured by nouns such as *power, energy, potential;*[30] *wield* typically collocates with *power, influence, clout, axe, sword*. The alliteration of *will . . . wield . . . wonders* is also a contributing factor to its strength. The interpretings can be seen in Table 2.5.

The interpreters find positive terms but without the metaphorical or attitudinal intensity of the ST. This is especially the case for the translations of *wield* which use the everyday *usar* or *utilizar* ('use'); TT2's translation of *harness* uses the strong *captar* ('capture'), while TT1 selects the relatively common verb *aprovechar*, a strong collocate of *recursos* ('resources') and *energía* ('energy'), which perhaps explains its selection. This is not a phenomenon restricted to interpreting. TT4, the translation posted on the White House blog, also chooses *utilizaremos* and *aprovecharemos*.

One final example, describing the hardships of earlier generations of Americans, epitomizes the invoked judgement in this text and links to the frame of remembrance

TABLE 2.5 Translation of non-core verbs *wield* and *harness*

	wield technology's wonders . . .	*harness the sun . . .*
TT1	*Usaremos las maravillas de la tecnología* [We will use the wonders of technology]	*Aprovecharemos los recursos del sol* [We will make the most of the resources of the sun]
TT2	*Vamos a usar las maravillas de la tecnología* [We are going to use the wonders of technology]	*Vamos a captar la energía del sol* [We are going to capture the energy of the sun]
TT3	*Utilizaremos la tecnología* [We shall use technology]	Ø

of the past discussed with regard to deictic positioning in Section 2.3 below. The four elements in the sentence are marked for ease of reference:

> For us, they [1] toiled in sweatshops, and [2] settled the West, [3] endured the lash of the whip, and [4] plowed the hard earth (41–2).

These are oblique allusions that will nonetheless trigger a reaction to anyone with knowledge of American history, and so very clear to the national audience. Each is an example of tenacity and expanded capacity: *toiled in sweatshops* indexes the hardship of the early small-scale industry of the east coast, *settled the West* refers to the pioneers who travelled West in search of land, *endured the lash of the whip* points to the suffering of the slaves and *plowed the hard earth* the tough conditions of the settler farmers of the Midwest. Interestingly the lexical evaluation is realized by various parts of speech: the verb *toiled*,[31] the nouns *sweatshops*[32] and *lash*[33] and the adjectival inscription in *hard earth*. Comparing TT1 and TT2 (TT3 gets rather lost here and mentions only the whip and 'difficulties'), we see the following:

> **TT1** For us they [1] worked in factories, [2] conquered the West … [3] endured … difficulties.[34]

> **TT2** For us they [1] struggled in workshops and factories, [2] colonized the West; [3] suffered the lash of the whip and [4] plowed the hard earth.[35]

TT2 manages to achieve closer textual equivalence. TT1 gets stuck on element 3 and the problems in resolving it cause the interpreter to omit the fourth element (or to subsume the two together under the very timid 'difficulties'). This may suggest that this point is the main evaluative problem, but it could very well also be that the problem of finding an equivalent for *lash* produces a temporary block. However, as far as evaluation is concerned, element 1 is certainly problematic: TT1 chooses the common and neutral verb 'worked' [*trabajaron*] and the neutral 'factories' [*fábricas*]; TT2 chooses the positive verb 'struggled' [*lucharon*] and adds 'workshops' [*talleres*] to 'factories', but neither has the strongly negative meaning of *sweatshops*. On the other hand, the translations of element 2 strengthen the neutral *settled the West*, which probably invokes positive connotations for the majority of ST readers: both TT1 and TT2 shift the frame of the process with *conquered* and *colonized*, placing it within a narrative of conquest or colonization, which may be true but is not the traditional US representation.[36] What we end up with in TT1 is a story of capacity and conquest in the face of unspecified difficulties, and in TT2 a fuller picture that may suggest union activism (element 1) and a colonial attitude (element 2). Some of the translators of the written Spanish TTs, benefiting from welcome time for reflection, opted for explicitation here:

> For us they worked in subhuman conditions … (TT4)
> For us they worked without rest in despotic factories …[37]

In both these translations the evoked evaluation of *toiled in sweatshops* has been heavily inscribed in the epithets 'subhuman [conditions]' (*infrahumanas*) and 'despotic [factories]' (*déspotas*). That such explicitation of evaluation is produced by a shift from evoked ST noun to heavily inscribed TT epithet is worthy of further research. For example, does evaluative explicitation generally occur through the use of the most archetypal form of evaluation, the epithet? Similarly, since explicitation is less readily deployed by the simultaneous interpreter processing co-terminously with the speaker's input, it seems plausible that this is more likely to be a feature of written translation (perhaps also consecutive interpreting). The question remains as to what alternative strategy might be adopted by the simultaneous interpreter.

2.2.3 Appreciation

The examples of appreciation occurring in the speech are given in Table 2.6, in which it can be seen that appreciation occurs more often than affect in this speech, but much less frequently than judgement. This is a result of the speech's focus on the ethical values associated with responsibility, and the values that bind the nation together, rather than on presenting a more obvious evaluation of the

TABLE 2.6 Examples of appreciation in the Obama inaugural

Appreciation

+reaction
rising tides of prosperity (07), *still waters of peace* (07), *better history* (31), *better life* (45), *bigger . . . greater [America]* (45–6), *unmatched [power]* (76), *grandest capitals* (88), *old [things/values]* (140), *quiet [force of progress]* (141), *magnificent mall* (150)

−reaction
gathering clouds (08), *raging storms* (08), *stale [political arguments]* (66), *bitter swill of civil war and segregation* (108), *dark chapter* (108), *darkest hours* (135–6)

+composition
unity of purpose (26), *full measure of happiness* (33), *undiminished [capacity]* (50), *patchwork heritage* (105), *stronger and more united* (108–9), *the world grows smaller* (110), *clean waters* (120)

−composition
too costly (17), *Less measurable* (20), *not . . . be met easily [challenges]* (24), *narrow interests* (51)

+valuation
no less profound (20–1), *our better history* (31), *precious gift* (31), *greatness [nation]* (34), *better life* (45), *bigger . . . greater [America]* (45–6), *no less inventive* (48–9), *new jobs* (55), *rightful place* (57), *surest route to our common good* (81), *great gift of freedom* (167)

−valuation
America's decline (22), *real, serious, many [challenges]* (23), *petty grievances* (27), *worn-out dogmas* (28), *childish things* (30), *their memories are short* (63)

political situation. While some realizations of appreciation are 'simple' epithets or comparators (e.g. *our better history*), others are much more complex (e.g. *old*, *patchwork*, which I shall return to below). The table does show that there is more positive than negative appreciation; the negative examples generally relate to the crisis and challenges facing the country. The two are sometimes juxtaposed for contrastive effect (e.g. *rising tides of prosperity* and *still waters of peace* vs *gathering clouds* and *raging storms*, which I shall discuss in Section 2.2.4).

Close analysis of the Spanish interpretings reveals some omissions of appreciation, but seemingly these are non-systematic. The underlined omissions are mainly of positive appreciation: <u>*raging*</u> *storms* (TT1, TT2, TT3), <u>*quiet*</u> *force of progress* (TT1), <u>*precious*</u> *gift* (TT1), <u>*great*</u> *gift of freedom* (TT2, TT3), <u>*full measure*</u> *of happiness* (TT1, TT3). In addition, there is noticeable variation in interpreting around negative metaphors of appreciation: **gathering** *clouds* (which I shall deal with in Section 2.2.4), **stale** *political arguments*[38] and **bitter swill** *of civil war and segregation*.[39] But the most interesting instances relate to invoked evaluation, where the lexical item depends almost completely on co-text and context for its value. I shall restrict myself to looking at two of these: *old* (140) and *patchwork* (105).

As we saw in Chapter 1, Section 1.3.1, *old* is an example of a culturally loaded word and was at the heart of the debate over the values and portrayal of the political divisions of modern Europe. While nominally descriptive (e.g. *an old system*), it associates with the subjective values of the speaker. (How old is 'old'? Is an 'old' system one which has proven its worth or one which needs updating? and so on.) In the Obama speech, *old* is most certainly positive:

> *honesty . . . and hard work, courage and fair play, tolerance and curiosity, loyalty and patriotism –* . . . *these things are* **old** . . . *These things are true* . . . (139–41).

Old evaluates the intense cluster of judgement words and furthermore works in parallel with the powerful judgement epithet *true*. *Old* in this sense is thus imbued with a value of sturdiness, resilience, veracity, becoming a hybrid judgement-appreciation. The CNN and Telemundo interpreters understand this, translating it as 'immanent' (*inmanentes*, TT1) and 'ancient' (*antiguos*, TT2). By contrast, TT3 and all the written translations studied use 'old' (*viejos*), the default TL equivalent. *Old* is a problematic word in other languages too. The Chinese CCTV written TT[40] explicates as 历久弥新 ('it is old, but remains new') and many Japanese TTs, interpretings and translations, use amplification and/or explicitation such as 'age-old', 'has never changed' or 'values we have inherited down the ages'.[41]

In Table 2.6, the *patchwork heritage* example is one of the most striking evaluative items in the whole speech, and a clear candidate for a critical point in translation. It occurs at the midpoint in the speech and directly relates to the cohesiveness of the multi-faith American people that Obama is seeking to portray:

> *For we know . . . that our patchwork heritage is a strength . . . not a weakness. We are a nation of Christians and Muslims . . . Jews and Hindus . . . and non-believers* (105–6).

Here, the modifier *patchwork*[42] is a marker of positive evaluation, but this positivity greatly derives from signalling in the co-text (*is a strength ... not a weakness*). The very explicitness alerts the reader to the unusual use of the term, and there is tacit acknowledgement that *patchwork heritage* might be perceived as a *weakness* by some. Typical dictionary definitions for this meaning of *patchwork* are neutral, supported also by the examples in the *Collins Cobuild English Dictionary* (1995: 1210):

> If you refer to something as a patchwork, you mean that it is made up of many different parts, pieces or colours. *The low mountains were a patchwork of green and brown ... this complex republic, a patchwork of cultures, religions and nationalities.*

An analysis of the collocation patterns of *patchwork*[43] shows extremely diverse realizations in the metaphorical sense. The most common use (74 per cent in our sample)[44] is *patchwork of* ... (e.g. *patchwork of several applications*), some examples of which make explicit their evaluation through premodifiers. This is negative evaluation with the premodifiers *confusing, feudal, hopeless, laborious, strange, unjustified, unruly, unwieldy* ... and positive evaluation with *elegant* and *vivid* (e.g. *an elegant patchwork of monochromatic shades*). Most interestingly, in some examples possibly neutral adjectives (e.g. *complex, vast*) which accompany *patchwork* are modified themselves in order to unambiguously highlight the negative evaluation:

> A **hugely** complex patchwork of pricing and regulatory systems.[45]
> Nerve center of a vast **and unruly** patchwork of security forces.[46]

On their own, the appreciation epithets *complex* and *vast* are not necessarily negative. They are attitudinally context- and reader-dependent, like the forms of provoked attitude discussed in Chapter 1. They have a propensity to vary in value and in these examples are fixed as negative (and strongly so) by the intensifying adverb *hugely* and the second epithet *unruly*.

Other, non-modified, instances absorb negativity from more distantly related co-text:

> the European Commission has proposed **sweeping away** this patchwork of national restrictions.[47]

The phrasal verb *sweeping away* would usually have a positive connotation,[48] countering the negative *patchwork of* ... *restrictions*. However, the wider context of the article, on the varying opinions of the diverse regulations on price-cutting in different European countries, does not unambiguously support this. Such uncertainty makes a term such as *patchwork* potentially critical for a reader or translator, even more so perhaps for an interpreter working in real time. In the Obama example, where *patchwork heritage* is clearly positive, the three Spanish-language interpreters all choose different realizations: 'legacy' (*legado*, TT1), 'inheritance/heritage' (*herencia*, TT2), and a reformulation with 'the fact that' (TT3).[49] These are all neutral and omit any direct equivalent for the item *patchwork*. The interpreters seem to prefer to avoid making a value-laden decision on how to translate this term, allowing the rest of the sentence to relay the message about strength and the mix of religions in the country. By contrast, the various Spanish written translations offer more specific equivalents based on collocates of the word *herencia* ('heritage/inheritance'): 'multi-colour heritage' (*herencia multicolor*, TT4), 'diverse heritage' (*herencia diversa*)[50], 'mixed heritage' (*herencia mixta*)[51] and 'multi-ethnic heritage' (*herencia multiétnica*).[52] These are again as neutral (or as positive) as ST *heritage*, but sometimes more specific in the rendering of *patchwork* in racial rather than religious terms ('multi-colour', 'multi-ethnic'). They have all had to make a decision on a potentially sensitive word. Omission is not really an option. Nor, in Spanish, is borrowing, although for some other languages it might be acceptable.[53] In such cases, explicitation is a procedure that carries some risk, since explicating one element may draw exaggerated attention to a feature that is not salient in the ST. TT4's 'multi-colour heritage' thus reveals the translator's interpretation through a frame of racial difference, perhaps taking the metaphor more literally as transmitting variation on colour rather than variation in religion. The ST is more subtle and wider-ranging.

Once again, the same term proves to be problematic in other languages too. Translation procedures include generalization, which neutralizes the evaluation:

> 'diversified heritage' (多元化遗产, Chinese CCTV), 'this heritage that we have' (我々がもつこの遺是 Japanese NKH network)

or explicitation, which turns invoked evaluation into direct inscription:

> 'the tradition abundant with diversity of our nation' (Japanese, Fuji Television Network).

2.2.4 Provoked evaluation – lexical metaphors

Lexical metaphors are one device that can 'provoke' an attitudinal response indirectly (Martin and White 2005: 64–5). Metaphors are a common device in inaugurals, designed 'both to make intelligible and to persuade the listener of the value of abstract social ideals such as peace, prosperity and justice' (Charteris-Black 2004: 109). In order to do this, metaphors establish common ground between the speaker and the listener based on what is assumed to be or presented as shared experience (Howe 1988). Part of the clarifying role is the use of clusters of similar lexical metaphors which operate hierarchically as conceptual metaphors (Charteris-Black 2004: 245).

For the purposes of analysis here, I shall discuss three main conceptual fields, associated with different sections of the speech: (i) meteorology, (ii) journey and movement and (iii) personification and reification. Each is classified according to the positive and negative evaluation provoked by the metaphor:[54]

(i) Meteorology

> +evaluation
> *rising tides of prosperity* (07), *still waters of peace* (07)
>
> −evaluation
> *gathering clouds* (08), *raging storms* (08), *endure what storms may come* (164).

Weather metaphors and others related to the physical environment are especially common in inaugurals (Charteris-Black 2004: 103). In Obama's speech they cluster at the beginning, where the President is setting out the difficulties the country faces:

> *Forty-four Americans . . . have now taken . . . the presidential oath. The words have been spoken during* **rising tides** *of prosperity . . . and the* **still waters** *of peace . . . Yet, every so often, the oath is taken amidst* **gathering clouds** *. . . and* **raging storms** *. . .* (ST: 6–8).

Comparison of the different Spanish-language interpreting reveals very different translation procedures:

> Forty-four Americans . . . have . . . sworn the oath to be president. The words have been spoken in **moments** . . . of prosperity and in **waters** of peace. Yet from time to time, the oath occurs in the middle of **dense clouds** and **storms** . . . (TT1: 6–8).[55]

> Forty-four Americans . . . have now taken . . . the presidential oath. The words have been pronounced during . . . **times** of prosperity and of peace . . . However, now and again . . . the oath is taken . . . amidst **dense clouds** and **storms** . . . (TT2: 6–8).[56]

> Forty-four . . . Americans have . . . taken the oath as president. During prosperity have been spoken certain words. However, from time to time the oath is taken in the middle of . . . **difficulties** and **storms** (TT3: 6–8).[57]

Here, all ST metaphors comprise adjective+noun combinations, where the adjective mainly provokes the evaluation. The first two (*rising tides* and *still waters*) are positive. In the TTs there is a general pattern of reduction of metaphorical strength and evaluation. *Rising tides* is omitted by all TTs and *still waters* by TT2 and TT3 (even TT1 only renders *waters*); the TTs use the basic, bland, non-metaphorical and very neutral terms 'moments' and 'times'. The second pair of metaphors (*gathering clouds* and *raging storms*) is strongly negative. *Raging storms* follows the pattern above; the basic part of the metaphor (*storms*) is rendered by *tormentas* but the most inscribed evaluative element (*raging*) is omitted. On the other hand, *gathering clouds* is perhaps slightly intensified by the more concise, single referent *nubarrones* ('large, thick clouds').

Greater attention is given to metaphor in the written TTs. *Rising tides* is translated as 'increasing waves',[58] *still waters* as 'peaceful and tranquil waters' (TT4),[59] 'tranquil waters'[60] and 'waters tranquil';[61] *fierce storms* is rendered as the equally strong collocations 'ferocious storms'[62] and 'furious storms'.[63] But it cannot be said that written translation will always preserve the strength and evaluative force of metaphor. For instance, TT4 reads as follows:

> They have done it during tides of prosperity and in peaceful and tranquil waters. However, on occasions, this oath has been sworn amidst clouds and storms.[64]

Here, the evaluative epithets *rising*, *raging* and *gathering* are omitted. Similarly, if we compare other languages, the Chinese CCTV written TT[65] very much generalizes the first part of the metaphor to 'prosperity and peace'. Interestingly, a different kind of standardization is also a feature of an online (possibly prepared) American Sign Language (ASL) interpretation of the speech: *rising tides of prosperity . . . and the still waters of peace* is interpreted as the more general and explicit *wonderful times . . . success*, while *gathering clouds . . . and raging storms* is rendered as *difficult times . . . hard times*.[66]

There therefore seems to be a variation in the sensitivity of the translator to the importance of metaphor (especially the axiological import), a variation that may be exaggerated in interpreting but is not straightforwardly a distinguishing feature.

(ii) Journey and movement

By far the most prominent metaphors are realizations of the conceptual metaphor of LIFE AS A JOURNEY and, related to that, other forms of movement and the bearing of the gift of freedom to future generations. In his analysis of all inaugurals from Washington to Clinton, Charteris-Black considers the journey to be the second-most common conceptual metaphor, after that of conflict.[67] The journey metaphor is particularly suited because of its depiction of progress towards a destination, often led by the politician him- or herself. It has a strongly positive evaluation (Charteris-Black 2004: 93). This metaphor permeates the whole Obama text, and almost all the linguistic realizations are positive:

+evaluation
our journey (35), *have carried us . . . up the long, rugged path towards prosperity and freedom* (39), *this is the journey we continue today* (47), *surest route to our common good* (81), *we seek a new way forward* (112), *the road that unfolds before us* (124), *how far we have traveled* (153–4), *we refused to let the journey end . . . we did not turn back nor did we falter* (165–6)

−evaluation
short-cuts (35), *path for the faint-hearted* (36), *seek only the pleasures of riches and fame* (37).

Generally, the basic metaphor poses few problems for the interpreters. *Journey* and *path* are translated as *viaje, trayectoria, camino, senda, vía* ('journey', 'trajectory', 'way', 'path', 'line'), all maintaining both the image and the conceptual metaphor. The verbs of movement, while they vary, also still realize the conceptual metaphor: thus *we have travelled* is interpreted as *recorrido, llegado* and *viajado* ('covered', 'arrived' and 'travelled'), while *have carried us* is *avanzado, llevado, llegado* ('advanced', 'carried', 'arrived'). The two major changes, which are therefore perhaps indicative of critical decision-making points, occur in the examples below, first:

> the **long rugged** path towards prosperity and freedom (39).

Here, TT1 explicates the highlighted adjectives as *difícil* ('difficult'), TT2 only translates *long* (*largo*) and TT3 merely makes implicit the length (*a lo largo de estos caminos*, 'over the course of these paths'). In other words, it is the evaluative element of the metaphor that tends to be downplayed in the interpreting. This is further evidenced by comparison with the *El País* written translation, which renders both adjectives − one quite literally and the other in explicated form as *el largo y arduo sendero* ('the long and arduous path').

The other shift occurs in the translation of the verb *unfolds* in *the road that* **unfolds** *before us* (124). All three interpreters adopt a similar procedure, namely 'the path we have before us' (*el camino que tenemos ante nosotros*, TT1, TT2; *el camino que tenemos frente a nosotros*, TT3). The core image of the road is retained, but it is the subtler active process of movement ('unfolds') that is weakened. It is unclear why this should be so. On the one hand, a more or less literal translation is possible, and is used in the EFE agency translation (*la ruta que se despliega ante nosotros*, 'the route which unfolds itself before us'). But the interpreters shy away from such a powerful choice, or they have decided that it is the element that may be most safely omitted. Other written TTs adopt a middle position, rewriting the verbal part of the metaphor but with less visual vividness than the ST: thus, 'the road that awaits us' (*el camino que nos espera*, TT4), 'the road that presents itself before us' (*el camino que se presenta ante nosotros*)[68] and 'that opens up before us' (*el camino que se abre ante nosotros*).[69]

Associated metaphors are those of gift-bearing (e.g. *we* **carried forth** *that great gift of freedom* [ST: 166–7]) and general movement (e.g. *we . . .* **emerged** *from that dark chapter*). Examples of negative evaluation support the trends identified above:

> But our time of **standing pat,** . . . has surely passed (51)

sets up an important contrast resolved by the determination to press on and 'remake' the nation. *Stand pat* is an informal expression, used in the US to mean 'to oppose or resist change'.[70] In TT1, the interpreter hesitates at this point, revealing that there is a processing or encoding problem, before he produces a slightly different image of passivity ('remain observing', *quedarnos observando*); TT2 similarly changes the image, but to a stereotypical one of opposition ('crossing our arms', *cruzarnos el brazo*); TT3 omits; written TT4 uses an abstract noun, *inmovilismo* (= 'immobilism', 'resistance to change'), which renders the function of resistance without the image.

Another example, later in the text, is a more active one:

> *we'll work . . . to . . . roll back the specter of a warming planet* (99–100).

TT2 omits this section perhaps because of the speed of delivery; TT3 condenses it to the more standardized *enfrentaremos el . . . los problemas que trae el . . . el calentamiento global* ('we shall confront the [sing.] . . . the problems that brings the . . . the global warming'); TT1 omits a translation of *roll back*, joining it with a previous clause governed by *lessen* (*reducir*). Only the written texts both maintain the image of the *specter* and seek a strong translation of the verb *roll back* (TT4, for instance, uses *hacer retroceder*, 'make recoil').

(iii) Personification and reification

There is also a considerable number (fifteen) of linguistic and conceptual metaphors that give living qualities to inanimate entities, e.g. *feed our commerce* (56–7), *our power grows* (94), *in the year of America's birth* (154). Such personification is translated more or less literally, as is the more powerful and less conventional metaphor *strangled our politics* (29).[71] More problems seem to be raised by strong and relatively unusual metaphors such as

> *the bitter swill of civil war and segregation* (108).

Again, in the TTs the pattern can be seen of retention of the basic semantic core of the negative evaluation (*bitter*), sometimes jettisoning or neutralizing the more complex *swill*. Hence, TT1 and TT3 give *la amargura* ('bitterness') and TT2 opts for *el trago amargo* ('the bitter sip').[72] All translations are negative, of course, but all again limit the negativity to a single core element of the metaphor. That this is indeed a trend, perhaps even for metaphor translation is a whole, is suggested by other examples, this time of reification,[73] such as:

> *We will . . . forge a hard-earned peace in Afghanistan* (98–9).

It is the non-metaphorical abstract noun *peace* that is retained in the TTs. This is the central semantic feature of the clause. *Forge* is translated as the more neutral and more basic *consolidar* ('consolidate') in TT1, *ganar* ('win') in TT2 and even the less optimistic *buscaré* ('I shall win') in TT3. None of the three interpreters translates the most obvious evaluative concept, the epithet *hard-earned*. That there is no need for the intensity of the TTs to be reduced is shown by the written TT4, which translates more closely as *forjar una merecida paz* ('forge a deserved peace').

But the key example is the critical double metaphor that has been perceived to be directed at Iran and which was censored in China and elsewhere (see 2.1 above):

> *To those . . . who cling to power through corruption and deceit . . . we will* **extend a hand** *if you are willing to* **unclench your fist** (117–18).

The first part of the metaphor (*we will extend a hand*) is relatively straightforward and is rendered by the interpreters as *le vamos a tender la mano* ('we are going to extend a hand to you [sing.]', TT1), *les vamos a extenderles las manos* ('we are going to extend [our] hands to you [pl.]', TT2), *les tenderemos una mano* ('we will extend a hand to you [pl.]', TT3). The variation in the articulation is mainly in the syntax and grammar (verb tense, number of the indirect object pronoun, singular or plural of *mano*). But it is the second part of the metaphor, *unclench your fist*, which is crucial, since it calls for action on the presupposition that the current position is of a menacing, clenched fist. The presupposition may explain the semantic variation in the interpretations:

> **TT1** (*abrir el puño*, 'open the fist') is as succinct and direct as the ST even if it employs a more basic verb ('open' for *unclench*);[74]

> **TT2** initially opts for a huge generalization (*cambiar*, 'change') which is so vague that it loses both metaphoricity and menace. Perhaps for these reasons, after a pause the interpreter adds a translation of the metaphor, *aflojar el puño* ('weaken the fist');

> **TT3** translates with a similar but less menacing image (*abrir sus palmas*, 'open your palms') and then adds explicitation (*para recibir nuestra ayuda*, 'to receive our help').

So, in interpreting the influence of metaphors is strong, there seems to be an urge where possible to retain or recreate the metaphor in the TT. However, what often happens in the more complex or creative metaphors is that there is variation in the degree of metaphoricity centred around the translation of the core element. Certainly, in TT2 and TT3 of the last example, the interpreter's move, when time and processing constraints permit, is to combine standardization with a refinement of the image or an explanation of the meaning. Written translation, with its looser constraints, is more likely to be able to retain or recreate the ST metaphor.

2.2.5 Indirect evaluation and the question of translation

The analysis so far has highlighted the different realizations of attitude and has shown that direct, inscribed evaluation (e.g. **humbled** *by the task before us*) is only part of the story. Indeed, most of the discussion has focused on indirect or invoked forms of evaluation. Thus, the lexical metaphors studied in the previous section, which may be woven into complex webs of conceptual metaphor, 'provoke' a response and play a key role in the leader's persuading the audience of the truthfulness of the message. 'Non-core' vocabulary items (e.g. *jobs shed*) may also connote rather

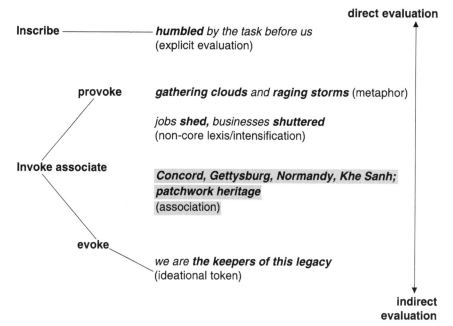

FIGURE 2.1 Illustration of the cline of direct and indirect evaluation in the Obama inaugural

than denote attitude (Martin and White 2005: 66, see Chapter 1, Section 1.3.1.4). A further strategy is to evoke evaluation by the presentation of ideational information without any overt comment: so, when Obama states that *we are the keepers of this legacy* [of previous generations] (96), this contributes to reinforcing the message of responsibility and enhances judgement attitude, even if no explicit evaluation is being made.

An illustration of the different forms of evaluation is given in Figure 2.1, based on the classification and depiction provided by Martin and White (see Figure 1.3). In this figure, the most direct, 'inscribed' evaluation is at the top; the most indirect, 'invoked' form of evaluation is at the bottom. The receiver's response is directed most obviously at the top of the figure, where the attitude is spelled out (*humbled by* . . .), but seems to have most freedom at the bottom, where the ideational selection evokes an attitude. This is only apparently the case, of course, since categorical statements of the *we are the keepers* type are very difficult to challenge, which is why they tend to be used to disguise evaluative points. Also, as we discussed in Chapter 1, Section 1.6, receivers may adopt different reading strategies (compliant, resistant, tactical) that will govern how they respond to individual instances.[75]

From a translation perspective, the analysis from the Spanish interpretings shows that it is the indirect forms of evaluation that are most subject to change in the TTs – generally towards a flattening or loss of intensification of the attitude realized in the ST through lexical metaphor and through non-core vocabulary. These will be further discussed below under graduation (this chapter, Section 2.2.6). Most intriguing, though, are those less direct forms of evaluation that depend on association. We saw this with the *patchwork heritage* example, where the positive evaluation was context-dependent and ran somewhat counter to the general use of *patchwork*. The interpreters used omission or reformulation to produce a neutral term, while the translators tended to (over)-explicate. Such terms seem to push the interpreter/translator to adopt a strategy of avoidance (in the case of the interpreters) or careful and overly-defensive explicitation (in the case of the translators). This suggests that the interpreters/translators may consider them to be sensitive (in our terms 'critical') points of translation. Furthermore, since they do not neatly fall within Martin and White's list of strategies (Figure 2.1), I am proposing a new category, that of '**invoke/associate**'. This would cover not only the context-dependent instances such as *patchwork* but also other, culturally sensitive triggers, the association of which may pass unnoticed by some sectors of the audience. In Obama's speech this is particularly the case with references to past history and remembrance (see this chapter, Section 2.3.2). It is most exquisitely illustrated in the list of key battles in American history that stand for moments of national pride or for historical landmarks – *Concord and Gettysburg, Normandy and Khe Sanh* (42–3). Thus, *Concord* stands for the American Revolutionary War and freedom from the British, *Gettysburg* the victory of the North in the American Civil War that kept the nation together, *Normandy* the American-led Allied landings in occupied France in World War II and *Khe Sanh* a major defensive battle by US Marines in the Vietnam War. Other references are to contemporary crises such as the New Orleans floods of 2005 – *the kindness to take in a stranger when the levees break* (133–44). This is triggered by a single word (*levees*), indissolubly linked to Hurricane Katrina. TT2 and TT4 translate this as the equivalent *diques*, but it is omitted by both TT1 and TT3, thus breaking the intertextual bond.

Such a style of presentation means that the individual event is triggered by association rather than direct naming. This also happens at the end of the speech, where the phrase *the father of our nation* (157) denotes George Washington without naming him in person. Sometimes, too, such associative attitude is combined with other forms of evaluation, such as non-core vocabulary. This happens with *toiled in sweatshops* (see this chapter, Section 2.2.2), alluding to the conditions of the East Coast migrants, and also to the oblique 9/11 reference:

It is the firefighter's courage to storm a stairway filled with smoke (136).

Here, there is a possible intertextual association with the iconic photo of fireman Mike Kehoe, ascending the stairs of Tower One of the World Trade Center, taken by one of the line of employees who was descending.[76] The interpretings are as follows:

It is the courage of a firefighter to enter in a stairway full of smoke (TT1).[77]
It is the courage of a firefighter who faces up to a stairway full of smoke (TT2).[78]
It is the spirit that often firefighters have when they help (TT3).[79]

TT3 obliterates any possible link by tamely generalizing both the referent ('often ... firefighters') and the specific image ('when they help'). Even the TT1 and TT2 interpreters, while rendering the denotative sense of the source, vary at two important points: the use of the indefinite ('a firefighter . . .') for the definite article (*the firefighter*), and the translation of the non-core verb *storm* to 'enter' or 'faces up to'. The specificity and intensity of the ST are erased.

2.2.6 Graduation

The types of non-core vocabulary and lexical metaphor discussed in Sections 2.2.1 and 2.2.4 function as intensifiers of evaluation and are therefore comparable to the resources of force in graduation (Martin and White 2005: 67; also see Chapter 1, Section 1.3.3). The findings above suggest some reduction in force in the interpretings into Spanish. If we turn to examine the more conventional forms of graduation in the ST, we see that there are 23 instances of intensification in the ST.[80] Of these, nine are intensifiers of positive evaluation (e.g. *our **better** history* [31]), ten of negative evaluation (e.g. ***badly** weakened* [14]) and three are more neutral indicators of strength (e.g. ***this very** hour* [125]). In the interpretings, the general trend, shown in the following 12 of the 23 examples (52 per cent), is to lessen or omit intensification:

> ***Well*** *understood* (13) (omitted by TT2, TT3)
> ***far-reaching*** *network . . . of violence and hatred* (13–14) (omitted by TT2, TT3)
> ***badly*** *weakened* (14) (omitted by TT2)
> *fail **too many*** (17) (*algunas* ['some'] TT2)
> *for **far too long*** (28) (*por mucho tiempo* ['for a long time'] TT1, TT2, omitted by TT3)
> *demand **even** greater effort, **even** greater cooperation* (97) (omitted by all TTs)
> *our spirit is **stronger*** (103) (comparative omitted by TT1)
> *old hatreds shall **someday** pass* (109) (change of point of view TT1, omitted by TT2)
> *lines of tribe shall **soon** dissolve* (109–10) (whole phrase omitted by TT1, intensifier omitted by TT2)
> *at **this very** hour* (125) (omitted by TT1)
> *the outcome of our revolution was **most** in doubt* (156–7) (omitted by all TTs).

In total, TT1 omits 5 and lessens 2 (32 per cent of the overall realizations of graduation), TT2 omits 7 and lessens 2 (39 per cent of the overall) and TT3 omits 5 (22 per cent of the overall). It is unclear why TT3 has the lowest score, especially as the interpreter omits much more propositional content. One possibility is that TT1 and TT2 prioritize obvious propositional content over interpersonal markers. Importantly, despite the examples of explicitation, there are no cases of intensification of graduation of evaluation using the traditional interpersonal resources listed above. In other words, intensification is lessened in around 35 per cent of cases and not increased in any. This is a potentially significant finding.

2.2.7 Counter-expectancy indicators

Another means of invoking attitude is what are termed 'indicators of counter-expectancy' (Martin and White 2005: 67), which include discourse markers such as *however*, modal particles such as *only, surely*, and attitudinal adverbials such as *indeed, really, even* (see Chapter 1, Section 1.3.1.4). These 'provoke' attitude and represent points in the text where the writer is adding in a value judgement, either by contradicting what has gone before (e.g. *however, on the other hand*) or by underlining a value that counters a potential challenge (e.g. *only, really*). They are thus deemed to represent an 'intrusion' by the writer into the text. Indeed, they may be considered the clearest form of intervention by the ST author and, by extension and especially when there is a shift in the TT, by the translator. Obama's speech lacks common sentence-initial discourse markers, but it does contain a number of modal particles and attitudinal adverbials:

> **not simply** *because of the skill or vision of those in high office* (09), *greatness is* **never** *a given* (34–5), *our journey has* **never** *been one of short-cuts* (35), *those that* . . . *seek* **only** *the pleasures* (36–7), *that time has* **surely** *passed* (51–2), **not only** *to create new jobs* (55), **no longer** *apply* (67), *cannot prosper* **long** (77), *favors* **only** *the prosperous* (78), *depended* **not just** *on the size* (78–9), *we can* **scarcely** *imagine* (83–4), *those ideals* **still** *light the world* (85), *we are ready to lead* **once more** (90), **not just** *with missiles* (91), *our power* **alone** *cannot protect us* (92–3), *demand* **even** *greater effort,* **even** *greater cooperation* (97), **not** *what you destroy* (115), **no longer** *afford indifference* (121), *it is* **ultimately** *the faith* (132–3), *that* **finally** *decides our fate* (137), *but* **rather** *seize gladly* (144–5).

All 22 items in bold show clear intrusion from the authors (Obama and his speechwriters), either countering alternative perceptions (e.g. *we can* **scarcely** *imagine;* **not** *what you destroy*) or reinforcing an unexpected point against challenge (e.g. *the time has* **surely** *passed; it is* **ultimately** *the faith*). In the interpreting texts, a high number of these realizations (7 of 22) are omitted in one or all of the TTs:

> *greatness is* **never** *a given* (34–5) (omitted by TT1, TT3)
> *the time has* **surely** *passed* (51–2) (omitted by all TTs)
> *cannot prosper* **long** (77) (omitted by TT1, TT3)
> *favors* **only** *the prosperous* (78) (omitted by TT1)
> *demand* **even** *greater effort,* **even** *greater cooperation* (97) (both omitted by all TTs)
> **no longer** *afford indifference* (121) (omitted by TT1, TT2).

Given that these elements are important indicators of attitude, an overall omission rate of 32 per cent (for TT1), 18 per cent (for TT2) and 23 per cent (for TT3) is quite striking. The interpreters have all reduced intrusion in the TT and, in three very prominent cases, all at the same point (*surely; even; even*). This reduction is only partially attenuated by the interpreter of TT3, who expresses positive attitude at one point through stress and slowed pace:

*we are ready to lead **once more*** (90)
estamos listos para liderar ... **u** ... **na** ... **vez** ... **má** ... **s**

In this way, prosody and voice quality reinforce or even convey the attitudinal position. This is an area that would seem worthy of much further investigation (cf. Iglesias Fernández 2010).

2.2.8 Engagement

As a rhetorical strategy, counter-expectancy indicators are part of engagement, indicating commitment to a value judgement and aligning the readers with that axiological positioning (Martin and White 2005: 120, Fairclough 2003: 41; see also this chapter, Section 2.1). Aside from such indicators, pronouns (this chapter, Section 2.3.1 below) and adverbial modals and evidentials, the most obvious form of engagement is through the use of modal verbs. A detailed list of modals, based on Halliday's categorization (see Chapter 1, Section 1.2), is to be found in Table 2.7.

With the exception of usuality, which is closely linked to markers of counter-expectancy and graduation, there is surprisingly little variation in the ST realizations

TABLE 2.7 Categories of engagement modals in the Obama inaugural

Category	Realized by
(i) probability	*the time has **surely** passed* (51–2), *the **surest** route to our common good* (81), *old hatreds **shall** someday pass* (109), *lines of tribe **shall** soon dissolve* (109–10), *our common humanity **shall** reveal itself* (110–11), ***might not** have been served* (151)
(ii) usuality	***every so often*** (07), *for **far too long*** (28), *greatness is **never** a given* (34–5), *our journey has **never** been one of short-cuts* (35), ***more often** men and women obscure in their labor* (38–9), *what this country has **already** done* (64), *the nation cannot prosper **long*** (77), ***even greater** effort, **even greater** cooperation* (97)
(iii) obligation	*so it **must** be* (12), *greatness ... **must** be earned* (35), *we **must** pick ourselves up* (52), *America **must** play its role* (111), *we **must** change* (123), *this spirit that **must** inhabit us* (131–2), *as much as government can do, and **must** do* (132)
(iv) inclination (including readiness and capacity)	*... so that we **might** lead a better life* (45), *we **will** build ... restore ... transform ...* (56–9), *we **can** do ... we **will** do* (60–1), ***cannot** tolerate* (63), ***cannot** prosper long* (77), *we **will not** give them up* (85–6), ***will** work tirelessly* (99–100), *we **will not** apologize/waver* (101), *you **cannot** outlast us* (103), *we **will** defeat you* (103–4), *we **cannot** help but believe* (109), *what you **can** build ... not what you destroy* (114–15), *we **can** no longer afford indifference* (121), *a **willingness** to find meaning* (129), *as much as government **can** do, and must do* (132), ***willingness** to nurture a child* (137), *nothing but hope and virtue **could** survive* (159–60)

of engagement: *can/could, will/shall* and *must* predominate. Likewise, there is general consistency in the interpretings and very little omission. These seem to be key and easily rendered elements in the argument, especially the modal auxiliaries, and raise the possibility that the more core realizations of evaluation are strongly enough embedded in the interpreter's mind to resist dilution. What TT variation there is may be indicative of speaker or interpreter idiolect: just as Obama consistently prefers *must* to alternatives such as *has to*, so TT1 chooses the auxiliary *deber* and TT2 generally *tener que*.

2.3 Deictic positioning

The lexical markers explored so far indicate the text's axiology or value orientation, and the resources of engagement have begun to show the relative alignment of speaker and listener. But there is a higher-level interpersonal feature that is central to analysis of this genre of political communication. It is the notion of what Chilton (2004: 56) calls 'deictic positioning', which conceptualizes the relationship of speaker to hearer as well as various situational features including physical location, point in the speech and development of the discourse. It is closely related to the appraisal resource of engagement (see Chapter 1, Section 1.3.3). Deixis is the most evident form of positioning, working in tandem with the other forms of evaluation set out in Chapter 1.

Chilton describes deictic markers that serve to locate the interlocutors along the three axes (or 'dimensions of deixis') of space, time and modality (see Figure 2.2). The 'deictic centre' (Verscheuren 1999: 20) shows the positioning of the speaker

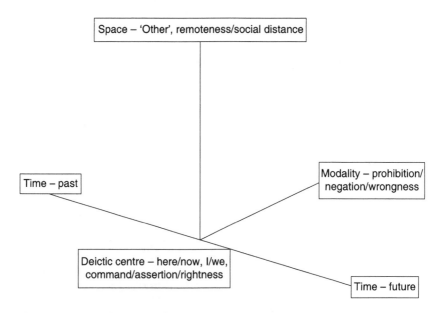

FIGURE 2.2 Dimensions of deixis (adapted from Chilton 2004: 58)

either as single *I* or as group *we*, at a central, present spatio-temporal point, the 'here' and 'now', and asserting moral rightness. The three axes allow a depiction of the distance from the Self along:

(i)   the **time** axis – past to future
(ii) the **space** axis – distance that is not only geographical but cultural, including social and power differences. Following Chilton, it is important to note that both time and space are often expressed using spatial deixis and conceptual spatial metaphor (e.g. *the end of the war is coming*, Lakoff and Johnson 1980)
(iii) the axis of **modality** – the political speaker typically allocates to him/herself the notion of moral 'rightness' and the truthful depiction of reality.[81] These are typically conflated with the speech acts of commanding and asserting (Chilton ibid.: 60). For example, the categorical statement (e.g. *we gather because we have chosen hope over fear*) is often used to project opinion as fact (cf. Martin and White 2005: 99).

The most fundamental linguistic expression of the positioning of the politician vis-à-vis the audience is the selection of pronouns, which reflects the speaker's mental representation of the receivers and classification of them, for example, with or against the speaker (see van Dijk 2008: 226). In systemic functional terms, these are indexical of Tenor, and negotiate the overall relationship of solidarity and distance between the interlocutors. For speaker projection, the key choice is between the personal *I*, to show personal investment in the statement, the plural *we*, which may be inclusive or exclusive, and a self-effacing impersonal style that may come across as formal. Each of these is potentially complex: thus, *I* may show not just personal investment in or 'ownership' of a statement but also potentially either a desire to hedge (e.g. *I think that*) or, by contrast, to 'sledgehammer' an argument home (e.g. *I am a hunter, I'm a gun-owner*, Pennebaker 2009).

At the very beginning of Obama's speech (See Appendix 2.1), the pronoun choices very carefully position the new president in respect to the public (actual and virtual):

> **My** *fellow citizens* . . . **I** *stand here today* . . . . . . *humbled by the task before* **us** . . . *grateful for the trust* **you've bestowed** . . . *mindful of the sacrifices borne by* **our** *ancestors* (2–3).

The first person singular possessive and personal pronouns (*My* . . . *I*) momentarily set Obama apart from the audience of *fellow citizens*, but immediately the two are joined *by the task before* **us** and *borne by* **our** *ancestors*. It should be noted that, in order to achieve this, the verb *bestowed* is used actively (*you've bestowed*) and without an indirect object, a very marked choice.[82] *You*, the audience, have given this trust to Obama. Having established this bond with the audience, in the rest of the speech Obama only twice more refers to himself directly when stressing the severity of the challenges to be faced: *Today* **I** *say to you* (23) and *the small village where* **my father** *was born* (88), which acts in contrast to *the grandest capitals* and alerts the public to Obama's humble origins.[83]

The overwhelming pronominal use by far is the first person plural. There are 58 occurrences of *we*, 67 of *our* and 3 of *ourselves*.[84] However, once again such uses of the plural pronoun cannot be placed in one catch-all category. Nor can they simply be qualified as a binary opposition between inclusive *we*, meaning 'all of us' (*we are in the midst of crisis*), and an exclusive *we*, meaning *I* (both the now-archaic Victorian *we are not amused* and the 'authorial *we*' of some academic writing, *as we shall show below*); likewise, they do not represent a simple opposition between an inclusive speaker+addressee and an exclusive speaker+third party/parties (Wales 1996: 58). In the context of the political speech, there is what Wales calls a blurring or 'useful ambivalence' in the choice of *we*:

> [T]he politician-speaker often uses *we* with the double reference and presumption that he or she is not only speaking on behalf of the party or government (exclusive), but also on behalf of the audience (inclusive).
>
> *(Wales 1996: 62)*

This common strategy by political leaders[85] allows the speaker to suggest that, irrespective of any party differences, there is an overriding national unity, what Wales (ibid.) calls the 'patriotic *we*'. In my view, it is better to consider the question as one of how Obama identifies with the audience(s) – the deictic positioning of Obama towards the audience(s). In this respect, analysis of the full speech shows three main categories of the pronoun *we* (see Table 2.8).

An exemplification of each of these categories is as follows:[86]

(i) **Spatio-temporally inclusive *we*** — Obama plus those physically present in the Mall listening to him.[87] Examples cluster as *we gather . . . we have chosen hope . . . we come to proclaim* (lines 26–7). Though striking in presence and creating a huge visual context to the broadcast, this category of audience was of course

TABLE 2.8 Categories of the use of the pronoun *we* in the Obama inaugural

Category of pronoun	Subcategory	Description
(i) Spatio-temporally inclusive *we*		Obama plus those physically present in the Mall
(ii) Identitary inclusive *we*	(a) Broader temporal *we* America	Obama and the nation and the people with a common history
	(b) Current temporal *we* Americans	Obama and the people, in the present
(iii) '*We* the government'	(a) Ambiguous *we*	The government and/with the people
	(b) Exclusive *we*	Acting distinctly from the people but for their good

dwarfed by the mass national and international TV/internet audiences which were temporally present but spatially remote.[88]

(ii) **Identitary inclusive** *we* – a unity of Obama and the American people and nation, which is by far the largest category since this is a main theme of the speech. This corresponds to Wales' 'patriotic we'. Some differentiation may be made here between:

    (a) **Broader temporal *we* America** – Obama and the nation and the people, with a common history. This focuses on the past end of the temporal axis, particularly the American Revolution and independence: *our nation* (04), *we . . . the people* (10), *our forebears* (10), *our founding documents* (11), *across our land* (21), *we remain a young nation* (29), *our enduring spirit* (30), *we have tasted the bitter swill of civil war and segregation* (107–8), *the outcome of our revolution* (156–7); and

    (b) **Current temporal *we* Americans** – Obama and the people, in the present. This *we* locates itself at the deictic centre of the communication (see Figure 2.2): *we are in the midst of crisis* (13), *our economy* (14), *our collective failure* (15), *our health care . . . our schools* (17), *ways we use energy* (18), *the challenges we face* (23), *stale political arguments that have consumed us* (66–7), *the question before us* (75), *when we were tested* (165), *our common dangers* (162).

Sometimes (iia) and (iib) are bound by the recurring metaphor of an ongoing journey (*the journey we continue* [47], *remembrance of who we are and how far we have traveled* [153–4]) or the upkeep of a tradition or value (*they saw America as bigger than the sum of our individual ambitions* [45–6], *we are the keepers of this legacy* [96]). Also, by the conceptual binding of past and present in which sacrifices of the past have been made for the benefit of present-day Americans: *For us . . . they . . . travelled across oceans . . . For us they toiled in sweatshops . . . For us, they fought and died . . .* (40–3).

(iii) **'*We* the government'**

    (a) an **ambiguous *we*, government and/with the people**, in the present: *we will act* (55), *we will build* (56), *we will restore science* (57), *we will harness the sun* (58), *we will transform our schools and colleges and universities* (59–60), *All this we can do. All this we will do* (60–1), *our ambitions* (62), *the question we ask today* (68), *we reject as false* (82), *we will begin to responsibly leave Iraq* (98), *we will extend a hand* (117), *we pledge* (119).

    (b) an **exclusive *we***, acting distinctly from the people but for their good: *those of us who manage the public's dollars* (71), *we intend to move forward* (70), *do our business in the light of day* (72–3), *only then can we restore the vital trust* (73), *we say we can no longer afford* (121) . . .

In (iiia) there is implied exclusiveness because the actions or decisions need to be taken by the government rather than the people. But there is also an invoked inclusiveness, assuming a unity of purpose of government and people, fostered by the breadth of meaning of the pronoun *we* (cf. Charteris-Black 2005: 175).

This point, that Obama is using an 'old-fashioned *we* the people', is made by Liberman (2009a, 2009b) as a counter to Fish's (2009) contention that Obama's was the aloof and distant royal *we*. The use of pronoun here is a critical point for the evaluation of the text as a whole – it is critical at text and discourse level, because upon it depends an interpretation of Obama's message. For Liberman, Obama is 'urging all citizens to "pick ourselves up, dust ourselves off, and begin again the work of remaking America" ' (Liberman 2009b);[89] for Fish, these are 'promises ... made to an America that is asked only to stand by while they are fulfilled' (Fish 2009). The fact that *we* generates these possible interpretations demonstrates its inherent ambiguity and the subjectivity of the response. Liberman's is a 'compliant' reading, Fish's a 'resistant' one (see Chapter 1, Section 1.6).

As a counterpart to these uses of *we*, there is also a range of addressees, classified into four categories (see Table 2.9). Such a classification is based on the proximity or remoteness of the audience both spatio-temporally and in terms of identity. This overcomes the problem that, from the perspective of audience design, almost

TABLE 2.9 Categories of addressees in the Obama inaugural

Addressees	*Location*	*Realizations*
(A) Those physically present	Spatially and temporally close	*thank you* (01), *President Bush* (04), *stand before you* (151)
(B) The American people or nation, in situ or viewing TV	Temporally and identitarily close, but proximity may be virtual	*my fellow citizens* (02), *the trust you've bestowed* (03), *today I say to you* (23), *know this America* (24), *recall that* (91), *the American people upon which this nation relies* (133), *let us mark this day* (153), *America* (162), *let us remember* (162–3), *let us brave once more the icy currents* (163-4), *thank you* (168), *God bless you* (168)
(C) Others within the United States – mostly opponents	Non-directly addressed and identitarily remote	*greed and irresponsibility on the part of* **some** (15), *the faint-hearted. . .* **those** *that prefer leisure over work* (36), *there are* **some** *who question* (62), *the cynics* (65–6)
(D) Peoples, governments and leaders outside the US	Spatially and identitary remote	*to all the other peoples and governments who are watching today ... know that America is a friend* (87–9), *for those who seek to advance their aims by inducing terror ... we say to you now that ... you cannot outlast us ... we will defeat you* (101–4), *to the Muslim world* (112), *to those leaders around the world who seek to sow conflict ... know that your people will judge you on what you build* (113–14), *to those ... who cling to power through corruption ... know that you are on the wrong side of history* (116–17), *if you are willing to unclench your fist* (117–18), *to the people of poor nations, we pledge to work alongside you to make your farms flourish* (119), *to those nations like ours* (120–1)

anyone might be a direct 'addressee' of this speech.[90] But, as shown above, different parts of the speech are directed at different addresses: to those present in the Mall, to the US people, to friend and foe, to the Muslim world, to those who cling to power, to the people of poor nations, and so on. This means that at some other points of the speech those specific listeners become 'auditors',[91] hearing Obama's comments to other addressees and perhaps, at those times, even identifying with him.

2.3.1 Translation of pronouns

Systemic differences between languages first means that what is expressed by a subject pronoun in English is conveyed by other means in what are known as 'pro-drop' or 'null subject' languages – by pragmatic inference in Japanese, Chinese or Arabic, or by verb inflection in most Romance and Slavic languages. Spanish generally drops the subject pronoun – so, Obama's *we are in the midst of crisis* may be translated as **estamos** *en medio de una crisis*. But the multivalency of English *we* and *you* may pose problems in translation. Some of the hidden relations may need to be explicated, for example in languages that have a *T/V* distinction. This may be concealed in, say, the French translations (where *vous* is the second person plural for both familiar and formal) and in the Latin American/US Spanish versions (the *ustedes* form is generally used for both familiar and formal plural). However, in the Italian translation in *La Repubblica*[92] and the peninsular Spanish translations available, including TT4, which was published in the prestigious daily *El País* and appeared on the White House blog, the informal plural is selected to address the range of audiences discussed in (i), (ii) and (iii) above. Amongst the Spanish written translations, the only intertextual discrepancy, indeed inconsistency, occurs in the Spanish financial news publication, *Cinco Días*:

> To those ... who cling to power through corruption and deceit and the silencing of dissent, KNOW that **you are** on the wrong side of history ... but that we will extend a hand ... if **you are** willing to unclench your fist (ST: 116–18).

> A quienes se aferran al poder a través de la corrupción y el engaño y silencian a los disidentes, SEPAN que **estáis** en el lado incorrecto de la historia, pero que extenderemos una mano si **estáis** dispuestos a deshacer el puño. (*Cinco Días*)[93]

In this example, where the translation is lexically very close to the source, the formal address forms are marked in CAPITALS in the TT, the informal address forms in bold, with the corresponding words in the ST similarly highlighted. In this way, it can be seen that the TT addresses the remote, corrupt leaders using the formal second person plural (*sepan que ... – know that ...*) before switching to the informal *estáis* (*you are ...*). The impression is one of uncertainty on the part of the translator and definitely no systematic attempt to differentiate the positioning of the different audiences along the social distance axis.

On the other hand, pronouns and forms of address are differentiated far more keenly in some languages. In Bahasa Indonesia, for example, there are two different first person singular pronouns, the formal *saya* and the informal *aku*. The translation of the speech produced by the Antara News Agency shows the high-status President unsurprisingly using the formal *saya* for himself. However, like other Austronesian and East Asian languages, Indonesian also has two first person plural pronouns, differentiated according to the crucial criterion of inclusiveness: *kita* (inclusive) and *kami* (exclusive). These become especially important choices in such a sensitive context and affect the positioning of the participants. Analysis of the Indonesian TT shows the overwhelming use of the inclusive *kita*, blurring the four uses of *we* discussed above. The exception is ***we*** *will extend a hand* [*to those who cling to power through corruption and deceit* . . .] (117); here, the use of the exclusive *kami* reveals that the translator read this offer as coming from the American government or administration and not the people as a whole. Pronouns show some shift in the Japanese too. The formal corporate 我々 (*ware-ware*) tends to have been preferred, but comparison of the simultaneous interpreting on the public NHK (Japanese Broadcasting Corporation) TV channel and the written TT in the Nikkei newspaper[94] show that the pronoun is very much suppressed (24 times) in the interpreting. On ten occasions it is changed to 'America', as in the example ***our*** *nation is at war* . . . ***Our*** *economy is badly weakened* (13–14).[95]

Pronoun choices in the American Sign Language interpretation are also illuminating. Here, even what seems to be one of the most explicit markers of deictic positioning (*we*) becomes more ambiguous. Thus, *On this day* . . . *we gather because we have chosen hope over fear* . . . is interpreted as:

> NOW [3rd person]-GATHER-TO-[1st person] TOGETHER 2nd-person-plural [small articulation] PICK HOPE [left side] MORE-THAN FEAR [right side]
>
> [Back translation: '(people?) come here; we choose hope more than we choose fear']

This is interesting because the null subject of GATHER seems to be marked for an unspecified third person, and GATHER is approximately located with the speaker, but it is not overly marked. Much information in ASL and other sign languages is marked non-manually by co-occurring movements of the face and upper body. In this example, the eye gaze seems to mark the unspecified nature of the people gathering rather than the clear spatio-temporally inclusive **we** of the ST.

2.3.2 Spatio-temporal deixis and identity

The other key positioning features in the speech are the temporal markers. Obama brings together past, present and future to link to the identitary representation of the American people drawn in Table 2.9 above. He does so in a way which goes far beyond what we might call inscriptions of time and place (*today, now*) to embrace a dazzling array of indirect tokens, brilliantly conjuring up historical and cultural references that fit deep into the shared American identity.

The most straightforward of these frames is the present.[96] This frame first gives the here and now of the President speaking to the people (*I stand here* **today** [02], **today** *I say to you* [23], *we say to you* **now** [102], *can* **now** *stand before you* [151], *let us mark* **this day** [153], *these* **timeless** *words* [163]). It also declares in the present tense the continuation with a past and the values it embodies, sometimes presented as a conceptual metaphor of the journey (*this is the journey* **we continue** *today* [47]), *remembrance . . .* **of who we are** *. . . and how far we have travelled* [153–4]). In the Spanish interpretings, it is the small deictic markers of time that are most prone to omission. The three **underlined** examples above are all omitted by TT3, while the *now* of *we say to you* **now** is omitted by the three interpreters in TT1, TT2 and TT3.

The future frame is realized through a combination of overt naming of those to come (**next** *generation [of Americans]* [22], *to the* **future** *world* [159], *our* **children's** *children* [164], **future** *generations* [167]) and the common use (11 examples) of the positively inscribed token *new* (**new** *life* [41], *a* **new** *way forward* [112]), **new** *era of responsibility* [142–3]). These are not immune from omission, as evidenced by the three underlined examples.

However, it is the past frame and the many allusions to history and remembrance that are most prominent, as can be seen in the full list:

> *our ancestors* (03), *our forbears* (10), *our founding documents* (11), *endured the lash of the whip* (41–2), *plowed the hard earth* (42), *Concord and Gettysburg, Normandy and Khe Sanh* (42–3), *our Founding Fathers* (83), *faced down fascism and communism* (91), *earlier generations* (91), *we are the keepers of this legacy* (96), *with old friends and former foes* (99), *we have tasted the bitter swill of civil war and segregation* (107–8), *old hatreds* (109), *fallen heroes who lie in Arlington* (126), *guardians of our liberty* (128), *levees break* (134), *workers who would rather cut their hours* (135), *the firefighter's courage to storm a stairway filled with smoke* (136), *whose father 60 years ago might not have been served at a local restaurant* (150–1), *in the year of America's birth* (154), *a small band of patriots* (154), *the father of our nation* (157).

These range through American history from the War of Independence and the founding of the nation (*in the year of America's birth; a small band of patriots; the father of our nation*) to slavery, the Civil War, the settling of the West, key battles of war (*Concord and Gettysburg, Normandy and Khe Sanh*) to contemporary crises such as 9/11 (*the firefighter's courage*) and the floods of New Orleans (*the levees break*). As discussed in Section 2.2.5 above, a characteristic of the speech (indeed, part of the magic) is that many of these references are implicitly invoked rather than directly inscribed and they work particularly through the association placed on them by the American audience.[97]

The result of the spatio-temporal markers is the presentation, as a coherent whole, of the history of the American people (the *we* [iia] and audience B in Tables

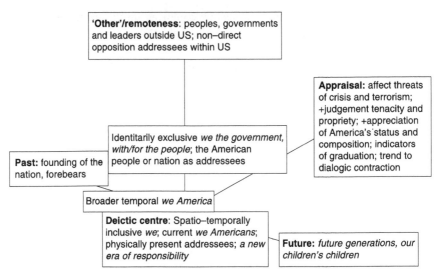

FIGURE 2.3 Deictic positioning in the Obama inaugural

2.8 and 2.9 above), from the founding of the nation to the present. This is further reinforcement for the central theme that each member of the group must assume his/her responsibility (the *we* [iib] in Table 2.8 above). Figure 2.3 shows the deictic positioning profile that may be deduced in the ST.

The strong deictic centre of *we Americans* in the present is strongly linked along the spatial cline from past to future. Into this profile, along an axiological axis from the deictic centre, has been inserted the expression of **appraisal**, replacing what Chilton calls 'modality' (see Figure 2.2). As we have seen throughout Chapters 1 and 2, appraisal extends well beyond modality to encompass core axiological values of affect, judgement and appreciation and, with the resources of engagement and graduation, dialogically negotiates meaning with the receiver.

2.3.3 Reading position and voice of the interpreter

The interpreters of TT1 and TT2 most probably worked from a written version of the speech, released in advance of the event (Dougherty 2009; see this chapter, Section 2.2 above). As well as reducing the cognitive demands on the interpreter, it should also be noted that in some ways Obama's erudite, academic delivery is easier to translate as the interpreter's conscious affective engagement with the subject may be minimal (Alarcón 2009). It is TT3, from the Peruvian Canal N, that provides the most unusual interpreting since the reporter covering the event also undertakes the interpreting. Such a condition brings together two roles and the result is a blurring of voices. The transition from one to the other frames the whole speech. Thus, the move from the swearing of the oath to the beginning of the speech is rendered as follows:

He makes a few mistakes as he swears the oath ... and I will do it to the best of my ability ... **Now he does begin the speech** ... My fellow citizens, **says Barack Obama**, I stand today here ...[98]

The bold highlights indicate the reporter voice (see p. 46) which gradually gives way to translator voice[99] as Obama moves into his speech. Note that this is a gradual process, not a clear-cut division between reporting and translating. Later in the speech, the reporter voice resurfaces, first of all as a simple *dice* ('he says'), and then more extensively as a strategy to cover the gaps in the interpreting caused by the journalist's inability to keep pace with the speech. Thus:

ST: Nor is the question before us whether the market is a force ... ~~for good or ill. Its~~ power to generate wealth ~~and expand freedom is unmatched~~. But this crisis has reminded us that ~~without a watchful eye ... the market can spin out of control~~. The nation cannot prosper ~~long~~ when it favors only the prosperous ... ~~The success of our economy has always depended not just on the size of our gross domestic product, but on the reach of our prosperity, on the ability to extend opportunity to every willing heart – not out of charity ... but because~~ it is the surest route to our common good ... ~~As for our common defense~~ ... we reject as false ... the choice between our safety and our ideals ... (ST: 76–83, ~~strikethrough~~ text is omitted in TT)

TT3: The question neither is if the market is a force ... we know that ... the power of ... the desire to generate money is clear, but this crisis has made us see that the country cannot prosper if it favors only the prosperous ... **Also he speaks about those sectors that remain on the margins of prosperity** this is the surest way to common good, **says Barack Obama, he makes reference to the economic crisis, to greed** and in these moments we reject ... we reject to have to choose between our ideas and national security.[100]

Here the journalist switches to mediated attribution (highlighted in bold), summarizing through reported speech what she has omitted (see ~~strikethrough~~ in the ST). However, close analysis of the two extracts shows that these summaries are in fact inaccurate and draw more on the overall frame of reception created by earlier arguments. So, *those sectors that remain on the margins of prosperity* relates to Obama's immediately preceding comments on employment, health care and retirement problems (ST: 69–70 and, earlier, 16–17), while *reference to the economic crisis, to greed* was mentioned much earlier (in ST: 13–15). This suggests the strong influence exerted on the interpreter by these phrases in those sections of the speech.

Once this strategy of switching voice has been established, it is used by the journalist on two other occasions when she produces text which goes as far as to border on the correspondent voice (Martin and White 2005: 178, 185; see also Chapter 1, Section 1.5), analysing and interpreting the message of the President. The passage where Obama states that America is a friend of each nation (ST: 88–89) is translated closely but the translator's voice then switches with the addition of the commentator's voice:

> *this is the message which Barack Obama directs to the whole world, he wants peace and so does the United States people, that is what he says in his inauguration speech.*[101]

Similarly, when Obama speaks of himself as

> *a man whose father less than 60 years ago might not have been served in a local restaurant can now stand before you to take a most sacred oath* (ST: 150–2).

a shift to correspondent voice is again made in the TT:

> my father 60 years ago might not have been served in a local restaurant, says Barack Obama, **but now yes and he is precisely representing this great change in US history on becoming president number 44 of the United States.**[102]

At the end of the speech, the journalist immediately moves back from translator voice, highlighting specific themes of citizens' responsibility, duty, service, etc. This marks a definitive return to the reporter voice. The speech act represented by Obama's words has ended even if, quite unusually, it has been blurred by the peppering of other voices with which the journalist has sought to distance herself from the deictic centre and from the translator's alignment with the speaker. In this way, she has afforded herself some freedom to evaluate the speech as a reporter or correspondent.

2.4 Conclusion

The very detailed analysis of the Obama speech has demonstrated the value of an appraisal-based analysis for understanding the construal and projection of value in the ST. Obama's speech is heavily saturated with lexical expressions of judgement, with indirect evaluation such as metaphor and with what we have termed invoked-associative attitude – *toiled in sweatshops ... endured the lash of the whip*, and so on. The TT Spanish interpretings have not obviously distorted the ST and the basic inscribed value patterns have been transferred. There are few cases of a shift in attitudinal category. However, the TTs have shown the omission of some epithets which occur with a value-laden noun (e.g. *hard-earned peace*) and especially of graduation, predominantly modal adjuncts and counter-expectancy indicators (*even greater, only . . .*) and non-core lexis (*ills* > 'problems', *wield* > 'use'). Suggested critical points, identified from their cultural prominence and range of translations, are context-dependent markers of invoked-associative attitude: *old*, which is explicated in some written translations to give the positive sense of *age-old*, and *patchwork heritage*. The latter is a potentially sensitive term as it relates to the variety of faiths in American society. The interpreters tend to standardize, omitting *patchwork*, while the translators explicate and/or standardize (e.g. *multi-ethnic heritage*). *Patchwork heritage* is seen to be problematic for translators in Chinese and Japanese too.

Another critical point in this speech was pronouns, which are used by Obama to position himself close to the listener and to create a bond of inclusiveness with the American people. Analysis incorporating the concept of deictic positioning (Chilton 2004) has been useful in describing this political move. In this model, attitude sits firmly on the axiological axis while the pronoun choice locates the speaker in regard to the listener. In some languages, such as Japanese or Behasa Indonesia, a translator/interpreter has to make a choice between an inclusive or exclusive first person plural, a distinction which English is able to skirt over by the ambiguity of *we*. At a strategic level, the reading position in the TT may shift: the Peruvian interpreter from Canal N goes so far as to switch between reporter and interpreter function, at times adopting a correspondent voice to relay Obama's words in reported speech. At a higher level still, the axiological and ideological message of the text may be truncated or manipulated by censorship or recontextualization of various forms.

APPENDIX 2.1

Transcript of Obama inaugural speech, 20 January 2009*

1   Thank you ... Thank *you* ...

2   My fellow citizens – I stand here today ... *humbled* by the task before us... grateful for the
3   trust you have bestowed ... mindful of the sacrifices borne by our ancestors.

4   I thank President Bush for his service to our nation – (applause) – as well as the generosity
5   and cooperation he has shown throughout this transition.

6   Forty-four Americans ... have now taken ... the presidential oath. The words have been
7   spoken during rising tides of prosperity ... and the still waters of peace... Yet, every so often,
8   the oath is taken amidst gathering clouds ... and raging storms... At these moments, America
9   has carried on not simply because of the skill or vision of those in high office, but because
10 we ... the people ... have remained faithful to the ideals of our forebears ... and true to our
11 founding documents.

12 So it has been ... so it must be with this ... generation of Americans.
13 That we are in the midst of crisis is now well understood. Our nation is at war... against a far-
14 reaching network ... of violence and hatred. Our economy is badly weakened, a
15 consequence of ... greed and irresponsibility on the part of some, but also our collective
16 failure to make hard choices ... and prepare the nation ... for a new age. Homes have been
17 lost, jobs shed, businesses shuttered. Our health care is too costly, our schools fail too many
18 – and each day brings further evidence that the ways we use energy strengthen our
19 adversaries and threaten our planet.

20 These are the ... indicators of crisis, subject to data and statistics ... Less measurable, but no
21 less profound, is a sapping of confidence ... across our land; a nagging fear that ... America's
22 decline ... is inevitable, that the next generation must lower its sights.

23 Today I say to you that the challenges we face are real. They are serious and they are many.
24 They will not met ... be met easily or in a short span of time. But know this America: They
25 will be met. (Applause.)

26 On this day ... we gather because we have chosen hope over fear, unity of purpose ... over
27 conflict and discord. On this day ... we come to proclaim an end to the petty grievances and
28 false promises, the recriminations and worn-out dogmas ... that for far too long have
29 strangled our politics ... We remain a young nation... but in the words of Scripture, the time
30 has come ... to set aside childish things. The time has come ... to reaffirm our enduring spirit,
31 to choose our better history, to carry forward that precious gift, that noble idea passed on
32 from generation to generation, the God-given promise that *all* are equal, *all* are free, and *all*
33 deserve a chance to pursue their full measure of happiness. (Applause.)

34 In reaffirming ... the greatness of our nation ... we understand that greatness is never a
35 given ... It must be earned. Our journey has never been one of short-cuts or settling for less...
36 It has not been the path for the faint-hearted ... for those that prefer leisure over work, or
37 seek only the pleasures of riches and fame. Rather, it has been the risk-takers, the doers,
38 the makers of things – some celebrated, but more often men and women obscure in their
39 labor – who have carried us ... up the long, rugged path towards prosperity and freedom.

40   For *us* . . . they packed up their few worldly possessions and traveled across oceans in search
41   of a new life. For *us*, they toiled in sweatshops, and settled the West, endured the lash of
42   the whip, and plowed the hard earth. For *us*, they fought and died . . . in places like Concord
43   and Gettysburg, Normandy and Khe Sahn.

44   Time and again these men and women struggled and sacrificed and worked till their hands
45   were raw so that we might live a better life. They saw America as bigger . . . than the sum of
46   our individual ambitions, greater than all the differences of birth or wealth or faction.

47   *This* is the journey we continue today. We remain the most . . . prosperous, powerful nation
48   on Earth. Our workers are no less productive than when this crisis began. Our minds are no
49   less inventive, our goods and services . . . no less needed than they were last week, or last
50   month, or last year. Our capacity remains undiminished . . . But our time of standing pat, . . . of
51   protecting narrow interests and putting off unpleasant decisions – that time has surely
52   passed. Starting *today*, we must pick ourselves up, dust ourselves off, and begin again the
53   work of remaking America. (Applause.)

54   For everywhere we look, there is work to be done. The state of our economy calls for action,
55   bold and swift. And we will act, not only to create new jobs, but to lay a new foundation for
56   growth. We will build the roads and bridges, the electric grids and digital lines that feed our
57   commerce . . . and bind us together. We will restore science to its rightful place, and wield
58   technology's wonders to raise health care's quality and lower its cost. We will harness the
59   sun and the winds and the soil to fuel our cars and run our factories . . . and we will transform
60   our schools and colleges and universities to meet the demands of a new age. All this we *can*
61   do. All this we *will* do.

62   Now, there are some who question the scale of our ambitions . . . who suggest that our
63   system . . . cannot tolerate too many big plans . . . Their memories are short . . . for they have
64   forgotten what this country has already done, what free men and women can achieve
65   when. . . imagination is joined to common purpose . . . and necessity to courage. What the
66   cynics fail to understand is that the ground has shifted beneath them, that the stale political
67   arguments that have consumed us for so long no longer apply.

68   The question we ask today is not whether our government is too big or too small, but
69   whether it works, whether it helps families find jobs at a decent wage, care they can afford,
70   a retirement that is dignified. Where the answer is yes . . . we intend to move forward. Where
71   the answer is no . . . programs will end. And those of us who manage the public's dollars will
72   be held to account, to spend wisely, reform bad habits, and do our business in the light of
73   day, because only *then* can we restore the vital trust between a people and their
74   government.

75   Nor is the question before us whether the market is a force . . . for good or ill. Its power to
76   generate wealth and expand freedom is unmatched. But this crisis has reminded us that
77   without a watchful eye . . . the market can spin out of control. The nation cannot prosper long
78   when it favors only the prosperous . . . The success of our economy has always depended not
79   just on the size of our gross domestic product, but on the reach of our prosperity, on the
80   ability to extend opportunity to every willing heart – not out of charity . . . but because it is
81   the surest route to our common good. (Applause.)

82   As for our common defense . . . we reject as false . . . the choice between our safety and our
83   ideals . . . our Founding Fathers – (applause) – our Founding Fathers, faced with perils that we
84   can scarcely imagine, drafted a charter to assure the rule of law and the rights of man, a
85   charter expanded by the blood of generations. Those ideals still light the world. . . and we will
86   not give them up for expedience's sake. (Applause.)

87 And so ... to all the other peoples and governments who are watching today, from the
88 grandest capitals to the small village where my father was born, know that America is a
89 friend of *each* nation, and *every* man, woman and child who seeks a future of peace and
90 dignity, and we are ready to lead once more. (Applause.)

91 Recall that earlier generations faced down fascism and communism ... not just with missiles
92 and tanks, but with sturdy alliances and enduring convictions. They understood that our
93 power alone cannot protect us... nor does it entitle us to do as we please. Instead they knew
94 that our power grows ... through its prudent use, our security emanates from the justness of
95 our cause, the force of our example, the tempering qualities ... of humility and restraint.

96 We are the keepers of this legacy ... Guided by these principles once more we can meet
97 those new threats that demand even greater effort, even greater cooperation and
98 understanding between nations. We will begin to responsibly leave Iraq to its people ... and
99 forge a hard-earned peace in Afghanistan. With old friends and former foes, we'll work
100 tirelessly to lessen the nuclear threat, and roll back the specter of a warming planet.

101 We will not apologize for our way of life, nor will we waver in its defense, and for those who
102 seek to advance their aims by inducing terror and slaughtering innocents, we say to you now
103 that our spirit is stronger and cannot be broken, you cannot outlast us, and we will defeat
104 you. (Applause.)

105 For we know ... that our patchwork heritage is a strength ... not a weakness. We are a nation
106 of Christians and Muslims ... Jews and Hindus ... and non-believers. We are shaped by every
107 language and culture, drawn from every end of this earth, and because we have tasted the
108 bitter swill of civil war and segregation and emerged from that dark chapter stronger and
109 more united, we cannot help but believe that the old hatreds shall someday pass, that the
110 lines of tribe shall soon dissolve, that as the world grows smaller, our common humanity
111 shall reveal itself, and that America must play its role in ushering in a new era of peace.

112 To the Muslim world, we seek a new way forward, based on mutual interest and mutual
113 respect ... To those leaders around the globe who seek to sow conflict, or blame their
114 society's ills on the West, know that your people will judge you on what you can build ... not
115 what you destroy. (Applause.)

116 To those ... who cling to power through corruption and deceit and the silencing of dissent,
117 know that you are on the wrong side of history ... but that we will extend a hand ... if you are
118 willing to unclench your fist. (Applause.)

119 To the people of poor nations, we pledge to work alongside you to make your farms flourish
120 and let clean waters flow, to nourish starved bodies and feed hungry minds. And to those
121 nations like ours that ... enjoy relative plenty, we say we can no longer afford indifference to
122 the suffering outside our borders, nor can we consume the world's resources without regard
123 to effect ... For the world has changed ... and we must change with it.

124 As we consider the role that unfolds before us, we remember ... with humble gratitude ...
125 those brave Americans who ... at this very hour ... patrol far-off deserts and distant
126 mountains ... They have something to tell us ... just as the fallen heroes who lie in Arlington
127 whisper through the ages.

128 We honor them not only because they are the guardians of our liberty, but because they
129 embody ... the spirit of service ... a willingness to find meaning in something greater than
130 themselves.

131 And yet at *this* moment . . . a moment that will define a generation . . . it is precisely this spirit
132 that must inhabit us *all* . . . For as much as government can do, and *must* do, it is ultimately
133 the faith and determination of the American people upon which this nation relies. It is the
134 kindness to take in a stranger when the levees break, the selflessness of workers who would
135 rather cut their hours than see a friend lose their job which sees us through our darkest
136 hours. It is the firefighter's courage to storm a stairway filled with smoke, but also a parent's
137 willingness to nurture a child. . . that finally decides our fate.

138 Our challenges may be new . . . The instruments with which we meet them may be new. . . But
139 those values upon which our success depends – honesty . . . and hard work, courage and fair
140 play, tolerance and curiosity, loyalty and patriotism – . . . these things are old . . . These things
141 are true . . . They have been the quiet force of progress throughout our history.

142 What is demanded, then, is a return . . . to these truths. What is required of us now is a *new*
143 era of responsibility . . . a recognition on the part of every American that we have duties to
144 ourselves, our nation and the world, duties that we do not grudgingly accept, but rather
145 seize gladly, firm in the knowledge that there is nothing so satisfying to the spirit . . . so
146 defining of our character . . . than giving our all to a difficult task.

147 *This* is the price and the promise of citizenship. *This* is the source of our confidence – the
148 knowledge that God calls on us to shape an uncertain destiny. *This* is the meaning of our
149 liberty and our creed, why men and women and children of every *race* and every *faith* can
150 join in celebration across this magnificent mall . . . And why a man whose father less than 60
151 years ago might not have been served in a local restaurant can now stand before you to
152 take a most sacred oath. (Applause.)

153 So let us mark this day with remembrance . . . of who we are . . . and how far we have
154 traveled . . . In the year of America's birth, in the coldest of months, a small band of patriots
155 huddled by . . . dying campfires on the shores of an icy river. The capital was abandoned. The
156 enemy was advancing. The snow was stained with blood . . . At the moment when the
157 outcome of our revolution was most in doubt, the father of our nation ordered these words
158 to be read to the people . . .

159 'Let it be told to the future world . . . that in the depth of winter, when nothing but hope and
160 virtue could survive . . . that the city and the country, alarmed at one common danger, came
161 forth to meet it.'

162 America: In the face of our common dangers, in this winter of our hardship, let us
163 remember these timeless words. With hope and virtue, let us brave once more the icy
164 currents . . . and endure what storms may come. Let it be said by our *children's* children that
165 when we were tested we refused to let this journey end, that we did not turn back nor did
166 we falter, and with eyes fixed on the horizon and God's grace upon us, we carried forth that
167 great gift of freedom and delivered it safely . . . to future generations.

168 Thank you . . . God bless you . . . And God bless the United States of America. (Applause.)[103]

3

THE VIEW FROM THE TECHNICAL TRANSLATORS

3.0 Introduction

In Chapter 2 we used appraisal theory for a very detailed analysis of the Obama ST and its various interpreting and written translations. The results were revealing of certain critical points and translation procedures and strategies in political speech. But the questions tackled in this chapter are: How far do critical points differ in technical texts? How conscious are technical translators of them? The investigation will employ two methods:

- phone and email interviews with 11 technical translators working in a range of languages and contexts (Section 3.1); and
- an analysis of two online forums where translators post queries and discuss translation problems and solutions. These forums are KudoZ™ (Section 3.2) and SENSE (Section 3.3).

In his presentation of a method for descriptive translation studies, Toury (1995: 65) claims that extratextual sources, such as comments from the translators themselves, may be incomplete and biased in favour of the informants. While it is clear such comments cannot give unfiltered access to the cognitive processing that has been undertaken, at the very least they do reveal what the informant thinks they should be doing (that is, what they think social and professional norms dictate). At best, the comments give real insight into the type of evaluation and criteria that guided the translator's or reviser's selection of the general strategy or specific procedures.

3.1 The perception of the professionals

The initial attempt to examine professionals' perceptions of critical translation points was through interviews with selected subjects. Each interview was preceded by email contact and a set of questions:

1. What really causes a translator/interpreter to stop and think, to change their minds, to agonize?
2. Which points in a text are really problematic, and why?
3. Where does the translator/interpreter/reviser feel that their subjective evaluation is most apparent?
4. Which points are more critical than others, and why?
5. How far do language, text-type, genre, purpose, audience, etc. affect the critical points?

These questions were designed to help the interviewee prepare responses but general enough to avoid the possibility of their being prompted to respond along lines predetermined by the hypotheses or interests of the research.

As can be seen, the specific goal of the research (the identification of 'critical . . . points') was highlighted, along with a vague definition ('points in a text [that] are really problematic' and 'where . . . subjective evaluation is most apparent'). Suggested general causes are listed (language, text-type, etc.) but no specific examples of critical points are given.

Seven telephone interviews were carried out in February 2011 and lasted an average of 10–15 minutes. Subjects were:

*   G1, a senior German>English translator for a large UK-based agency
*   G2, a German>English translator and reviser of legal and financial texts for a large UK-based agency
*   G3 and G4, in-house German>English translators for a solar energy company in the UK
*   NL, a freelance Dutch>English translator based in the UK
*   PT, a Portuguese>English translator of legal texts for a large UK-based translation agency
*   SC, an in-house translator for a large Scandinavian-based translation agency.

Four email interviews were also conducted with in-house translators of a China-based financial institution working between Chinese and English. These 11 subjects therefore cover a range of languages, text-types and professional situations, although there is no claim that they are fully representative of the profession as a whole. While all respondents were keen to take part, it quickly became clear that some were left a little disconcerted by the open-endedness of the questions and required further prompting before they were able to offer their own examples.

Four of the interviewees worked as German>English technical translators or revisers. Some of the problems they raised were common to each of them. Thus they mention the problem of false friends (e.g. *sognenannt*, where the calque *so-called* may sometimes be best avoided in favour of an equivalent such as *known as*) and embedded adjectival structures such as the following:

> *Sie versorgen unsere Kunden mit Informationen, die diese zur Bewertung der zum Verkauf oder Kauf stehenden Einheiten benötigen.*

['You supply our clients with information, which they for the evaluation of the for sale or purchase standing units need']

You deliver to our clients the facts that they need when negotiating the value of entities they plan to sell or acquire.

In this example, the difficulty is resolved by a syntactic shift in the second part of the clause from a German noun-based structure to an English verb-based structure (... *Bewertung* ... *Verkauf* ... *Kauf* ... to ... *when negotiating* ... *they plan to sell or acquire*). In more complex instances, the translator may need to split the German sentences in English. However, the sentence seems to be an important unit of translation and even of revision. Senior translator G3 commented that 'I generally operate on the sentence level. I can't see any other way.'

The most frequent problems noted by the informants were lexical items that occupy different semantic spaces in the two languages. Above all, where a single word in the SL (source language) corresponds to a range of possible correspondents in the TL (target language). Examples are the general English verb *to handle* or the German technical term *Stoßverbinder* (*joint connector, spigot, in-line splices*, and so on). The problem is one of finding a contextually and collocationally appropriate TT item or selecting amongst competing potential equivalents. An example of where this becomes a question of the interpretation of the ST meaning is the German *Aufwand*, which can mean *time spent, effort expended, cost incurred*, or any combination of the three. In more technical texts, the word *Belastung* causes headaches, because it means *loading*, both in the mechanical and in the electrical senses, but can also mean *impact, stress, strain*, amongst many others. Some of these are quite far from the core meaning. Polysemous words where the correct translation equivalent is contextually motivated were raised by informants as a frequent problem in translation revision. An example is the noun *Leistung*. Examination of dictionary or corpus equivalents shows these to be manifold, posing problems for both humans and machines. For instance, equivalents that appear in TTs cited on the linguee[1] website are:

> *service, performance, power, achievement, benefit, capacity, output, efficiency, effort, accomplishment, showing, payment, rating, merit, attainment, feat, proficiency, provision of services, power output, engine power.*[2]

With some terms, the distinction between competing equivalents can be critical. Thus, the German legal translators noted the common problem of differentiating between *lawyer, solicitor* and *barrister: lawyer* is a general term, a *solicitor's* work involves wills, property purchases and so on, while a *barrister* represents clients in the higher courts. The same problem occurs in other languages. The Portuguese legal translator pointed to the solution of using the same equivalent for each accompanied by the English term in parenthesis as a discriminator, for example, *advogado* (*lawyer*).

In this category of problem, there were a few examples directly related to attitude. Translator G4 gave the general example of the German adjective or adverb *anspruchsvoll*. Of a person or building, this can variously be translated as *sophisticated, complicated, discerning, discriminating*. Such disambiguation necessarily entails subjective evaluation from the translator, as in this example taken from a website for a Hungarian hotel, translated from German into English:

> *Das Hotel hält 13* **anspruchsvoll** *eingerichtete Doppelzimmer und 4 klimatisierte Suiten für die Gäste bereit.*[3]
>
> ['The hotel holds 13 'anspruchsvoll' equipped/appointed double rooms and 4 air-conditioned suites for the guests ready']
>
> There are 13 **fastidiously** furnished double rooms and 4 suites available for our guests.[4]

Here, the interesting point is that the translation equivalent, *fastidiously*, is also attitudinally ambiguous – hence, the entry for *fastidious* in the *Collins Cobuild Dictionary* (1995: 608) points to attention to detail or cleanliness but also 'to an extent that many people consider to be too fussy'. Yet the translator has opted for a domain-specific collocation, *fastidiously furnished*, which tends to be marked as positive.[5] Analysis of further German>English translations of *anspruchsvoll* in other contexts gives some remarkably different interpretations. Linguee allows these to be graded by contributors and readers. In order of preference, the equivalents are: *demanding, challenging, sophisticated, ambitious, discriminating, exacting, discerning, fastidious, upmarket, pretentious, taxing, highbrow.*[6] They congeal around certain points on a positive–negative cline of evaluation: thus, *pretentious* is obviously negative, and *discriminating* and *discerning* clearly positive. The others, which are context-dependent, are predominantly positive (*challenging, sophisticated*). *Anspruchsvoll* is also a gradeable concept: a common ST feature is an adverbial modification of the adjective in the ST, hence *sehr/recht anspruchsvoll* ('very/really demanding'). This tends to be further exaggerated in the TT equivalents, as in the following two examples:

> *Dass diese Forderungen* **anspruchsvoll** *sind und der Einstieg in die Zukunft nicht leicht werden würde, war auch im vergangenen Jahr jedem bewusst.*[7]
>
> ['That these requirements are **demanding** and the leap into the future would not be easy, was also in past years known to all']
>
> We were aware from the outset that these requirements were **extremely demanding**, and that this leap into the future wouldn't be easy.[8]

> *Die Anforderungen an die Städtefreundschaft sind* **anspruchsvoll**.[9]
>
> ['The requirements of city twinning are **demanding**']
>
> The requirements placed on the city friendship are **actually quite demanding**.[10]

Neither of the ST uses is adverbially modified. Yet in translation the force of the evaluation is intensified, as **extremely** *demanding* and, in the second sentence, by the double modifier **actually quite** *demanding*. Why this should be so is unclear.

One plausible explanation is that it may be part of a general translation move towards explicitation and disambiguation of attitudinally rich items.

Other forms of evaluation that were specifically commented on by the interviewees were discourse markers, which in appraisal theory are counter-expectancy indicators (see Chapter 1, Section 1.3.3 and Chapter 2, Section 2.2.7), and modal verbs (see Chapter 1, Sections 1.2 and Chapter 2, Section 2.2.8). Two examples of discourse markers were provided: *grundsätzlich*, which means 'in principle' but which is used for emphasis (e.g. 'you <u>must</u> do something'), especially in legal documents where the writer seeks to achieve clarity; and *bzw* [*beziehungsweise*]. According to senior agency translator and reviser G1, native speakers of German, when translating the latter to English, tend to choose the incorrect *respectively*. G1's preferred translation is the conjunction *or* (e.g. *Technologielinien bzw. Medizintechnikanwendungen* as *technology or technical applications used in medicine*). Alternatively, in a legal contract, it may mean 'and, if applicable'.

G3 highlighted German modal particles as causing particular problems and as requiring revision in translations made by less experienced translators who maybe overlook their importance. Such particles (*auch, doch, eben, einmal, ja, schon*, etc.) are stereotypical markers of interpersonal attitude since they indicate the speaker's evaluation of a phenomenon or event, and are a well-known and studied form in German (e.g. House 2008, 2011; see Chapter 1, Section 1.2.1). They are clearly crucial for the transmission of translator attitude.

The link with other forms of modality was also quite striking. G1 mentioned modal verbs in German, notably *dürfen*. Her explanation of the problem concerns ambiguity as follows:

> it means *may* in the sense of 'have permission'. However, the problem in English is that in some cases, if you put *may* it can be unclear whether you in fact mean 'might/could' rather than having permission to do something.

In theoretical terms, the problem is therefore one of the type of modality. *Dürfen* is a realization of modality of obligation (see Halliday and Matthiessen 2004: 147), at the lower end of the 'allowed to/supposed to/required to' cline. This is G1's 'may/ have permission' or 'be allowed to'. The following example, taken from a German text on human biobanks illustrates this:

> *Aus Gründen des Datenschutzes sind Proben getrennt von personenbezogenen Daten aufzubewahren und **dürfen** auch an Dritte nur pseudonymisiert weitergegeben werden.*[11]
> ['For reasons of data protection samples are stored separately from personal data and **dürfen** also passed on to third parties only pseudonymised']
> Samples are to be stored separately from personal data and **may** only be passed on to third parties if they are pseudonymised for data protection reasons.[12]

Here, the sense of *dürfen* is quite clearly that of permission for the transfer, subject to the specific conditions. Potential problems could arise since in English *may* is also an expression of modality of probability/possibility (e.g. 'it may be difficult to determine the cause'). As G1 says, in a legal document this difference can be crucial and clarity is paramount. Consider the following extract from the German and English versions of European Commission Regulation 50/2000 on the labelling of foodstuffs:

> ... *die Richtlinie 89/107/EWG des Rates vom 21. Dezember 1988 zur Angleichung der Rechtsvorschriften der Mitgliedstaaten über Zusatzstoffe, die in Lebensmitteln verwendet werden* **dürfen** ...
>
> ['... Directive 89/107/EEC of the Council of 21 December 1988 on the approximation of the legislation of the Member States concerning additives, which in foodstuffs be used **dürfen** ...']
>
> ... Council Directive 89/107/EEC of 21 December 1988 on the approximation of the laws of the Member States concerning food additives **authorised** for use in foodstuffs intended for human consumption ...[13]

The drafting of EC legislation is a complex, multilingual and multilegal process in which each language version has equal legal status (see Biel 2007, European Commission and Directorate-General for Translation 2011). Here the English version avoids *may* and clarifies the sense with the term *authorised for use*, clearly showing that this means that prior permission must be granted. G1 notes that she deals with certain configurations of *dürfen* differently. Thus, in negative sentences she usually chooses *must not*. ST combinations with *nur* (the counter-expectancy indicator 'only') also serve to constrict possible interpretations (e.g. *Gedruckte Zeichnungen* **dürfen nur** *für einzelne Aufträge verwendet werden*, translated as *Printed drawings* **may only** *be used for individual orders*). Such observations show that intensification of ST attitudinal indicators is useful for translators for disambiguating potentially confusing realizations and that translators devise batteries of ready-made solutions to cope with these problems.

3.1.1 Text-type and explicitation

Text-type is also important. In advertising and promotional literature, G3 perceived that German tended to be 'long-winded', whereas in UK English such texts were shorter and more intense. She worked from an evaluation of the impact that needed to be made on the reader. G4 also considered marketing texts to be more challenging than more technical texts, since they require an ability to 'write well' in English and a sensitivity to TL conventions. The latter, he said, was the fruit of experience although some areas of good practice, such as terminology mining and rereading, could be taught. G4 made interesting points about the role of different translators and how this impacts on translation choice. Thus, he posited that, for marketing texts, in-house translators may grant themselves more latitude since they are more familiar with the image the company wishes to project and have more opportunity to check possible translations for acceptability with management.

Even so, when the translator has doubts, the tendency is to 'hedge your bets' and to opt for something that 'can't be wrong'.

In some cases, a value-laden culture-specific term requires either explicitation or standardization to correspond to the receivers' inferencing needs. An instance of explicitation given by G4 relates to the typical character traits of East-Westphalians which are associated with the success of a company. The German adjective *hartnaeckig* can be rendered either as *stubborn* or *tenacious*, both realizations of judgement (specifically tenacity) and both stressing determination. In the example, the option *tenacious* is preferred because of the positive association; *stubborn* would be equivalent to 'unreasonably refusing to change one's way or mind'. On the other hand, standardization is used in the deletion of information considered to be superfluous to the receiver. An example given was the reference to the home town of the company's celebrity sponsor golfer: thus, ST *Bernard Langer (Anhausen)* becomes the standardized TT *the German Bernhard Langer*. This type of evaluative decision is made according to the perceived needs of the receiver and by instinctive judgement as to the cues that are informationally relevant (Gutt 2000).

3.1.2 The Chinese context

Some of the same problems were noted by the informants in China, translators in both directions between Chinese into English for mainly internal business purposes. For example, in a banking environment terminology, consistency and accuracy are much more important than in other domains. A mismatch of semantic space is also a problem, thus one respondent gave the example of 落实 (*luò shí*), a commonly used word in Chinese reports, which may be translated as *implement, carry out, decide, establish, fulfil*, etc. But higher-level considerations were prominent amongst the four respondents. These relate first to cohesion (part of Halliday's Mode and textual metafunction, see Chapter 1, Section 1.2) and discourse organization, which is considered to be much more explicit in English. An example provided was the following:

> [1] 为建立健全本行整体内部控制体系, [2] 保证内部控制措施的有效运行, [3] 提高内部控制水平, [4] 加强合规意识, [5] 明确内部控制责任, [6] 防控案件风险, [7] 根据YYY有关要求, [8] 本行2010 年度继续实行案件防控工作目标责任制。
>
> [[1] To perfect the overall internal control system of XXX, [2] ensure the effectiveness of the internal control measures, [3] improve its internal control level, [4] build up the compliance awareness of staff, [5] clarify internal control responsibilities and [6] prevent/control case risks, [7] pursuant to relevant requirements of YYY, [8] this bank in 2010 will continue to carry out the case prevention accountability system.]

In the respondent's explanation, on the surface the six clauses may seem equal. But on closer analysis, 1 and 2 can be seen to be more general, while 3, 4, 5 and

6 are more specific. The ST is also structured so that the 'new' information about the bank's future actions is located in the prominent final position. The informant's suggested wording for the translation involves a major shift in the hierarchy of the clauses and in the presentation of information:

> [1] To perfect the overall internal control system of XXX and [2] ensure the effectiveness of the internal control measures, [8] this Bank will continue to carry out the case prevention accountability system in 2010, [7] pursuant to relevant requirements of YYY, so as [3] to improve its internal control level, [4] build up the compliance awareness of staff, [5] clarify internal control responsibilities and [6] prevent/control case risks.

The main clause 8 (*this Bank will continue to . . .*) is promoted in the organizational hierarchy, which arranges the message more conventionally in English. However, it means that there is a shift in the information structure with elements 3–6 now occurring in final position. Here, the translator configures the information to match what he/she perceives to be cultural and processing differences between the source and target audience. Thus, one of the respondents explicitly stated that this type of example represented 'different ways of thinking and of expressing ideas (linear analysis for English-speaking people and circular synthesis for Chinese) . . . Quite frequently, you have to figure out the logic between sentences first before putting them into the target language.' This perception of differences in cognitive processing was reinforced by the higher-level cultural differences that the same respondents say affected their translation. This particularly manifested itself in the perception that Westerners were more direct, and blunter. It contrasted to what one respondent indicated was a 'Chinese mindset' of 'be polite, non-aggressive, and avoid confrontation in the translation process'. The effect on the translation process is a tendency towards understatement and implicitation. For instance, if an apparently complaining email arrives, care is taken in the translation not to offend the receiver or to create problems between sender and receiver.

The interviews with the various informants were useful in extracting some examples of what the technical translators consciously considered to be problematic points. As we have seen, these were often technical and, with the exception of the Chinese examples, mainly located at the lexical and technical level. However, it was also clear that direct interviews were sometimes not able to elicit detailed information about the working processes of the translator. This was either because of the very general nature of the questions, the lack of familiarity of the respondents with this type of empirical research or, most crucially, because many critical points become most apparent at the moment they are encountered in a text. In order to circumvent these problems, a more detailed source of examples and a more indirect form of observation was employed – the study of online forums KudoZ™ (Section 3.2) and SENSE (Section 3.3).

3.2 KudoZ™

Proz.com, created in Syracuse, New York, by Henry Dotterer in 1999, is perhaps the best-known translation industry website. By 2010 it had at least 389,000 users. A total of some 224,000 jobs and 2.3 million translation queries had been posted on the site (Goddard 2010: 20). Many of the queries relate to terminology issues. They are posted on the part of the site known as KudoZ™[14] and receive replies from members. Respondents grade their own replies according to their confidence in their correctness (4 being the most confident), while other members may indicate peer agreement with the suggestions. The querier then selects the preferred response and awards 'KudoZ points' to the answers that are deemed worthy.[15]

In its own online description, 'the KudoZ network provides a framework for translators and others to assist each other with translations or explanations of terms and short phrases'. For the researcher it gives a certain insight into the lexical difficulties encountered in texts. Although Dotterer himself states that 'KudoZ is a terminology resource of last resort, and the vast majority of professionals who come upon it immediately understand it as such' (Goddard ibid.: 21), it is clear from investigating it that there is also a considerable number of queries posted which occur as the translator is in the process of drafting the TT. The level of the participants also varies, since membership is open to professional and non-professional translators. This is openly indicated in members' self-classification and in the flagging of queries. Thus, a query about the meaning of the phrase *dissolve and dilute* (in a pharmaceutical text) is marked 'UN-PRO' (non-professional).

For the purposes of analysis, a random sample was chosen, comprising those queries posted on 9 May 2011. The great majority of the hundreds of difficulties concerned technical terminology, for instance the translation of *pitch regulated upwind turbine with active yaw* into Romanian, or of *retea electrica de distributie* (electrical distribution network) from Romanian into English. Despite the terminological focus, variation was still evident in the translation equivalents. The proposed solution for the first example was a lengthy explicitation, *turbine montata in amonte, cu system de orientare a palelor si system activ de orientare a nacelei* ('turbine mounted upwind, whose pitch-drive system is an active yaw-drive system'). For the second example, alternative suggestions were *electricity (or power) distribution network* and *power grid*.

For technical texts, concrete technical terminology is central but is usually resolved by subject- or domain-specific knowledge, supplied by a more expert member of the online community. It is other problems that may be more difficult to resolve, and some of the most interesting of these concern the interpersonal nature of evaluation. These seem quite closely related to text type/genre, since they occur in promotional texts of different kinds. Thus, there are cases from texts on gastronomy and high-class restaurants:

1. the Russian **авторские рестораны** (*avtorskie restorany*, 'celebrity chef restaurants'). The suggested translation was *signature restaurant*. The respondent gave links to two Moscow restaurant websites that use this term and also to

bilingual restaurant websites where the Russian авторская кухня (*avtorskaya kuhnya*, 'celebrity chef cuisine') is translated as *signature cuisine*. Both these English collocations are supported by online searches, which are a common though crude way often used by translators to gauge relative frequency (see Section 3.3 below): so, *signature restaurant* has 309,000 hits on Google™, while *signature cuisine* has 99,700. The interesting point is the positive appreciation exuded by the modifier *signature*, which has spread from the earlier novel collocation *signature dish* (now more common, with 1,590,000 hits). The effect of the earlier collocation seems to colour the translator's thinking when seeking an equivalent for the new term.

2. *dull mouthful.* This query is taken from an English-language review of a Catalan restaurant:

> *If ever there was a classic Catalan eating institution, it's XX. Yes, you have to queue, and service can be brusque. And some will moan that it's become TOO well known, attracting hordes of excitable gastro-tourists. But in the four or five times I've visited, I've barely had a* **dull mouthful**.

The querier, translating this into Italian, initially appears to misunderstand the highlighted expression and interprets it as *ho mangiato appena un boccone* ('I've barely eaten a mouthful'). Seven possible translations are suggested by respondents:

> *l'esperienza (gustativa) non è stata mai banale* ('the [taste] experience has never been banal'), described by the poster as 'more appropriate for the jargon of food criticism'. The respondent grades his confidence as 3 out of a maximum of 4, and the response also receives 9 peer agreements.
> *è sempre stata una delicia del palato* ('it's always been a delight for the palate'). Graded 4, with 5 peer agreements. This was the selected option.
> *le mie papille gustative non son rimaste mai deluse* ('my taste buds have never been disappointed'). Graded 3, with 5 peer agreements.
> *non ne sono mai uscito meno che esaltato* ('I have never come out less than elated'). Graded 3, with 0 peer agreements.
> *null di insípido/scipito* ('nothing insipid/flavourless'). Graded 4, with 0 peer agreements.
> *non ho mai mandato giù un boccone insípido* ('I have never had an insipid mouthful'). Graded 4, with 0 peer agreements.

The final respondent makes two crucial comments. First, he emphasizes a preference for a close translation that retains the 'freshness' of the original, at the same time casting doubt on the extent to which an explicatory paraphrase might be acceptable:

> I always prefer to remain as close as possible to the original terms: if the terms can be rendered 'one-to-one', maintaining the freshness of a spontaneous

> expression, I never venture into paraphrases that end up 'intellectualizing' content that is much more 'ruspante' ['free-range']. (my translation)

His second comment, added at a later date, shows the focus of his translation:

> Attention: for the translation I concentrated on *dull mouthful* as requested. When translating the whole sentence, note the fact that it uses *barely*. (my translation)

This is very important, as it shows that the initial tendency of this translator is on the informational content – Halliday's ideational metafunction (see Chapter 1, Section 1.1). The word *barely*, a key counter-expectancy indicator of attitude (see Chapter 1, Section 1.3.1.4) and intensification, is overlooked to begin with, though picked up by the respondent at the revision stage. This omission of adverbials of graduation tallies with the findings in the study of the Obama interpreting text in Chapter 2.

There are also a number of queries that have to do with innovative language of what might be categorized as hybrid texts (Reiss [1971] 2000) – in particular, texts on technical subjects that have a combined goal of informing but also of persuading. One is a press release from a mining company, announcing its expansion programme:

> *The increase in labor is part of an overall expansion plan and **blue sky exploration potential**, which will increase the company's gold production at its flagship 'XX' mine.*

The query concerns the expression *blue-sky exploration potential*, which has 5680 hits on Google™. The number of noun collocates of *blue-sky* is wide but they fall generally within a semantic field of positive appreciation, specifically an intellectualized forecasting of the future: the most common (and perhaps the 'original' metaphorical use) is *blue-sky thinking*. Also frequent is *blue-sky potential*, and others are *blue-sky approach, assumption, planning* .... The asker accepts a suggested translation into German as *optimistisches Förderpotential* ('optimistic promotion potential'), which seems to be a completely new collocation in German. Other translations suggested are explicitations: *positive Erwartungen in Bezug auf das Erschließungspotenzial* ('positive expectations in relation to exploration potential') and a generalization (*sehr*) *hohe Höffigkeit* ('[very] high hopes'). The sender of the latter acknowledges that this sense really needs to be rendered in subject-specific terminology.

This kind of newly coined term of appreciation makes severe demands on the translator, first to understand precisely what the evaluation is (because it relies on evokedness and crosses over between the interpersonal and ideational) and, second, to find a creative and forceful means of reproducing it in the TL. Another example of this type comes from a software manual to be translated from English to Portuguese:

> *All these features are planted firmly on the **bleeding edge** of web design, and none of them works in versions of Internet Explorer before IE 9.*

The metaphorical expression *bleeding edge* is a form of appreciation, of positive valuation (Martin and White 2005: 56). One respondent notes the meaning of the more common generic term *bleeding edge technology* as 'technology that is so new that the user is required to risk unreliability, and possibly greater expense, in order to use it'.[16] His suggestion, *nova tecnología (não aperfeiçoada)* – 'new technology (not perfected)' – is a generic term plus explicitation. The preferred suggestion (with 6 peer agreements) is *vanguarda absoluta* ('absolute vanguard'). The Portuguese expression has some 573 Google™ hits, 418 of them in the proximity of *tecnologia* ('technology'), and even appears in an online dictionary as the equivalent of *bleeding edge technology*.[17] So, although the Portuguese selection is not a new term, some attempt is made to find a generalizing term that is suited to the text-type.

More evidence for the difficulties posed by appreciation (specifically of valuation or composition) is to be found in the same document, where the same translator queries *new-fangled* in the following example:

> *That means you can write HTML5 documents right now (as you will in this book), without using any of the **new-fangled** features that browsers don't yet support, and everything will work out just fine.*

New-fangled is quite informal and negative. Five potential translation candidates are suggested: *recém-criados* ('newly created'), *inovadoras* ('innovative'), *modernas* ('modern'), *novíssimos* ('very new'), *novas firulas* ('new frills'). Here the dispute is between interpretations of the ST epithet, and definitions of *new-fangled* are used to reinforce the argument. Hence, the suggestion *novíssimos* is supported by the neutral definition 'of the newest style or kind, "had many newfangled gadgets in the kitchen" '. On the other hand, the most daring suggestion, *novas firulas*, reproduces a definition supplied by a contributor to the online *Urban Dictionary*: 'An object, device, any product of mankind, which is deemed futuristic, unnecessary, and occasionally gay.'[18] While idiosyncratic, the definition does home in on the key negative association of *new-fangled* in its range of collocates related to new technology (*contraption, doodah, gadget, technology* . . .).[19] The choice finally made by the translator, *de última geração* ('latest generation'), actually fails to capture this since it prefers the neutral, and arguably positive, interpretation.

This type of item seems to cause problems irrespective of language pair and direction. Thus, another example is from the online details of a Spanish hotel:

> *El hotel Balneario XXXX cuenta con 2 piscinas al aire libre rodeadas de tumbonas, y un lujoso spa que recoge la tradición del histórico balneario fundado en 1898 y la* **proyecta hacia la vanguardia** *en un Spa de referencia mundial.*
>
> ['The XXXX Resort hotel counts on 2 open-air pools surrounded by sun loungers, and a luxurious spa which takes the tradition of the historic resort founded in 1898 and **projects it towards the vanguard** in a world reference Spa.']

Three suggestions are made for the highlighted phrase:

- *brings to the fore/forefront*
- *brings completely into the twenty-first century*
- *makes them one of the most innovative (and technologically advanced) spas in the world.*[20]

All the suggestions move away from the lexical structure of the original in rendering the key elements that need to be communicated: 'project towards' + 'vanguard'. Here, 'vanguard' represents highly positive direct appreciation along the lines of the *skyscraper gleaming with the wealth of modern life* in the London text in Chapter 1. The first suggested equivalent paraphrases 'vanguard' as *fore/forefront* and provides a less forceful verbal element (the core verb *brings to* rather than the non-core Spanish 'projects towards'). The other two suggestions show a difference of interpretation of *vanguard*, either as 'very modern' (*completely into the twenty-first century*) or as *innovative*.[21] That there is some overlap between the two is apparent from the respondent's addition of the bracketed '*(and technologically advanced)*' to complement *innovative*. For this third suggestion, the peer comments are informative. Three point out that the bracketed explicitation is redundant, especially if the text contains a later description of the new technologies. Another comment proposes the addition of *whilst being one of the most innovative*. This counter-expectancy indicator conveys a contrast with the founding of the hotel back in 1898, but at the same time binds the strengths of tradition and innovation. Such comments indicate discrepancies amongst translators over the amount of explicitation that is required or acceptable. They either remove an interpretation that is overspecific (*projects towards the vanguard* may not actually equal *technologically advanced*, or the information may be explained elsewhere in the text and therefore redundant here) or they recommend an explicitation at the discourse-rhetorical level (setting up the 'historic-yet-innovative' contrast). Such obvious differences of approach show, at a simple level, that explicitation cannot be considered a general universal of translation.

The preferred translation in the Forum was the third (... *innovative* ...). However, it is the second that appears in the published translation:

> The XXX Balneario has two outdoor swimming pools surrounded by sun loungers and a luxurious spa that reflects the tradition of the historic seaside resort founded in 1898 and **brings it completely into the 21st century** as a global leading Spa.[22]

This later alteration suggests that the translation of this expression continued to exercise the translator (or editor/commissioner). For this genre of promotional text, it is somewhat surprising that the published solution should have been an instance of standardization. It is a case of disambiguation that explicates, but in engagement terms constrains, the level of reader interpretation.

Matters of attitude are closely linked to culture and also to text Field (in the Hallidayan sense). Thus evaluation spans the ideational as well as the interpersonal.

Translators are sensitive to this. So, in a text about athletes and the motivational power of superstitions during the game, a translator into Arabic highlights the problem of translating the culture-sensitive term *superstitious*, an example of affect (–security).[23] The asker initially suggested معتقداتهم الخرافية (*mu'taqudatihim al-xurafiya*) with the sense of 'superstitious beliefs', but admitted dissatisfaction because of its negative connotations. The accepted solution was a generalizing term, يتفاءل (*yatafael*), 'to feel optimistic'. Another Field-specific example occurs in a legal judgement on a commercial dispute, where the Danish term *ubillig* is used. The querier offers the range of equivalents featuring in *Gyldendals Røde Ordbøger* (Danish–English dictionary): *unfair, unjust, inequitable, unreasonable* and *unconscionable*. He is fully aware of the domain-specific nature of the query: 'Now, in American law some of these have very different meanings from each other. I'd like to have an expert recommendation for the right one here.'[24]

Here, we are dealing with an example of Martin and White's judgement category (–social sanction, since it refers to ethics), but more importantly of Field-specific legal terminology; the overlap between interpersonal (ethical) and ideational is clear. It requires very sensitive treatment for the reasons noted by the querier – all the proposed equivalents realize negative judgement but not all are acceptable ideationally in the context of target culture law. In the end, the adjective *unfair* is chosen because one respondent pointed to its use in an unofficial translation by a Danish law professor. Just as case law is based to a greater or lesser degree on precedent, so translation equivalents too depend on intertextual translation selections, and not always in a formal computerized translation memory system. *Unfair* also happens to be the least forceful and most core of the proposed equivalents, which is perhaps safer than intensification through a non-core selection (e.g. *unconscionable*).

3.3 SENSE

The sheer number of queries and variety of languages on KudoZ™ are a rich source for the translation analyst, but introduce multiple variables. For this reason, a more focused forum, SENSE, limited to one language pair (Dutch<>English) was chosen for the final part of the research for this chapter. SENSE was founded in the Netherlands in 1990 as a society of English native-speaking editors.[25] At the time of writing, it boasts nearly 400 subscribers,[26] including some Dutch native speakers, many of whom also work as translators and copywriters. Some of its members hold informal workshops and its online members' forum also serves as a daily means of seeking help for queries related to translation and editing. For the analyst, the forum offers an unusual opportunity to see the formulation, discussion and resolution of real-life translation queries by highly qualified and experienced professionals. For the purposes of the current research, analysis was made of the archive of messages posted online between 1 July 2010 and 30 September 2010. These messages comprised the initial query followed by feedback on responses that was collated a few days later by the poster.

In the forum, a coding system is used by senders in the subject lines of the queries, as follows: T: terminology, V: vacancy/assignment, P: Professional practice issues, C: computer-related, M: miscellaneous, U: urgent. In practice, most queries are classified as terminology related. And, of these, the vast majority concern technical terms. Like KudoZ™, predominantly the query solicits a TL equivalent of an ST term, such as: What is the Dutch equivalent for the English *fudge factor*? Is *pencil stub* or *pencil stump* to be preferred for the Dutch *potloodstompje*? However, some queries ask for an explanation of what a concept is: e.g. What is the difference between *beautician, beauty therapist* and *beauty specialist*? What does the legal term *immovable property* actually denote? A smaller number of queries concerns TL grammar: Should the verb be singular or plural after a collective noun such as *company*? Should one say *sold in* or *on a market*? Is it *leverage in* or *into*? Spelling conventions are also debated (*–ise* or *–ize*?, *decision making* or *decision-making*?, *immovable* or *immoveable*?).

In some cases, these questions may have a single, objectively correct response: in a list of ingredients for an energy-boosting supplement, Dutch *malaatzuur* should be translated as the English *L-malic acid*, for instance (response to query of 8 July 2010). However, as we saw in Section 3.2 above, even the translation of terminology may be subject to variation. A prototypical example is *warmteterugwininstallatie*, for which the proposed TL equivalent was *heat recovery installation/system/plant* (query 26 August 2010, responses 27 August 2010). Here the variation is in the generic noun component of the term. Sometimes, the favoured response values clarity and generalization above commitment to more precise terminology. Hence, a query on a health care document (30 July 2010) preferred *community-care support centre* for *Zorgsteunpunt* ('care point') and *housing for the elderly* for *Seniorenwoningen* ('elderly housing'), since these were terms that would be understood by the target readership.

Indeed, perceptions of readership ('audience design') are often the reason given for a selection. A notable example is the translation of *schenkkring*, a small-scale and partly informal fund to which individuals make regular contributions and which pays out in the event that one of the participants is unfit for work (query 1 July, responses 2 July 2010). In the absence of a corresponding concept in English, the querier himself proposed three possibilities – *gift circle, contribution circle, support circle*. Thirteen other suggestions were submitted:

> *support scheme, self-insurance scheme for disability allowance, self-insurance scheme for work incapacity, private disability scheme, funding pool, contributions fund pool, contingency disability fund, mutual support fund, circle of contributors, financial support circle, solidarity circle, donor circle, donor group.*

As can be seen from the list, these range from huge generalizations, such as *support scheme* and *donor group*, to greater explicitation, such as *self-insurance scheme for disability allowance*. But the most interesting point was the question posed by the querier in the follow-up: 'Should I pitch my translation at "alternative/green/ left" self-employed people who don't like what insurance companies do with their money, or at more conventional self-employed people who simply can't afford conventional [incapacity insurance]?' Some of the suggestions were felt to be more appropriate to a specific audience. Thus, *support scheme, mutual support fund, financial support circle, solidarity circle*, etc. for the 'alternative' group, would value the idea of supporting fellow citizens; these suggestions take their wording from the area of ethical behaviour, relating to appraisal's realm of judgement (social sanction, +propriety). The more formal terms (e.g. *private disability scheme, self-insurance scheme for work incapacity*) would fit the colder, more conventional, more ideational frame. The choice, therefore, is not between a correct or incorrect term, one that describes a foreign concept more or less precisely, nor even between one that is more or less common. Online searches will show that some of the suggestions have no hits at all and even some that seem intuitively 'mainstream' are in fact very infrequent (only three hits for *private disability scheme*, for instance). The options contain indirect, associated evaluation, and that is dependent on target audience rather than on context.[27] The choice in fact revolves around the translator's ethical positioning of the organization in relation to that audience. This is a subjective decision, affected by the translator's evaluation of the reading position of the target audience, an issue which needed to be raised with the commissioner. Thus it is a clear case of tactical reading by the translator, since he or she is second-guessing the audience's stance and aligning the translation to that, thereby forcefully constraining the text's resources of engagement.

Technical queries are therefore far from devoid of attitudinal value. Another query from 19 August 2010 asked for help with the translation in a museum text of the term *oude Kunst* ('old art'), which had been rendered as *Old Masters* and *old art*. The desire to avoid any possible negative connotation of *old* (compare Chapter 1, Section 1.3.1.1, and Chapter 2, 2.2.2 and 2.2.3) leads to the initial suggestion of *antique art* and the solution of the more directly positive *fine art*. In another query (6 September, responses 10 September 2010), related to ethical considerations of nursing care, the reviser was concerned about two terms that had been translated literally: *Waardeverwerkelijkend handelen,* translated as *value-actualizing treatment* and revised to *value-generating action*, and *Uitdrukkingshandeling*, translated as *expression measure* and revised to *expressive care*. The perceived problem was that these were extremely rare wordings in English – it was pointed out that the first example (*value-generating action*) only produced one hit in a Google™ search. The reviser, in conjunction with the translator, opts for what she describes as a 'simple but sure' translation.

The number of Google™ hits in a particular language or variety was quite often used as an explicit criterion for judging between competing equivalents. A query of 26 August 2010 asked whether *base flood elevation* is a good translation for *uitgiftepeil*. This is the level above which buildings are supposed to be constructed in order to protect them from flooding. The summary of responses (27 August 2010) concludes, 'I finally went with *base flood level* (more UK hits on Google™) with the options of *base flood elevation* (which I feel has a more American bias) and *base flood depths* (which I found later on), with an explanation.' However, above a certain, unspecified threshold the number of hits is not always the overriding criterion. The hits for *pencil stub* and *pencil stump* (as a possible translation for *potloodstompje*, 1 August 2010) were 203,000 and 340,000 respectively. Despite this, the respondents came down 50 to 3 in favour of *pencil stub*, which was also favoured by the querier.

If terminology is the main bugbear of the technical translator, a decontextualized list is considered to be even more problematic. One poster (8 August 2010) points out the problems:

> There is a saying that the hardest thing to translate is a list of words or terms, and I can confirm this. Having just spent several days on a list of products from a supplier of office supplies etc, I am now stuck with the following terms:
>
> • *rekeningstaten*, this has something to do with invoices and could possibly be something like numbered invoice books.
> • *draaizuilen voor ringmappen*. Something to do with ringbinders, but what?

The question is first to identify what the ST object is and then to find a TL text that contains the equivalent. One suggested means of doing this (respondent of 8 August 2010) is to search online for an image of the object (using the Dutch term) and then to search for similar images in the hope that one of these would contain a description of the item in English. However, one drawback with this technique, pointed out by the respondent, is that it does not work for verbs and abstract nouns. This critical point, therefore, depends on word class – it is easiest to find equivalents for concrete nouns. This is a curious finding that should not be dismissed as simplistic. Even the formulation of responses sometimes hints at something similar. A query (26 July, responses 27 July 2010) asks for the English equivalent of the Dutch *bezetting*, 'in the context of a particular combination of musical instruments which may be required to perform a certain piece of music'. Nine of the 11 suggestions are nouns (*orchestration, instrumentation, line-up* and the terminologically most exact *forces*). The other two suggestions are adjectives: *scored for . . .* and *well-balanced/properly balanced orchestra*. The intriguing question is why the latter should be qualified by an adverb of graduation (***well/properly*** *balanced*) and why the more concise translation *balanced orchestra* was deemed insufficient. The force of this instance of appreciation (+composition) is intensified in the proposed TL equivalent. Given that this is a sole example, it is not possible to go beyond presenting the hypothesis that epithets, because of their prototypically evaluative nature, occupy a prominent place in the translator's subjective reasoning. More neutral epithets (such as *balanced*) may be more susceptible to graduation in translation in order to fit into the overall evaluative prosody of the text.

Sometimes the more subjective queries seek a more dynamically equivalent translation. One (24 August 2010) relates to part of a promotional text that had been provisionally translated into English by a Dutch native speaker. The native English reviser wanted to make the text 'more punchy'.

ST

De wereld draait door en dat is maar goed ook. Sterker nog, de wereld lijkt wel steeds sneller te gaan draaien. Wij merken dat aan de eisen die vanuit zowel de nationale als de internationale arbeidsmarkt aan onze XXX afgestudeerden worden gesteld.

['The world keeps turning and that is well also. More strongly still, the world seems to spin ever more rapidly. We see that in the demands which are placed on our graduates from XXX by both the national and international labour market.']

Draft TT (by Dutch writer):
The world turns and sometimes it seems to spin faster than ever. This phenomenon can be seen in the demands that national and international labour markets pose upon XXX graduates.

The reviser's reply of 29 August 2010 summarizes the responses received and gives keen insight into the process of identifying and resolving the critical points. The description of the revision process highlights that some points, such as incorrect or unusual collocations (*demands that markets . . . pose upon*) are very evident and easily identified and resolved based on the revisers' experience of the TL (*demands that markets . . . place upon*). Obvious syntactic shifts, such as the active to passive shift in transitivity in the last sentence ('We see that . . .' > *This phenomenon can be seen . . .*), part of the ideational function of language, are also identified. However, the critical point for the respondents revolves around the allusion to a TV show and the pun in *de wereld draait door* ('the world goes round' and 'the world goes mad'). Several solutions are suggested to improve on the draft TT procedure of circumvention of the allusion:

> As for the problem of transmuting the flavour of 'de wereld draait door', B. suggested that the translator sensibly choose to circumvent the allusion to the popular TV show/pun – 'doordraaien' also meaning 'to go mad' – by merging the first two sentences. Most of you agreed and offered less than literal translations. I liked C.'s 'Life goes on. And sometimes apace' as well as A.'s variation: 'Life goes on, and that is a good thing too, in fact it seems to be racing away with us.' But being an incorrigible punster, I couldn't resist D.'s attempt to catch the original flavour: 'The world keeps turning and that's just as well.' Even if the allusion is only subliminal, you never know, some[one] might get it. I also liked his version because of its rhythm; not to be sniffed at in the opening line of a brochure directed at students.
>
> This is what I'm offering the client: 'The world keeps turning and that's just as well. Nowadays, however, the world seems to be racing away with us. We see this in the demands that national and international labour markets are placing on the graduates of our University.'

It seems that in such an instance there is considerable motivation to translate creatively in order to 'catch/transmute the flavour' of the pun and its rhythm and to admit the possibility that this will trigger a response in the more perceptive readers. The type of attitude here is invoked-associative. In terms of engagement, the choice is heteroglossic, inclusive of other voices and avoiding contraction (see Figure 1.4). When the same querier switches to a technical query, she considers this to be 'on a more serious note'. Perceptions are clearly that technical terminology is a more substantial matter than the overall stylistic rewriting of a section, which perhaps explains the joy with which respondents dealt with the pun query. By contrast, in the technical example that followed, uncertainty about the meaning led to the adoption of the safest and most generic solution: 'No one (least of all me) seemed to know how to tackle "handelingsindicatoren" so I plumped for the safe option of "indicators", clarifying this with "competence indicators" where appropriate.'

As well as puns, metaphors are instances of indirect and provoked evaluation, and a form of intensification (see Chapter 1, Section 1.3.1.4). They generate a wealth of suggestions for translation equivalents. Another querier seeks an idiomatic translation of the standard metaphor *een lege huls* in the sentence *Daarmee lijkt het maken van bezwaar **een lege huls** geworden* ['It seems that this has made **an empty shell** of objecting'], with the meaning 'The possibility to object is offered, but is in fact of no use.' Such a generalizing explicitation is rejected by the querier, since 'it seems a bit too literal'. Fourteen suggestions were discussed in the follow-up. These range from: explicitation (e.g. *a purely formal procedure, seems to make the possibility of raising any objection futile right from the start*) to fixed expressions or strong collocations (*a moot point, a pointless exercise, a fait accompli*) and different idioms or metaphors (*an empty gesture* [x3], *empty vessel* [x2], *empty possibility, a dead letter, a paper tiger*). These differ according to the degree of metaphoricity and at the same time the intensity and directness of the evaluation – the more metaphorical, the more indirect. The querier acknowledged the strength of the relatively popular *empty gesture* solution but opted for the metaphorical *paper tiger* for its thematic coherence for a text about paperwork. This example suggests that metaphor is an attitudinal feature that is prominent in the perception of translators and the desire to retain some metaphorical link is strong.

3.4 Conclusion

The findings from the different investigations informing this chapter are illuminating. For the informants, some of the conscious critical points were polysemous words (e.g. *Belastung*), a discordance of semantic space (e.g. *Leistung*, which covers much more ground than any English equivalent) and some culture-specific terms (*lawyer/solicitor*). These were generally, but not always, technical terms. Thus, one of the informants noted problems with what we would call evaluation and specifically mentioned the attitude transmitted by German modal particles and modal auxiliaries (*dürfen*). Text-type is also a consideration, legal texts being highlighted as a type where careful consideration is needed and where sometimes ambiguities in the ST (e.g. English *may*) cannot be retained in the TT. So, different translations were proposed for *dürfen* depending on the syntactic construction. Extralinguistic factors affecting choice are the audience, as would be expected, but also the position of the translator – in-house translators were perhaps able to be more creative and use adaptation more if they were able to negotiate directly with the ST producer. In translation between distant languages and cultures in the Chinese<>English pair, more adaptation was used to reduce the directness of overly aggressive rhetorical conventions that may otherwise upset the receiver.

In the online forums observed, queries of technical terminology predominated, the solutions requiring the assistance of subject experts with informational knowledge. Here there is some overlap between the ideational and interpersonal functions of language. While technical terminology is ideational and part of Field, it also contributes to the construction of solidarity between users and is therefore part of Tenor (see Chapter 1, Section 1.3.1). Some examples show this in the use of evoked attitude. When they are also neologisms, their creativity and concise encapsulation of evokedness represent a real critical point. The epithets *blue-sky* and *bleeding-edge* are outstanding examples of this phenomenon and generally they become more standardized and less intense in translation. The critical point depends to a degree on part of speech, too. One tentative hypothesis to be tested from the findings is that epithets, being the prototypical realization of evaluation, are more prone to graduation and manipulation by the translator's subjectivity. Concrete nouns seem to be more stable. This would tie in with the perception from some translators that technical queries are somewhat more 'serious' than what are more subjective interpersonal features.

4

THE LITERARY TRANSLATOR AND REVISER

4.0 Introduction

In this chapter, the methodology for the investigation of critical points centres around the possibilities offered by the study of archive material related to literary translation. Specifically, these comprise manuscripts of the drafting process and correspondence between two or more of author, translator, editor and reviser. The key feature under investigation is revisions made at different stages and the explicitly stated reasons for these.

Three case studies are described:

- (4.1) the revisions of the Penguin translation of a key text by the first-century Roman historian Tacitus. The interaction of the higher-level context and ideology with translation poetics (cf. Lefevere 1992) allows study of another level of evaluation. The paratexts and extratextual factors play an especially important role in determining translation strategy.
- (4.2) the translations and revisions of novels and essays of the Peruvian Nobel-prizewinner Mario Vargas Llosa, where detailed correspondence exists between the different participants, each of whom may present a different interpretation.
- (4.3) the translation and self-revision by translator David Bellos of the fiercely intertextual novel *Life: A User's Manual* by Georges Perec. Bellos left multiple drafts as well as preliminary notes and readers' comments and corrections.

All three studies are of high-profile authors and texts and all are supported by an unusually rich wealth of archival documents. To date such documents have been underutilized in translation studies. Their analysis actually offers a detailed retrospective insight into the decision-making processes, an observation of the different participants in action without the constraining effect of the researcher's presence.[1]

4.1 Revisions of a classical text – *Agricola* and *Germania*

The Penguin Classics series was launched at the end of World War II with the aim of reaching a wider audience with affordable books in 'readable' (rather than 'scholarly') translations. The first title was the bestselling translation of Homer's *Odyssey* (1946) by E.V. Rieu (1887–1972), who was the influential editor of the series. It was Rieu who commissioned and edited books for the series until his retirement in 1964, when he was succeeded by another outstanding editor, his colleague Betty Radice (1912–1985). One of the books in the series, containing *The Agricola* and *the Germania*, brought together two minor works by the Roman historian Tacitus (c. 56–c. 117 CE) written in 97–98 CE (Rives, in Tacitus 2009: xiv). Penguin published this in H.B. Mattingly's translation (*Tacitus on Britain and Germany*, 1948), revised controversially by S.A. Handford (*The Agricola and the Germania*, 1970) and more recently again by J.B. Rives (2009). The existence of two revisions at different times enables statements to be made as to possible contextual factors that may have influenced the decisions of the different revisers.

The circumstance of legal challenge over the Handford revision was fortuitous because it caused the draft provided by Handford to be sent to Penguin's solicitors. They only returned it later once the matter had been resolved and it was then retained in the editorial files and passed to the archive. This valuable and unusual manuscript therefore allows detailed insight into the process of alterations undertaken by Handford to the Mattingly text. The manuscript[2] contains the printed pages of the original Mattingly text pasted into the centre of the sheets[3] with emendations indicated with proofing marks in both margins.

The initial Penguin Classics translation of the books was commissioned by Rieu at the very beginning of the planning for the series. The translator, Harold Mattingly (1884–1964), was a renowned numismatist of ancient Rome who worked at the Department of Coins and Medals at the British Museum. In a letter to another major expert contributor, Humphrey Kitto (1897–1982), Professor of Greek at the University of Bristol, Rieu describes how the translation strategy was agreed:

> On the matter of translation … Mattingly and I thrashed it out at my club [The Athenaeum, Pall Mall, London] the other day over a protracted lunch and he went away keen as mustard and in a few days sent me some samples of Tacitus which are not only done in sound modern English but capture much of the sombre grandeur of the original.[4]

Mattingly's translation was published in 1948, selling 27,000 copies by the end of the year[5] and remaining popular, since it was often a set text for school examinations. After Mattingly's death in January 1964, the decision was taken to commission Stanley Handford (1898–1978) of King's College London, to revise the translation. The failure to negotiate at an early stage with Mattingly's estate led to huge problems, since his sons Stephen and Harold (a classical scholar himself) initially refused to allow Handford joint authorship and insisted that the 1948 translation remain in print, stating that they were seeking to protect their father's reputation.[6] This was eventually resolved by the splitting of an increased royalty and by a signed legal agreement which stipulated both the wording of the title page (where Mattingly was named as 'the translator' and Handford as 'the reviser')[7] and the text of a short preface in which Handford and Penguin 'acknowledge their indebtedness, and that of all classical scholars, to Harold Mattingly'.[8] This preface was included when the revised translation first appeared in 1970 and continues to appear in those copies of the work that are still on sale. Only in 2009 was a new revision published, undertaken by James Rives, Kenan Eminent Professor of Classics at the University of North Carolina at Chapel Hill.[9]

Another important consideration in the translation of ancient texts is the instability of the ST itself. Textual variants have occurred as a result of the copying of manuscripts by hand over centuries. The loss of the earliest documents has meant that the accuracy of the source is often a matter of historical and scholarly interpretation, with new scholarship and findings displacing what previously were considered to be the most reliable STs. Thus, although each translator used the Oxford Classical *Cornelii Taciti Opera Minora* as a source, the editions differ: Mattingly based his work on the text established by Henry Furneaux in 1898 and revised by J.G.C. Anderson in 1938; Handford used R.M. Ogilvie's 1967 text for *Agricola*; Rives, for his Oxford and Penguin translations, used the 1975 edition for both Tacitus texts.[10] Even then, Rives notes that '[i]n some places I have deviated from the latter [the 1975 texts], often simply in order to provide a coherent translation' (Rives, in Tacitus 2009: xlviii). These deviations are all relatively minor. They include spelling variants of names (e.g. *Ingaevones* > *Ingvaeones* in *Germania* 2.2), the addition of what seem to be missing words and the correction of corrupted grammar. Sometimes both the alternative readings make complete contextual sense: for *Germania* 22.3, Rives used Winterbottom's reading *licentia loci* ('in the licence of the occasion') even though he admits that most manuscripts have the equally sensible *licentia ioci* ('in the licence of jesting') and relegate Winterbottom's alternative wording to a marginal note (Rives in Tacitus 1999: 213).

For the translator, coherence and 'intelligibility' are thus paramount criteria, yet so also is an awareness of the importance of retaining the style of the ST author, because of his status. For Rives, the goal was 'to give even more of a sense of what it is like to read these works in the original Latin' (see Rives in Tacitus 1999: 76). This chimes with the original reception of the Mattingly translation as 'preserving, as far as any English can, the peculiar mordant, epigrammatic quality of the Roman'.[11] For this reason, Rives (in Tacitus 2009: xlviii) states that he had preferred to return to Mattingly's earlier translation for his revision of the Penguin edition since Handford had quite often explicated what had remained implicit in the Latin.

4.1.1 The manuscript revised

It is very rare to find a draft manuscript in the Penguin Classics archive. General editors Rieu and Radice both worked from home and seem to have discarded the various drafts.[12] Even the final version rarely survives in the form in which it would have been sent to the typesetter. The manuscript which Handford submitted to Penguin in 1967 represents the result of the revision rather than a catalogue of the different stages of the revision process. There is no way of knowing if earlier drafts of the translation existed, which might have given insights into earlier decision-making. Given the neatness of the manuscript (i.e. few crossings-out and very clear handwriting) and what is known of translation processes in general, it might be surmised that it was based on a preparatory draft, which would have been discarded before submission.[13] Occasional modifications appear to have been made in the course of the initial drafting of revision, since the initial selection has been crossed out and is followed immediately by the amended wording. For example:

> *He had learned the lesson of obedience and ~~taught himself~~*
> *~~to do his duty without injuring his own interests.~~ schooled*
> *himself to subordinate ambition to duty.*
>
> *(Agricola 8, Handford mss p. 4)*

There are also a few places (every few pages, more on the handwritten sheets) where at a later stage Handford has crossed out his original choice and altered his own translation. Some of these necessitated a squeezed addition, such as the following:

> *Yet ~~Agricola~~ ʰᵉ never sought to glorify himself by bragging of*
> *his achievements*
>
> *(Agricola 8, Handford mss p. 58)*

Critical micro-level points of the text include the results of Handford's overall strategy of explicitation of contextual information, later reversed by Rives (personal communication). The following example (from *Agricola* 6), is one of many where Handford's manuscript deletes and replaces a section of the Mattingly:

> **ST** *Tum electus a Galba ad dona templorum recognoscenda diligentissima conquisitione*
> *effecit, ne cuius alterius sacrilegium res publica quam Neronis sensisset.*
>
> *(Agricola 6)*

['Then chosen by Galba that he of the gifts of the temples a review through the most diligent search should effect, so that the state no other sacrilege other than Nero's should feel']

> **TT1** He was then chosen by Galba to check over the gifts in the temples ~~and,~~
> ~~by his searching scrutiny, achieved a striking success; the State experienced no~~
> ~~permanent loss from any sacrilege but Nero's.~~
>
> *(Tacitus 1948 (Mattingly): p. 5)*

> **TT2** He was afterwards chosen by Galba to check over the gifts in the temples; *and by diligently tracing stolen objects he repaired the losses inflicted on the State by all the temple-robbers except Nero.*
>
> *(Handford mss p. 3)*

Here, Mattingly's *searching scrutiny* (for *diligentissima conquisitione*) is explicated by Handford through the calqued judgement (+tenacity) adverb *diligently* and the added reference to *tracing stolen objects*. Furthermore, Mattingly's abstract judgement noun *sacrilege* (+propriety) is explicated in Handford with the addition of the specified agent, *temple-robbers*. This supplements the Mattingly endnote, retained by Handford, which gives further contextual information about Nero's pillaging of the temples after the Great Fire of Rome of 64 CE (Mattingly in Tacitus 1948: 56, Handford in Tacitus 1970: 143).

When it comes to such paratextual notes, the critical points may vary hugely according to individual perspective. Correspondence between Mattingly's heirs and Penguin shows that the status of the original TT was a very delicate matter. The Mattinglys' intent was to ensure that their father's reputation was not harmed and they thus argued to keep the TT intact. For them, the integrity and attribution of the text was critical. Penguin's interest, on the other hand, was to secure an agreement that enabled them to improve the version of one of their bestselling texts. If this meant accommodating the Mattinglys, they were prepared to do so. Thus, while in private Penguin Director Dieter Pevsner declared that 'Harold Mattingly's translation of TACITUS was now … manifestly inadequate',[14] the suggestion from Penguin's lawyer Michael Rubinstein for resolving the conflict involved finding a wording for the preface that would 'mak[e] it clear what an almost perfect translation the late Harold Mattingly's was, so as to maintain, if not enhance, his reputation!'[15] Handford's own response to the proposed preface was not to argue for his status as co-translator but to insist on what to most would seem the most minor alteration to the punctuation: 'We simply MUST have a stop after "books", and I think it should be a semi-colon. Please see that no one interferes with my instruction on this.'[16]

Here Handford's concern was over the syntactic correctness of a pause. At another point in *Germania* (chapter 46), the description of the Peucini tribe, punctuation is critical in understanding the racial, and racist, stereotypes employed by Tacitus, typical of ancient thinking that intermarriage between ethnic groups led to degeneration (Isaac 2006: 141–2, Rives in *Tacitus* 1999: 127). Tacitus declares that he is unsure whether to consider the Peucini to be Germani, whom they resemble through speech, way of life and settlements, or Sarmatians, whose characteristics are said to be much inferior:

> *Sordes omnium ac torpor procerum; conubiis mixtis nonnihil in Sarmatarum habitum foedantur* (*Germania* 46)
>
> ['Squalor all and indolence the nobles; through mixed marriages somewhat in Sarmatian condition they are defiled']

They are a squalid and slovenly people; the features of their nobles get something of the Sarmatian ugliness from intermarriage (Mattingly in Tacitus 1948: 139)

Squalor is universal among them and their nobles are indolent. Mixed marriages are giving them something of the repulsive appearance of the Sarmatians (Handford in Tacitus 1970: 140)

All of them are squalid and their nobles slovenly; as a result of intermarriage they are taking on something of Sarmatian ugliness (Rives in Tacitus 2009: 57).

This example again forcefully illustrates the critical problems of the instability, or dispute, of the source. The placement of the ST semi-colon has been particularly debated. In some versions, including that used by Mattingly, it precedes *procerum* ('nobles') to give a reading that all of the Peucini are indolent and that it is the intermarriage of the nobles with the Sarmatians that is negatively viewed. However, Handford's and Rives' readings are based on the location of the semi-colon after the noun. The cohesion is altered, aligning *procerum* with *torpor* ('indolence') while *conubiis mixtis* ('intermarriage') is deemed to refer to the Sarmatian people as a whole. In all cases, however, the extreme attitudinal negativity of *sordes* (*squalid/ squalor/filthy*, negative appreciation) and *torpor* (*slovenly/indolent/inert*, all negative judgement) are rendered in translation.

There is further evaluative interpretation in the second clause, most notably the translation of *foedantur*, a passive form of the verb *foedare*, meaning (a) 'make foul/filthy, defile, disfigure' or (b) morally, 'dishonour, disgrace', which might be considered to be a metaphorical extension of (a). These senses map on to what in attitudinal terms is (a) negative appreciation and (b) negative judgement. The TTs opt for *ugliness* (Mattingly, Rives), *repulsive appearance* (Handford), all examples of (a) though it should be added that Rives' 1999 Oxford translation, *debased*, is an interpretation that aligns itself with (b). Mattingly also adds an extraordinary endnote that explains this by the imposition of racial stereotyping: 'The ugly Sarmatian "features" mean the gaping nostrils and slanting eyes of the Mongolians' (Mattingly in Tacitus 1948: 159). The collocation *gaping nostrils* and *slanting eyes* are extremely negative and have racist connotations.[17] Equally astonishingly, 20 years later Handford intensifies the evaluation in the text itself by adding the hugely strong epithet **repulsive** *appearance* (negative appreciation) and otherwise only slightly moderates the note: 'Referring to the wide nostrils and slanting eyes of some Asiatic peoples' (Handford in Tacitus 1970: 160). Both Mattingly and Handford use an overarching colonial analogy to project a contemporary image of Tacitus: 'We may think of Tacitus as something like an officer in the Indian army and Indian Civil Servant rolled into one' (Mattingly in Tacitus 1948: 159).[18]

4.1.2 Evaluative keys and reading position

It is possible to speak of a cluster of clines of evaluation – an 'evaluative key' (Martin and White 2005: 161) or 'voice'. The combination of negative attitude, heightened graduation and explicit paratextual commentary link evaluation and ideological underpinning in a very clear way, serving to extend it. Interestingly, this is further strengthened with what can only be termed a very tactical reading by Mattingly. Writing at the end of World War II, he is very conscious to emphasize the earlier tactical reading of *Germania* by the National Socialists as 'a sort of Bible of German patriotism' that harks back to an imagined purity of the race. Mattingly does this both in the introduction, where he explicitly states that 'The National Socialist talk of "Blut und Boden" ["blood and soil"] was just mystical nonsense' (Mattingly in Tacitus 1948: 27), and in the note to chapter 4, where Tacitus gives his opinion that 'the peoples of Germany have never been tainted by intermarriage with other peoples, and stand out as a nation peculiar, pure and unique of its kind' (ibid.: 103). Mattingly's note concludes: 'Tacitus can never have dreamed of the terrible abuses which would grow out of his simple statement.' In this note, tactical reading positions the translator in relation to the author and at the same time attempts to condition the reader's response. Thus, Mattingly both disarms Tacitus' own racial stereotyping by terming it 'simple' (negative appreciation, with reduced graduation) and highlights the modern abuses through an evoked connection with Nazi Germany. Even in Handford's revision, these comments in the introduction and the endnote remain. Rives' 1999 Oxford edition is much more scholarly, with very detailed notes. His textual reading of *foedantur* as 'debased' tallies with his historical reading of this point elucidated in the notes, namely that Tacitus' criteria are based on cultural features (language and way of life) rather than on the physical characteristics (Rives in Tacitus 1999: 322). Rives' more popular Penguin edition of 2009 includes a completely new introduction and notes, reflecting a new positioning and reading of the work even if the text itself is broadly the same as Mattingly's. This raises the interesting question of whether a hierarchy of evaluation is in operation. The paratextual commentary, by the explicit expression of its positioning of the reading position of the translator, is the most visible and most intense form of evaluation; but subjective textual shifts, hidden to the monolingual reader, may covertly affect the attitudinal values.

4.2 Revision between author, translator and reader – Mario Vargas Llosa

The second case we shall consider is modern-day and involves more players: a complex scenario of high-profile author, translator and, in some cases, expert reader or editor. The author is the Peruvian novelist and politician Mario Vargas Llosa (b. 1936), one of the premier Latin American authors of the so-called 'boom' of the 1960s and 1970s and winner of the Nobel Prize for Literature in 2010.[19] Translations of the boom authors (Borges, Cortázar, Fuentes, García Márquez, Vargas Llosa ...) was a major project often supported by funding from private and state bodies in the United States (see Rostagno 1997, Cohn 2006, Munday 2008). Importantly for this study, archival material of this body of authors is rich.[20] In particular, I shall look at correspondence between translator and author and revisions suggested on draft manuscripts.

4.2.1 Correspondence and queries

Gregory Rabassa (b. 1922) was the very prominent translator of two key novels of the boom, Julio Cortázar's *Hopscotch* (1966) and Gabriel García Márquez's *One Hundred Years of Solitude* (1970). Rabassa also translated two of Vargas Llosa's early works, including *La casa verde* (1966), *The Green House* (1968) and *Conversación en La Catedral* (1969), *Conversation in The Cathedral* (1975). In the detailed correspondence between translator and author, the conscious critical points that appear are overwhelmingly culture-specific items. From the start, Rabassa has general concerns about the Peruvianisms in the text,[21] and later specifically about flora and fauna, food and so on.[22] One problem is of encoding (what to do when there is no equivalent in English), but another, perhaps even more pressing, is decoding something as basic but crucial as knowing whether a given word refers to a plant or an animal.[23] Long before the advent of the internet, this type of problem could only be solved by time-consuming research in specialist libraries, by resort to experts where available or, as in this case, by asking the text producer.

As the translation of *La casa* progresses, Rabassa sometimes sees the need to distinguish plants and to explain cultural artefacts to the reader: for example, he suggests a strategy of translating first by what we know as borrowing plus explicatory intratextual gloss (e.g. *her intípak, her Indian tunic*) and, for subsequent occurrences, by generic gloss alone (*tunic*).[24] Yet it should not be thought that it is simply a question of whether or not to borrow. There is also the typographical matter of whether or not to use italics. While such marked borrowings are a common procedure, Vargas Llosa and Rabassa agree to remove the italics because of the sheer number of items: italicization of all would produce an 'ugly' page, which Rabassa notes had happened with the UK translation of Miguel Angel Asturias' *El viento fuerte*.[25] The decision is not the translator's alone. It may be the editor's or, for *La casa verde*, the author's himself. Rabassa (1975: 17) comments that Vargas Llosa was 'very conscious of the problem of local color and often worried that the commonplace thing in Peru, just by its definition, was going to be exotic somewhere else'. Rabassa has since pointed out (2005: 78) that details of the Peruvian jungle would be as exotic to the reader in Madrid or Lima as in the United States. In order to avoid, or reduce, such default and undesired exoticization, Rabassa recommends translation procedures oriented towards what in translation theory terms is standardization or generalization (see Chapter 3, Section 3.1.1):

> If you wish to eliminate as far as possible the folkloric and exotic, in some cases it would be possible to eliminate the precise word and use the generic one, <u>monkey</u> simply instead of <u>frailecillo monkey</u>, for example.[26]

Rabassa's queries develop into a pattern, so much so that by 1972 he is able to state: 'My questions are always the same, an odd expression that I can't find in the dictionary (although now I have the Collins) ... Naturally, many Peruvianisms that are not to be found in other varieties ...'[27] To the twenty-first-century eye, it may seem quaint that such a remarkable translator should have to rely on a paper dictionary, even one as good as the new *Collins Spanish–English, English–Spanish Dictionary*, edited by Colin Smith (University of Cambridge, UK), that made such an impact upon publication in 1971. But that was the truth of the matter. Translators were limited to what now seem crude tools, and the existence, or non-existence, of encyclopedic and other resources including reliable native-speaker informants. The resources of the professionals in Chapter 3 were not available to the same degree.

The queries that occur with regularity, and that can be considered to be consciously critical points, are the sense of unknown individual items, regionalisms, swear words and racial terms,[28] characters' names and the title of the works themselves. This can be seen in the correspondence not just of Rabassa but also of other major translators, such as Ronald Christ, who was Director of the translation programme of the Center for Inter-American Relations (later, the Americas Society). The solutions to such problems need to be decided at a higher, strategic level than the individual instance. Thus, Christ, co-translating Vargas Llosa's *Pantaleón y las visitadoras* (1973) with Gregory Kolovakos (1952–1990), expresses uncertainty over whether to translate the name *Malecón Tarapaca* ('Tarapaca Boulevard/Promenade') of the city of Iquitos. He notes that the Havana *malecón* was left untranslated in Suzanne Jill Levine's translation of Cabrera Infante's *Three Trapped Tigers* (1971, from the source text *Tres tristes tigres*, 1967).[29] The awareness of intertextual solutions – that is, procedures adopted in other translations by other translators – is salient and practically constrains the translator's choices. The constraint, however, is not monoglossically constrictive in engagement terms (see Chapter 1, Figure 1.4). It actually places heteroglossic demands on the translator to dialogically expand the relation of the text to its precursors.

4.2.2 Indirect, associative evaluation

Christ and Vargas Llosa also discuss for over a year the translation of a key term in the title – *visitadora* ('visitor', f.). On 4 January 1976, Christ had gone into meticulous detail about the various possibilities:

> We have to decide on the title and the phrase to use for <u>visitadora</u> in your novel and I'd like your advice. As you know, Gregory Rabassa had been considering <u>Visitationist</u>, on the model of orders of nuns here like the Resurrectionist. The idea is a good one – of course – but the word itself seems a little too formal, a little too out of the way to work in the same or a comparable sense. I think the word <u>service</u> ought to be kept because it is accurate, because it translates the Spanish perfectly, because it is common and everyday and because it is a double enendre [sic] in English, the verb to <u>service</u>, meaning to satisfy the sexual needs of. Therefore I'm more inclined to one of the following: <u>Helping Hand Service</u> or <u>Visiting Aide Service</u>. The first has obvious advantages: it is easily understood and has the same euphemistic quality as <u>lavandera</u> ['washerwoman']. A <u>helping hand</u> is someone who assists

you to do something usually in a friendly way. The word <u>hand</u> in the phrase also supplies something of a double entendre. <u>Visiting Aide</u> is more neutral, less colloquial, but comes closer to the term Visiting Nurse, the term we use in the U.S.A. to name women who come to your house to care for you during an illness. As for <u>Women's Brigade</u>, I see the appropriateness for the title but find it useless in the text itself where neither <u>Women</u> nor <u>Brigade</u> can do the work of a <u>visitadora</u>. (<u>Brigade</u> of course can serve for <u>Service</u> but to no great advantage except for an initial military connotation, which, however, goes against the text itself, which stipulates repeatedly that the Service is to have no identification with the military.)[30]

This amount of detail enables access to the criteria used by the translator in arguing the point. Here, considerations include the formality of the word (the reason for rejecting *Resurrectionist*), the highly sensitive concept of accuracy (*service* is 'accurate', though accurate to what is unclear), its rendering of connotation (a double meaning of *service* with sexual connotations) and its functional equivalence and operational suitability (*Women's Brigade* is rejected because it is 'useless in context'). The desired equivalent should ideally meet all these criteria. But translation is about balancing different constraints. The two suggested solutions each work better by fulfilling one or more criteria to a greater degree: *Helping Hand Service* is at the same time more comprehensible, euphemistic and suggestive; *Visiting Aide Service* fits the target culture domain better but is seen to be deficient because of its neutrality and formality. The expectation is certainly of a more intense yet preferably indirect evaluative form for the title. In the end the editors opted for a different title that retains the connotations but underlines the genre of the light-hearted detective novel *Captain Pantoja and the Special Service* (1978).

4.2.3 The reader–author relationship

The translator of a literary author does not only work on fiction, of course. Some of the richest sources of information on translator decision-making are to be found in the translations of non-fiction essays and biographies. Vargas Llosa's memoirs *Un pez en el agua* (1993), published within three years of his unsuccessful Peruvian presidential election campaign of 1990, were translated by the experienced Helen Lane (1921–2004) and published in English as *A Fish in the Water* (1994a). Very detailed written feedback on the draft TT manuscript was given to Vargas Llosa by reader Robert Hemenway, Chair of the University of Kentucky English Department. In his notes, Hemenway too brings up the title of the work:

> The title!! The English equivalent of <u>Como el pez en el agua</u> is 'like a fish to water': 'He took to it like a fish to water'. The title <u>A Fish in the Water</u> … suggests … a poor fish, an easy target, to be shot at … a sitting duck … maybe that's right.[31]

Connotation is again crucial, and the function of the title is to trigger evaluation, either positively ('like a fish to water') or negatively ('a fish in the water'). However, despite Hemenway's cautions and his suggestion, which would have preserved the connotation that the author seemed to have taken to politics as easily as to writing, 'A Fish in the Water' was retained in the published version.

Hemenway provides thorough comments on the whole manuscript and, importantly for our purposes, explains very clearly the reasons for what he perceives to be key questions. He particularly notes a thematic problem affecting the whole structure of the narrative; namely, what to do with the translation of the school system, which adds coherence to the story of the young and growing Vargas Llosa. The difficulty is not only that there is no exact conceptual or terminological equivalence between the Peruvian and the US systems, but also that establishing such a link (e.g. 'first grade') would be problematic for TT readers in the UK and other systems. Hemenway suggests the addition of a footnote ('but at what point?') to clarify correspondence. The solution eventually selected involves a standardization to non-culture specific terms such as 'first year at primary school'.

Further concerns of Hemenway's were to remove inaccuracies in the text and also to provide sufficient background information for the TT reader to understand the motives for the author's actions. Thus, he notes (for ST p. 429) that the criticism levelled by Vargas Llosa against certain Peruvian intellectuals for accepting positions in the US is that they are hypocritical – they criticized the US but were happy to earn a good living there. Hemenway cautions that, unless this is made clear, the same charge could be levelled at Vargas Llosa himself, who has even signed the manuscript of the book from Princeton University. This is one of many examples where Vargas Llosa clarifies the ST in the light of the TT reader's suggestions.

The relationship between Vargas Llosa and his fellow Peruvian intellectuals proves to be a central sticking point in the text. Hemenway recommends changing the TT title of one of the critical chapters, from *Cheap intellectual* to *Cut-rate intellectuals*. The Spanish *El intelectual barato* is an intertextual reference to a series of articles written by Vargas Llosa for the Peruvian magazine *Caretas* in 1979. In these articles, he attacked those intellectuals whom he considered to have supported the left-wing dictatorship (1968–1975) of General Velasco. Hemenway's concerns have to do with the background knowledge of the TT audience, which would not recognize the intertextual reference, and with the connotation of the collocation:

> The Anglophone reader will have no association with the original articles in *Caretas*. 'Cheap intellectual' can mean simply that the ideas are cheap, trivial. 'Cut-rate intellectual' clearly implies that the intellectuals are up for sale. And the plural has more bite.

Since the rejected term *cheap* is a conventional translation equivalent of the Spanish *barato*, this is further evidence that evaluation, even in obviously inscribed tokens such as evaluative epithets, is provoked and nuanced by collocation, co-text and intertextuality. At the same time, inscription (*cut-rate*) wins out over the more subtle evaluative role played by the link to the *Caretas* articles. The recommendations made in the revision therefore prioritize the direct realization of attitude over any explicitation of intertextuality. The TT is constrictive in engagement terms (no recovery of the intertextual voice) even if this means, ironically, that there is potentially more freedom in the reader's interpretation (not restricted to the specific Peruvian context).

In the same chapter, the notes and modifications give clear indications of the way in which this overall interpretation or schema influences specific textual choices:

ST (Vargas Llosa 1993: 317)
El Perú es una prueba, más bien, de lo frágil que es la clase intelectual y la facilidad con que la falta de oportunidades, inseguridad, escasez de medios de trabajo, ausencia de **un status social** y **también la impotencia** para ejercer una efectiva influencia, la vuelva vulnerable a la corrupción, al cinismo y al arribismo.

['Peru is a proof, rather, of the fragile that is the intellectual class and the ease with which the lack of opportunities, insecurity, scarcity of means of work, absence of social status and also impotence to exercise effective influence, makes it vulnerable to corruption, to cynicism and to self-advancement']

Draft TT (Lane ms p. 441)
Peru is a proof, rather, of how fragile the intellectual class is and the ease with which the lack of opportunities, the insecurity, the scarcity of means to carry out its work, the absence of **social status** and **also powerlessness** to exercise any sort of effective influence, make it vulnerable to corruption, to abandonment of its ideals, to cynicism, and the use of language and thought for self-advancement.

In this example, Hemenway first makes four handwritten alterations to the draft TT (highlighted in bold in Lane's translation above). These are:

social status (ST 'social status') is changed to *any accepted status in society*
also powerlessness (ST 'also impotence') is replaced by *the inability*
commas are deleted after *influence* and *cynicism*.

The changes in the abstract nouns both involve judgement (social esteem) and both rework the phraseology away from calques of the ST. The first is intensified by the addition of *any*, the second is weakened by the more general *inability*. Hemenway then crosses out the whole sentence and replaces it with an insert at that point in the text, which includes further changes (highlighted in the example below):

Peru is a **demonstration**, rather, of how fragile the intellectual class is – of the ease with which the lack of opportunities, the insecurity, the scarcity of means to carry out one's work, the absence of any accepted status in society, and the inability to exert any sort of effective influence make **intellectuals** vulnerable to corruption, to abandonment of their ideals, to cynicism and **careerism**.

There is minor variation of lexis (*a demonstration* rather than *a proof,* both constraining forms of engagement) and syntax (the pause created by the punctuation dash which replaces the conjunctive *and* in the first line). But the really crucial turning points are explained clearly in Hemenway's accompanying explanatory note. In particular, he discusses his choice of the terms *intellectuals* rather than *intellectual class* and *careerism* as a translation of *arribismo.* The latter replaces Lane's explicitation *use of language and thought for self-advancement,* which Hemenway describes as 'awkward'. It is noteworthy how, in the interests of readability, *careerism* sacrifices the specifics of the means by which the intellectuals achieve their alleged aim. They remain implicit in the new TT, as they were in the ST – what *careerism* actually involves, we are not told. Although there is a tension in the TTs between Hemenway's readability and Lane's explicitation, it cannot be simply reduced to this. In the use of *intellectual class* (rather than *intellectuals*), it is Hemenway who leans towards explicitation, but he bears in mind its limitations and the need for avoiding misinterpretation of authorial intent:

> It's not clear to me whether you mean by the intellectual class here intellectuals in general – in the developed countries like France, Britain, Germany, and the United States as well as in the Third World – or mean to limit your observation to the latter. I was on the edge of making it 'how fragile the intellectual class is in the Third World' but I can't be certain of your intent.

Here, as Hemenway seeks to bring out the underlying argument, he notes the risk of over-explicitation of the concept. Is Vargas Llosa speaking only about the difficulties of intellectuals in the 'Third World' or does the argument relate to all intellectuals? The reviser might see a logical inference that it is restricted to the former, since security, resources and some status are certainly accorded to intellectuals in many more developed countries. But the ST does not make this absolutely clear. Explicitation by *how fragile the intellectual class is in the Third World* would thus run the risk of distorting the message. Without authorial approval, this change cannot normally be justified. Hemenway goes on to emphasize the importance of the decision, for author as well as translator: 'This is a fairly crucial sentence in the chapter. You may want to revise a bit.' Although the subsequent correspondence does not appear in the archive, we can deduce that Vargas Llosa accepted Hemenway's reading, because *in the Third World* is inserted into the published TT (Vargas Llosa 1994a: 313). This is thus an example of negotiated reading between author and reviser (Hall 1980 [1999]; see Chapter 1, Section 1.6). It also again shows an overlap between the ideational and interpersonal: both noun phrases, *clase intelectual* and *arribismo,* belong to Field and are an expression of the ideational metafunction of language, but the choice of translation also helps to align the TT reader interpersonally with the author's ideas and affects the reading of the whole passage.

As far as specific recurring textual decisions are concerned, Hemenway points out the difficulty of the translation of the term *criollo*, a word which may have ethnic and racial implications. This tallies with some of the major critical points highlighted by Rabassa (see Section 4.2.1 above). Originally used to mean a person born in the Americas of European or African descent, other senses of *criollo* include indigenous/distinctive/characteristic of a Spanish American country.[32] The very breadth of meaning and the partial dislocation implied by the English cognate *creole*[33] make this word problematic, as Hemenway discusses in his letter:

> *Criolla* – A chameleon of a word in Latin American Spanish that can't be translated as creole in any of the fourteen instances in this ms., so far as I can see. I've suggested 'homegrown', 'homespun', 'indigenous', 'grassroots', and 'dyed in the wool' in varying contexts.

None of these translations is likely to be given as an equivalent in dictionaries, which tend to restrict themselves to *Creole*, *native* or the adjective corresponding to the particular Latin American country (Peruvian, Colombian, Ecuadorian . . .).[34] In Lane's draft translation, she tends to use *creole*. Hemenway's creative alternative suggestions include *slangy* (*picardía criolla* ST 135, for Lane's *creole impudence* draft p. 184), *street-wise* or possibly *homegrown* (*político criollo*, ST 405, for Lane's *creole politician* draft p. 564) and *popular* (*música criolla* ST 134, *creole music* draft p. 181). Hemenway discusses this last example on one of his sticky notes:

> *El compositor de música criolla Augusto Polo Campos* ['the composer of criolla music, Augusto Polo Campos']: 'criolla' here means not 'creole' but 'native, indigenous, vernacular, authentic Peruvian.' (A note in Larousse saying this is often the case in Latin America). Aaron Copland would be a US parallel, perhaps. Not easy to say that crisply in English, and just 'popular' will do?[35]

This explicit statement of the problem highlights again competing constraints: first, of the breadth of meaning and connotation in the Spanish; and second, of the need to say it 'crisply', as Hemenway puts it, in English. The reviser is clearly aware of the 'loss' involved in the more standardizing *popular* but the overriding criterion of concision may make this a sufferable loss in his eyes. Furthermore, it is clear that the reviser is basing his corrections on his understanding of the English and only resorts to consultation of the ST when he has a doubt as to its accuracy. Hence Hemenway states: 'I've vetted the translation to some degree by going to the Spanish when the English didn't sound right . . . If there were time, it would be good to vet the translation line by line.' But such a reading is complemented by a close comparison of ST and TT by Vargas Llosa, answering translators' and editors' queries and making suggestions or decisions himself.[36] In two of the examples of *criollo*, the TT phrasing chosen in the final publication is *scoundrel of a politician* (Vargas Llosa 1994a: 397) and *the composer of traditional Peruvian music* (ibid.: 130). Both of these are more precise and more intensely attitudinal than either the Lane or Hemenway versions.

4.2.4 Lexical alternatives in the essay genre

The translation of another minor essay by Vargas Llosa gives a very clear identification of lexical doubts and choices and how these may be resolved by translator–author consultation. It is the text of a talk given by Vargas Llosa in Georgetown University Library on the occasion of the 'Two millionth volume celebration', on 4 May 1984, entitled 'El Paraíso de los libros' (Vargas Llosa 1991) and translated by George Davis as 'The Paradise of Books' (Vargas Llosa 1994b).[37] The subject is the town of Hay-on-Wye in Wales, famous for its multitude of bookshops and its annual international book festival. The typescript draft of the translation appears with translation queries for the attention of Vargas Llosa, marked by Davis as specific alternatives at different points in the text. This is a particularly valuable source, as (i) the alternatives are spelled out so clearly and (ii) the text is compact enough for us to be able to examine *all* 53 queries from an ST of 1843 words.

The following example, from the beginning of the essay, shows how Davis indicates the alternative choices at marked points in the text:

> *El pueblecito galés de Hay está al pie de una cordillera misteriosa* . . .
> *The little/small/tiny Welsh village/town of Hay is at the foot of a mysterious chain of mountains* . . .

Davis presents the queries as TT alternatives separated by a forward slash (*little/small/tiny; village/town*). It is unclear how exactly these were resolved (whether by Vargas Llosa himself, by the translator or by a combination of the two) but it is possible to see the result by comparing it with the published TT of the speech: *The tiny Welsh village of Hay* . . . In this instance, the doubts concern relatively minor synonym differences relating to two features of a single lexical item, *pueblecito*: the denotative element of the noun *pueblo* (*village/town*) and the realization of the diminutive suffix *–ito* (*little/small/tiny*). Classification of all the translator queries in this text reveals that 20 (approximately 38 per cent) of the 53 comprise such synonym doubts, for instance:[38]

> *más seguro* > *safer/**more secure***
> *las escaleras* > ***staircases**/stairways*
> *regularmente* > *regularly/**often***
> *desaniman* > *dishearten/**discourage***
> *No me arrepiento de haberlo hecho* > *I am not sorry for having done so/**I do not regret having done so.***

These are all quite minor stylistic alternatives and none shows obvious subjectivity on the part of the translator, not even any noticeable shift in intensification.

Some 18 other queries (approximately 34 per cent of the total) concern the accuracy of comprehension and rendering of the ST content. Three (5 per cent) are formulated as direct questions, the translator seeking help with understanding *un esquinero* (= *shelf*), *un rabdomante* (= *dowser*) and the phrase *si alguien le gana la mano en un ejemplar* (= *if anyone beats him to a copy*). Of the remainder, seven (13 per cent) relate to verifiable external phenomena:

> *granjeros* > ***farmers*** / *merchants* / *traders*
> *grabados* > *engravings* / ***prints***
> *husmean el armario* > *smell out* / ***pry into*** *the cabinet*
> *el invisible lindero que separa Gales de Inglaterra* > *the invisible edge* / *landmark* /
> ***boundary*** / *line which separates Wales from England*
> *su empanada mansión sobre el río Wye* > *his lofty mansion on* / *above* / ***over*** *the river Wye*
> *la terraza de su castillo* > *the terrace* / ***veranda*** *of his castle*
> *Richard Booth había pasado por la Universidad de Oxford* > *Richard Booth had gone through* / ***attended*** / *graduated from Oxford University*

In all these examples, the translator is checking his understanding of the real-world phenomena which the author is describing. Without access to the original scene, or information about it, it is simply not possible for the translator to know whether the object described as a *grabado* is an engraving or a print or what exactly was the nature of Richard Booth's studies in Oxford. In the last example, the Spanish *había pasado por* ['had passed through'] is a general, core verb that, in the absence of a similarly generic term in the TL, almost forces the translator to be more specific. It is this difference in the way the two languages cover the semantic space, and precisely the need for specificity (a form of explicitation in itself), that requires the involvement of the author or another authority with situational knowledge. Interestingly, literary translation here coincides closely with the findings from Chapter 3 — in interviews, technical translators identified examples of similar difficulties in determining equivalents, while the majority of queries on online forums related to terminology that could only be answered with subject-specific expertise. Lacking that knowledge, the default option may be for the translator to select the most neutral TT rendering. Just as the Spanish *había pasado* is non-specific, so the preferred English *had attended* avoids declaring the precise nature of the studies. Booth did actually graduate from Oxford,[39] but the Spanish does not confirm that, so neither can the translation.

Eight examples (15 per cent) seek clarification for subjective representation of external phenomena. Amongst these are:

> *las librerías que recorrimos* > *the bookstores we* ***went*** / *looked through*
> *palpando* > *going through* / *touching* / ***feeling*** *[prints, papers . . .]*
> *el azar* > ***chance*** / *fate* / *destiny*
> *Acaba de extender sus redes bibliográficas a un pueblecito al sur de Francia* >

*He has just extended his bibliographic chain/**dynasty**/empire/network to a small town in the south of France*

These are representations from the author/narrator's point of view. Each of the proposed translations would evoke an attitudinal response to the ST event or entity.[40] Take *recorrimos* in the first example. This is literally *went through*, but the actual details of the event remain unclear. It is unlikely that it means simply walking through the stores, but, presuming that the narrator and his companion did look at the books, it is equally uncertain how carefully this was done. Refocusing as *looked through* could be justified if the narrator's attention was on the books, but then we enter a cline of intensification that would potentially encompass the non-core *browsed*, *studied*, *examined*, etc. and a cline of adverbial intensification such as *slowly, carefully, meticulously* (see Chapter 1, Section 1.3.1.4).

The first three examples in the list above are resolved in the TT by the less risky choice of a neutral and literal translation (*went through, feeling, chance*). It is the last example which involves a notable subjective shift in representation. Richard Booth has opened two bookstores in a town in France, and it is the metaphorical representation of this event that is marked: whereas the ST talks of his extending his 'bibliographic networks' (*sus redes bibliográficas*), the translator doubts between *bibliographic chain/dynasty/empire/network*. Of these, both *empire* and the eventual TT choice *dynasty* impose on the event a more aggressive, neo-colonial conceptual framework in which Booth would be seen to be acting more out of concern for his status. This in fact fits in with the general Tenor of the rest of the text. However, it is a potentially risky alternative because of the increase in intensification and the highlighting of the negative connotation. This is a dangerous combination if the assumption is flawed. The translator would need to depend on the ST writer's approval, hence Davis' query.

The points of evaluation that most closely relate to attitude in appraisal terms are to be found in 11 queries (21 per cent of the total). Of these, three are verbal processes:

hurgando > **stirring up**/inciting
la prensa se ocupó de [las fiestas] > *the press preoccupied/**occupied** themselves with [the parties he threw]*
ponerme a llorar > *to weep/lament/moan/**cry***

In the first example, both translation alternatives for *hurgando*, indicative of strong affect, are in fact incorrect.[41] In the second and third examples, the chosen alternatives are the weaker *occupied themselves* and *cry*. These do happen to be the more literal translations of the ST, but it is still interesting that the stronger evaluative alternatives (e.g. *weep, lament, moan*) are rejected. The alternatives to *cry* are non-core words that again reflect a subjective representation of the event. But this time they are proposed by the translator himself. They are alternative scenarios that offer different degrees of affect. In this way, they are an index of graduation, which is also a key factor in a query of judgement: *bebedor océanico* > *excessive/exorbitant/* **compulsive** *drinker.* Here, the novel ST metaphor[42] is rendered by the less marked collocation *compulsive drinker.*[43]

Davis' negotiation with Vargas Llosa revolves around narrowing down the semantic space occupied by the ST items and very often adjusting the graduation in the TT. It is interesting that often the TT wording that is selected (presumably by or with the agreement of Vargas Llosa) is the most standardized and least intense.

4.3 The practice of self-revision – David Bellos' translation of Georges Perec

The third high-profile case study in this chapter is that of the translator David Bellos and his translation of *La Vie mode d'emploi* (1978, translated as *Life: A User's Manual*, 1987) by French author Georges Perec (1936–1982).[44] The groundbreaking novel, describing in detail a single moment (around 8 p.m. on 23 June 1975) in the lives of the inhabitants of a Parisian apartment block, won the prestigious Prix Médicis and established Perec's international reputation. Perec was a member of the experimental writing group *Oulipo* (Ouvroir de littérature potentielle), founded in 1960 and which also saw Raymond Queneau and Italo Calvino amongst its members.[45] Their style was marked by 'constrained writing' techniques, which included complicated mathematical problems and puzzles.[46] In *La Vie*, for example, the storytelling technique is governed by the movement of the Knight on a chessboard, and the 'squares' where it lands dictate the obligations for that chapter.

The complexity and range of *La Vie's* narrative, characterization, wordplays and puzzles pose huge obstacles for its translation (Bellos 1987). The early Italian translation (1984) by poet and translator Daniella Selvatico Estense (1936–1999) tended to explicate the sense of the original regardless of how hidden it might be. On the other hand, the prolific German translator Eugen Helmlé (1927–2000), who was able to work closely with Perec,[47] aimed at functional equivalence. This was particularly so of the passages that imposed severe formal constraints, such as the apocopated acrostic of chapter 51 where the letter *e* appears in a different position in each line to form a diagonal on the page, from top right to bottom left. A related question concerns the web of subtle intertextual references in the form of concealed quotations from a myriad other authors. These references and quotations[48] account for around 10 per cent of the ST. Yet they passed almost unnoticed by the first critical readers because they were concealed by techniques of what Bellos (1987) terms 'truncation' and 'embedding'. Their translation was also the source of an exaggeratedly scathing attack in *META* by Bernard Magné, Perec expert at the Université du Mirail-Toulouse. The crux of this criticism is that Bellos explicates allusions and references that are deliberately implicit in the ST, in engagement terms constraining the reader's response. For Magné, this 'textual exhibitionism' (Magné 1993a: 399) is unjustifiable and clumsy, destroying the sophisticated ploy by which Perec makes certain readings visible to only a select few readers. This élite, for example, would realize that:

Après sa mort, sa fille unique, Irène, publia son roman inachevé, Les Cent-Jours.

is a reference to Louis Aragon (1897–1982), whose pseudonymous erotic novel was entitled *Le Con d'Irène* (1928) and who published an autobiographical collection of poetry called *Le Roman inachevé*. Bellos' translation makes the authorship more explicit, but still demands effort on the part of the English language reader:

> After his death his only daughter, Irena Ragon, published his unfinished novel, *Les Cent-Jours* (Perec [1987] 2003: 289).

Magné does not view this translation procedure as a question of filling in the linguistic or cultural gaps in the reader's knowledge. The original is more a 'contrat de lecture' ['reading contract'] (Magné 1993: 401), where Perec obliges active reading in order to uncover the hidden treasures. We might say that such a contract envisages a form of compliant reading (Martin and White 2005) because the reader will need to discover the meaning intended by Perec, but it actually involves a dialogic expansion of TT voices to recover the intertextual link. Bellos' reading might be called tactical. It makes the allusion explicit and is therefore more constrictive of response. That Bellos took note of Magné's criticisms is evidenced by the fact that his papers contain a copy of the *META* article – a copy made by hand apparently by Bellos' research assistant Patrizia Molteni.

In Bellos' notes to the US editor, in which he explains the modifications he has introduced (e.g. US usage such as *humor, elevator*), he also discusses the overall strategy of compensation: 'Compensation has been attempted for the loss in translation of a significant number of jokes and allusions, and for the greater obscurity of some of the salvaged allusions'.[49] One of these specifically concerns the Aragon example above: 'the name "Irena Ragon" has been inserted as a clue or shifter to Albert de Routisie – the pen name of Louis Aragon'.[50] It is unclear whether Bellos is using compensation as a general term or as a theoretical procedure from translation theory (cf. Klaudy 2008, Munday 2009c: 174). What is clear, however, is that he describes conscious decision-making strategies to overcome specific critical problems.

4.3.1 The detail of self-revision

Bellos' translation is very well documented thanks to the preservation of draft translations and other material which he donated to the University of East Anglia, Norwich, UK. Specifically, this material comprises:

- folders containing the original French text, pasted on to A4 sheets, which were used by Bellos to mark up intertextual references. Of crucial assistance were Perec's working notes at the Perec archive in Paris and the annotated copy used by German translator Hemlé. Here, indeed, those references and their sources are literally made visible on the page by Bellos' notes.

- the first draft translation, neatly handwritten, that Bellos produced in 1985–1986 in a year's unpaid sabbatical before he took up his Chair at the University of Manchester.[51]
- a notebook in which Belloc briefly noted queries and translation problems, many associated with the location of published translations of source references.
- galley proofs of the first edition of the TT, on which are marked Bellos' later corrections by hand.
- correspondence from Bellos with various helpers and informants who assisted him in tracking down source quotations or in locating extant translations of those quotations.[52] In the case of Jacques Beaumatin (a retired English teacher in Bedoin, Provence), the help amounted to reading substantial parts of the text and pointing out translation errors or doubts, which informed the 1988 revision of the published TT.

I shall restrict myself to one chapter, 87 (entitled 'Bartlebooth 4'), which stands out for the larger than usual number of corrections, some of which were clearly made in the course of writing the first draft rather than as later corrections (e.g. *sketched with such brillia* is altered to *so brilliantly sketched with such brillia*, chapter 87/mms p. 5; *in Porte Ri* becomes *in Porte Ri Puerto Rico*, 87/6). This shows that the draft gives us access to some real-time translation decisions, though not all, of course, since those that were automatic (and hence did not undergo a redrafting) or not verbalized obviously do not appear. The section of the chapter that contains most corrections is shown in Table 4.1 as a transcription of the handwritten first draft.

TABLE 4.1 Sample of Bellos' revision of the translation of Chapter 87 of Perec's *Life: A User's Manual*

ST: Beyssandre était un homme sincère, aimant la peinture et les peintres, attentive, scrupuleux et ouvert, et heureux lorsqu'au terme de plusieurs heures passées dans un atelier ou une galerie, il parvenait à se laisser silencieusement envahir par la présence inaltérable d'un tableau, son existence ténue et sereine, son évidence compacte s'imposant petit à petit, devenant chose presque vivante, chose pleine, chose là, simple et complèxe, signes d'une histoire, d'un travail, d'un savoir, enfin tracés au delà de leur cheminement difficile, tortueux et peut-être même torturé. (ST 525)

['Beyssandre was a sincere man, loving painting and painters, attentive, scrupulous and open, and happy when at the end of several hours spent in a workshop or gallery, he managed to let himself silently be invaded by the unalterable presence of a painting, its existence tenuous and serene, its compact evidence imposing little by little, becoming something almost living, something full, something there, simple and complex, signs of a story, a work, a knowing, finally traced beyond their difficult, tortuous passage and perhaps even tortured.']

(continued)

TABLE 4.1 Sample of Bellos' revision of the translation of Chapter 87 of Perec's *Life: A User's Manual (continued)*

Beyssandre was a sincere man, who loved painting and painters, an

attentive, scrupulous and open man, who was happy when λ ~~after~~   *at the end*

~~spending~~ *many hours in a studio or a gallery, he* λ ~~succeeded in~~   *of a session of*   *managed to let*

~~allowing himself to be overcome by~~ *the unchanging presence of a*

painting λ *, by* ~~its precarious and serene~~ λ λ *existence, as its*   *invade his soul, to be filled*   *the work's calm and fragile*

λ ~~compact obviousness~~ *imposed itself on him little by little,*λ ~~becoming~~   *concentrated clarity*   *transforming the canvas into*

an almost living thing, a thing λ ~~of plenitude~~*, a thing* <u>*there*</u>*,* λ *simple*   *bodied forth*   *both*

and complex, λ *the signs of a past history,* λ *of a labor of*   *bearing*   *and*

a knowing, finally λ ~~drawn out beyond their~~ *difficult, tortuous and*   ~~brought~~*brought into a shape transcending its*

maybe even tortured paths of becoming.
(Draft Chapter 87: 18–19)

Here, the revisions have been inserted after the writing of the initial draft. Bellos (personal communication) tells that his schedule was to produce the first draft of a section in the mornings, which he would pass on to an assistant to type up for him. He would then revise by hand the following afternoon. The crossings out, additions and other rewritings in this example were thus part of that revision process. Below is an analysis of each in order of appearance:

(i) *after spending many hours > at the end of a session of many hours*
The change brings the TT closer to the French *au terme de* ('over the term of') and strengthens the graduation of time. This tallies with the move in the TT to translate *plusieurs heures* ('several hours') as the more intense *many hours*.

(ii) *he succeeded in allowing himself to be overcome by the unchanging presence of a painting > he managed to let the unchanging presence of a painting invade his soul*
Here the changes show a more informal *managed to let* (from *succeeded in allowing*) and a move away from the structure of the ST. This is achieved by the shift from pronominal verb plus passive (*allowing himself to be overcome by . . .*) to an active form plus the addition of an object (*let . . . invade his soul*). The critical core of the restructuring is the lexical move from *overcome* to *invade* – *invade* here is again lexically closer to the French *envahir*.

(iii) *by its precarious and serene existence > to be filled by the work's calm and fragile existence*

Three major changes are noticeable here: the lexical and word order shift from *precarious* to *calm* and *serene* to *fragile*, both of which preserve the positive appreciation in slightly less formal terms. In the case of *calm*, the move is also away from the calque of the French *sereine*. The two epithets are reversed, which could be classed either as a syntactic change or, perhaps more reasonably, as a prosodic shift to a more natural rhythm in the English. In addition, there is the syntactic explicitation with the added phrase *to be filled* at the beginning of the clause.

(iv)   *compact obviousness > concentrated clarity*
The ST is *évidence compacte*. As well as distancing itself from the calque of French *compacte*, the revision chooses synonyms that strengthen the naturalness of phraseology and collocation and add alliteration. This is demonstrated by a Google search[53] that reveals just three hits for *compact obviousness*, compared with 1270 for *concentrated clarity*. Of these, some 98 occur in the context of painting.

(v)   *becoming an almost living thing > transforming the canvas into an almost living thing*
Again, there is a move away from the common translation equivalent of *devenant* and a shift from intransitive (*becoming*) to transitive (*transforming*). As in (ii), this involves the addition of an object (*the canvas*), which was the unstated subject of the intransitive structure.

(vi)   *A thing of plenitude > a thing bodied forth*
This is another shunning of lexical calque (of the French *pleine*, 'full'), here with the substitution of an unusual non-core verb form (*bodied forth*) which adds intensity.

(vii)   The addition of *both . . . bearing . . . and*
These three all add cohesion to a ST sentence that holds together without conjunction.

(viii)   *Drawn out beyond their . . . paths of becoming > brought into a shape transcending its . . . paths of becoming*
The lexical and syntactic calque of the beginning is again removed (the initial *drawn out beyond* closely resembles the French *tracés au delà de*, 'traced beyond') and there is syntactic explicitation with the transitive verb *transcending* taking over the function of the preposition *beyond*. This example may have caused more problems for the translator, indicated by his choice of *brought*, which he crosses out before rewriting it anew.

The patterns of revision discernible from the analysis of this brief but illuminating passage suggest that the criteria behind the revision are less to do with any change in evaluation, except for the intensification of the time period in example (i) and the use of the non-core *bodied forth* in (vi). They are more to do with the avoidance of lexical calque and standard translation equivalents, the shift towards natural collocation, the restructuring towards the use of active and transitive forms and increased cohesion, common moves in a domesticating translation. However, the example of *bodied forth* should not be underestimated. It is a bold move by the translator to choose such a strong, non-core item. Such moves, I have claimed elsewhere (Munday 2008), may be characteristic of more high-profile, experienced and competent literary translators who are confident of their creative abilities in the TL.

Space here prohibits a detailed treatment of all 242 revisions to the chapter, but these may be classified as follows, with illustrative examples:[54]

Lexical 110, of which 19 are technical terms (e.g. *a little pocket-desk in shagreen* > *a little shagreen writing case* chapter 87/mss p. 1, *Trebizond* > *Trabzon* 87/28); and 91 are non-technical rewording (e.g. *covered in* > *draped in* 87/3, *to appeal to* > *to have recourse to* 87/4, *customer* > *client* 87/20)

Syntax and grammar 39 (e.g. *had sketched with such brillia* > *had so brilliantly sketched* 87/5)

Addition 33 (e.g. *a style of hotel* > *a style of tourist hotel* 87/4)

Cohesion 29 (e.g. *and Smantf read the letter* > *so Smantf read it* 87/23)

Word order change 19 (e.g. *an open-neck gray shirt* > *a gray open-neck shirt* 87/3)

Omission 15 (e.g. *his art investments* > *art investments* 87/17, *a banknote for one hundred thousand pounds sterling* ... > *a one hundred thousand pound banknote* 87/20)

Modality 6 (e.g. *without going outside* > *without having to go outside* 87/7)

Corrected information 3 (e.g. *the right hand one* > *the left-hand one* 87/2)

In broader terms, the revisions tend to involve either the substitution of individual non-technical lexical items (91 instances) or some syntactic or cohesive reworking (81 instances cover syntax, grammar, word order and cohesion). Some overlaps involve cohesion and either omission (**the** *construction work* > *construction work* 87/16) or addition (*artists and dealers* > *artists and* **their** *dealers* 87/24). As in the earlier list, cohesion is a major preoccupation at this revision stage.

More fine-grained analysis enables some greater understanding of the trends encompassed by the individual lexical items and additions. Of the 91 non-technical lexical changes, some 23 have some obvious relation to evaluation. The majority of these involve the replacement of one evaluative synonym by another, hence:

supremely sophisticated > *supreme sophistication* (87/6)
admirably systematized > *an admirable degree of systematization* (87/9)
urchins > *ragamuffins* (87/11)
glory > *magnificence* (87/15)
rather puerile > *somewhat puerile* (87/18)
new postings > *fresh estimates* (87/29)

There are six instances of intensification of evaluation in lexical choice. In five of these the revision employs a non-core item and/or a stronger metaphorical use:

covered > *draped* (87/3)
this idea had been **basic** > *this idea had been* **fundamental** (87/7)
disappeared > *subsided* (87/18)

showed > *proved* (87/28)
put > *invest* [capital] (87/29)

The other case involves an intensifying adverb, combined with a reversal of point of view (cf. Vinay and Darbelnet [1958] 1995: 252).

only a banknote > **absolutely nothing except** a banknote (87/20)

Intensification of evaluation through adverbial strengthening of graduation is also a pattern in the additions, as the following examples show:

with a single entrance > *and **only** a single entrance* (87/3)
a special place of relaxation > *a **very** special place of relaxation* (87/6)
the number of slaves . . . > *the **authentic** number of slaves* (87/15)
had given up writing > *had **entirely** given up writing* (87/21)
all the papers he had worked for > *all the papers he had **ever** worked for* (87/21)
gave him > ***generously** gave him* (87/22)
it had never occurred to him > *it had never **even** occurred to him* (87/26).

In each case, the added TT word has no counterpart in the ST. Such a trend towards intensification is highly interesting. It suggests that evaluation may not be a prime concern in the initial drafting process but does feature more prominently later at the revision stage. It also raises the possibility that intensification of evaluation is a major component of the procedure of explicitation. The translator's awareness of this is debatable. Bellos (personal communication) indicates that the most conscious changes at the drafting stage were primarily structural, which would explain the large number of syntactic, word order and other cohesive changes.

Supplementary analysis of the reasoning behind the conscious decisions is facilitated by the translator's notebooks for this translation, which make visible specific problem areas. In his notebook entitled 'Running queries',[55] Bellos refers mainly to quotations and references where the English published version needs to be researched (e.g. 'p. 33 RABELAIS infill when transl. found'; 'p. 63 English titles of paintings') and to technical or cultural terms where either he is unsure of the referent of the original ('p. 178 What is Pain perdu?') or the appropriate English term ('72/3 cowrie-coins: common name of cypraea moneta'; '101 chef d'entreprise: tln [translation] not obvious'). His awareness of Hemlé's German TT is proven in his resolution of two problems late in the notebook: '[ST 520] bal-à-Jo G[erman] gives Apachenball/suggest street parties' and '[ST 518] Matmata G[erman] gives die Matmata'. Bellos also keeps a brief list of 'hyphenation queries' (e.g. 'tea urn/tea-urn') and 'Terminology' of frequent terms and the translation equivalents used (e.g. 'quartier: quartier, block p. 9 district'). It must be admitted that in none of the conscious critical points of quotation and technical/cultural terms are there obvious forms of appraisal from the translator, except for some indecision over whether to preserve the foreignness of, for example, *quartier*.

4.3.2 Revision and evaluation at different stages

The result of the detailed above revisions is the almost published version of the text. At the subsequent, galley proof, stage, the only additional revisions to the text in Table 4.1 were the typographical change of *labor* to *labour* (for the UK edition) and the replacement of *a knowing* by *a craft* (ST *un savoir*).[56] Nevertheless, modifications continued to be made at other stages in the life of the TT. Bellos' correspondence with reader Jacques Beaumatin[57] and others was designed mainly to eliminate errors in the English after first publication. The majority of these minor corrections relate to terminology (e.g. *wrought-iron coatstand* to replace *cast-iron coatstand*, TT 27; *Ever Young* > *Evergreen*, TT 330) or figures (e.g. 1956 becomes 1955, TT 27; *five hundred* changes to *one hundred and five*, TT 192), and the rectifying of typographical errors (e.g. *Phillip III* > *Philip III*, TT 204) and omissions (e.g. *harissa*, TT 153). Minor correction of an already published text is complicated by the desire to avoid significant (and costly) pagination changes. This is of course particularly a problem with the filling in of omissions, exemplified by Bellos' handwritten addition to the typed list of amendments in which he states that an addition of two clauses on page 29 amounted to '50 characters+spaces more'.

A small number of translation errors are also corrected. A few of these are slips that may occur in any translation, or indeed any piece of original writing. They are perhaps provoked by a subconscious confusion of items in the same semantic field (*a French town* > *a French quarter* [TT 267], *arms akimbo* > *arms folded* [TT 311]) and/or with the same collocational behaviour (*right hand* > *left hand* [TT 311, TT 436], *Mademoiselle Lafuente* > *Madame Lafuente* [TT 451]). There remain three that pose specific problems of ascertaining exactly what the ST means. These are:

1. *besace*, translated as *knapsack* (TT 208), which Bellos defends since the definition in the *Collins English Dictionary* is 'virtually identical' to *Le Petit Robert*;
2. *Marabout*, again Bellos defends his *bell tent* rather than the suggested *shrine*, but is forced to concede by Beaumatin's response that the prime function of the Marabout in Algiers is indeed as a shrine (TT 374); and
3. *jambon persillé*, initially translated as *sprinkled with parsley*.

In each case, Bellos had relied on solid dictionary definitions, but in all three the question relates to understanding the exact visual and functional form of the referent. Thus, what is the form of a *besace*? In *Le Petit Robert* the main sense is 'a long bag, open in the middle and the ends of which form two pockets'.[58] Is this the same as a *knapsack*, which, according to the *Collins English Dictionary*, is 'a canvas or leather bag carried strapped on the back or shoulder'? Today, a translator would probably seek to resolve this by conducting an online search for images of the words and comparing the results (compare Chapter 3, Section 3.3). The same goes for the other queries, *Marabout* and *jambon persillé*. Visual identification reduces the possibility of a skewed interpretation. Combined with the accompanying text, it would doubtless have reassured Bellos that his *sprinkled with parsley* was a justified equivalent: English versions such as *ham hock terrine or jambon persillé (parsley ham)*[59] are common. Beaumatin's concentration on the aspic, and not the parsley, in the dish distracts Bellos into accepting his suggestion of *ham dotted with fat* (TT 414), a curious collocational neologism and generalization. Intervention in this regard has led to an overexplicitation of one visual feature to the detriment of arguably a more important one.

Interestingly, in his same letter to Beaumatin, Bellos' justifications for two of his choices reveal a higher-level translation strategy: for *panier à salade*, he retains *salad bowl* (TT 317) rather than the more correct *salad shaker* because '[f]ew English readers have or use or know what a salad shaker is. The translation is approximate to avoid unwanted bizarreness.' On the other hand, he defends his translation of *cendrier de faïence* as *porcelain ashtray* (TT 264), rather than *china*, *earthenware*, etc., since 'only porcelain seems to have a genuinely technical specification'. So, the critical element is again the technical term, although the solution is not to select the closest technical English equivalent but instead to aim for some kind of functional equivalence. Such equivalence is orientated to achieving or avoiding a certain contextual effect on the audience (the avoidance of an estranging term such as *salad shaker*; the selection of a relevant technical term in *porcelain*).

Twenty years after the publication of the translation, Godine published a corrected edition of the TT in the United States (Perec 2008). The changes that were made for that edition are explained in Bellos' 'Notes on the revised edition' (Perec 2008) and in an interview given by editor Susan Barba (Esposito 2010). Barba indicates that Bellos worked from new editions of the French, prepared by Magné, and had benefited from other scholarship in the intervening period. While Bellos comments on the importance of 're-readings' of the text and new interpretations, Barba notes that most of the changes were relatively minor: 'The changes we made were mostly of the variety that copyeditors and proofreaders make: spelling mistakes, mistakes in terminology, inverted colophons, incorrect page references in the index, and even the omission of a paragraph in the final chapter!' (in Esposito 2010).

4.4. Conclusion

The three case studies have served to reveal some of the wide range of critical points in literary texts. In the case of the classical Tacitus text, it was the instability of the ST and the role of the paratextual features (preface and endnotes) in imposing a compliant reading on the reader. The exaggeration of negative attitude towards the Peucini and Sarmatians came through subjective interpretation and intensification of the abstract noun *habitum* as highly negative appreciation *ugliness* and *repulsive appearance*. It involved racial stereotyping, not only by Tacitus but also, in a form of tactical reading, by the translators Mattingly and Handford, who in their notes recontextualize the negativity and project it towards modern-day 'Mongolians' and 'Asiatic peoples' and in the context of mixed marriages.

Race and racial descriptions are highly sensitive critical points in literary texts and, in the naming used, likely to be revealing of translator ideology and subjectivity.

Rabassa mentions these in his correspondence with Vargas Llosa. Other points he highlights are Peruvianisms and technical terms for flora and fauna, which tend to become more standardized in the TTs. At a higher level there is always much discussion about the titles of the books, of great importance because they send out a message that attracts readers and creates expectations. As far as attitudinal expressions are concerned, subtle indirect invocation-association, such as through intertextual reference, is sometimes turned into direct inscription in a process of explicitation. But there are competing constraints of readability, concision and the desire to avoid loss of the original sense. The result of the negotiated meaning between author, reviser and/or translator is blurred. So, the technical term *criollo*, very context-dependent for its attitudinal value, is intensified in the Hemenway-Vargas Llosa revision of *A Fish in the Water* as *a **scoundrel** of a politician* and **traditional Peruvian** *music*. On the other hand, the negotiation between George Davis and Vargas Llosa over a relatively minor essay shows a trend towards a loss of intensification, core words being preferred to non-core ones.

David Bellos' translation of Perec has to tackle highly complex puns, word puzzles and dialogic intertextual references in an extremely heteroglossic text. The intertextual critical points in a literary text constrain translators to reproduce quotations from other published texts, but the plays on words tend to generate disagreement between translators and other experts. Analysis of the self-revision shows Bellos' focus to be mainly on syntactic and lexical changes to make the TT more idiomatic, avoiding calques of the French ST. One very interesting finding is the pattern of increased intensification of graduation through the addition of adverbs (e.g. *a **very** special place*). Adjustment and refinement of evaluation therefore seems to have been an important consideration at the revision stage even if it was neglected during the initial drafting. Since Bellos was both translator and reviser, this may be an idiosyncratic characteristic of his own working process.

5

TRANSLATION VARIATION AND ITS LINK TO ATTITUDE

5.0 Introduction

This chapter describes an empirical study to examine the concept of variation in multiple TTs of the same ST and the subjectivity that this may entail. Although the main object of study are translation products (i.e. the TTs themselves), it is motivated by a keen interest in the translation process, in the differences that exist between translators, and, the other side of the same coin, in what characteristics translators share and how this can be traced in their work. The investigation centres on the small linguistic variations between different target versions of the same source text and on the extent to which those elements that are most open to shifting are expressions of attitude and feelings. This will shed further light on the question of 'legitimate translation variation', which is 'the fact that independent human translations of the same text often use different words and structures to convey the same content' (Babych and Hartley 2004: 833). In the context of statistical calculation of the quality of machine translation output measured against TTs produced by human translators, Babych and Hartley analyse two human translations of a French legal text into English. They find that the stability of units across the human translations is related to the salience of those units in the text:

> Highly significant words, which are consistently used within a single translation, were found to be the most unstable across different translations. The possible reason for this fact could be that translation of significant units typically requires invention of some novel translation strategy.
>
> *(Babych and Hartley 2004: 836)*

In their small-scale experiment, the two human translators each translated salient terms consistently within a text; for example, one translated the word *requêtes* as *petitions* throughout. However, variation occurred between the translation equivalents of these terms produced by the different translators – the other translator used *requests*. Babych and Hartley suggest that in some instances such variation occurs because no obvious, ready-made translation solutions are available and greater creativity is demanded. On the other hand, more stability is seen with less salient words.

The present chapter is a more qualitative experiment based on a literary text. Extracts from Jorge Luis Borges' short story 'Emma Zunz' (first published in 1948) are first analysed against the published English translations by Donald Yates and Andrew Hurley and then against a corpus of translations by trainee translators. A Borges story is chosen because of the importance attached to his style, and the existence of more than one TT allows more effective comparison of translation strategies. More importantly, the tale centres on the emotional and mental perspective of the protagonist, therefore lending itself to the study of attitude.

5.1 The texts: Borges and his translators

Although translated into French by Roger Caillois in the 1950s, the Argentine author Jorge Luis Borges (1899–1986) only achieved widespread international fame in 1961 with the award of the prestigious Formentor literary prize, shared with Samuel Beckett. The following year saw two collections of his short stories rushed through publication in English translation: *Fictions*, edited by Anthony Kerrigan, and *Labyrinths*, edited by University of Michigan graduates Donald Yates and James Irby and in which Yates's translation of 'Emma Zunz' appeared (Borges 1962). In the 1950s Irby had started translating the (then) relatively unknown Borges in order to 'get a feel for his style' (Yates 2002: 14). At the time publishers such as Alfred Knopf and New Directions had rejected opportunities to publish the work in English. According to Yates, Irby adopted what could be described as a deliberately marked or 'deviant' (Leech and Short 1981) form of English, with the justification that 'since Borges's language does not read smoothly in Spanish, there is no reason it should in English' (Irby, cited in Yates 2002: 17). Yates (ibid.) agrees with giving priority to the ST, and again, like many literary translators, provides a non-technical description of his aims: 'if the original has warts and blemishes, a translator should not try to cover them up with cosmetic touches, but rather attempt to give them a faithful rendering in another language'.

The second TT of the story was by Andrew Hurley, then Professor of English at the University of Puerto Rico and teacher on the university's translation programme, translator of over 30 works of history, poetry and fiction. His 'Emma Zunz' appeared in the volume *Collected Fictions* (Borges 1998a), new translations of almost all of Borges' literary work, published in advance of the centenary of the author's birth. Hurley's broad description of his translation strategy also focuses on style: 'My approach to translation . . . is that I attempt to reproduce in the translation the markers of style that I identify in the source text' (Hurley 1999: 289). But for Hurley, Borges' style is 'plain':

Quietness, subtlety, a laconic terseness – these are the marks of Borges' style
... Borges' sentences are almost invariably classical in their symmetry, in their
balance. Borges likes parallelism, chiasmus, subtle repetitions-with-variations;
his only indulgence in 'shocking' the reader (an effect he repudiated) may be
the 'Miltonian displacement of adjectives' to which he alludes in his foreword
to *The Maker*.

(Hurley 1998: 518)

This 'displacement of adjectives' challenges the naturalness of a text that is achieved
by the use of common collocations, a psychological association that is linked to the
way words are 'primed' to occur in certain genres (Hoey 2005: 5). Hurley (1999:
297) highlights 'etymologized adjectives and adverbs' such as the famous *unánime* in
the first sentence of the 'Las ruinas circulares' (1940, 'The Circular Ruins') – 'Nadie
lo vio desembarcar en la **unánime** noche' rendered by Hurley as the similarly
etymologized and calqued adjective *unanimous*: 'No one saw him slip from the boat
in the **unanimous** night' (Borges 1998a: 96).[1] I shall argue below that the choice
of adjective, or 'evaluative epithet', and collocation is a strong bearer of attitude in
such narrative texts.

Before proceeding to the analysis of the published 'Emma Zunz' translations,
it is important to note two points. First, coming to the task over 30 years after
the Yates publication, Hurley obviously had public access to Yates's translation and,
potentially, could have restricted himself to modifying only those passages where
he felt improvement was possible. However, the existence of prior translations,
by other translators and with different publishers, meant that variation might be
essential in order to avoid any accusation of plagiarism, of simply reproducing
what had been translated before.[2] Not that Hurley would necessarily have made
a specific lexical choice in his translations for the mere sake of variation. What is
more often emphasized by literary translators is the importance of finding and
recreating the narrative voice of the author. Margaret Sayers Peden, who worked as
'an outside editor' (Hurley 1998: 524) on the project, expresses this in the following
terms: '[t]o me the overall most important key to the translation is to find its voice.
Who is telling? Who is narrating?' (Peden 2002: 76). This narrative voice is more
nebulous, less easy to pin down, than what we have discussed as the evaluative
voice or style (White and Thomson 2008: 13; see also Chapter 1, Section 1.5).
The collaboration of Peden, closely reading and commenting on a draft, and of
Carter Wheelock of the University of Texas at Austin,[3] 'who read word by word
through an "early-final" draft of the translation, comparing it against the Spanish
for omissions, misperceptions and mistranslations, and errors of fact' (Hurley 1998:
523–4), shows that the linguistic choices of a TT are very often the amalgam of
decisions made by what has been termed the 'implied translator' (Schiavi 1996), an
abstract narratological construct that is useful for indicating the nature of literary
translation (see also Munday 2008: 12). By contrast, it is rather surprising to learn
that Yates and Irby's translations for the *Labyrinth* collection had been published by
New Directions without any editing or revision at all of the manuscript submitted
by the translators (Yates 2002: 15).

5.1.1 Analysis of the Yates and Hurley translations of 'Emma Zunz'

The title 'Emma Zunz' comes from the name of the protagonist, who, learning of the suicide of her shamed father, seeks and exacts revenge on Aaron Loewenthal, her father's former business partner. Emma Zunz had been told by her father that Loewenthal had concocted the evidence that had brought a damning charge of embezzlement against him. In order to exact revenge she arranges a late-night meeting with Loewenthal, where she shoots him with his own pistol. She then claims to the police that he had raped her. In the days before DNA testing, she is able to justify her story because, earlier that day in the guise of a prostitute, she had premeditatedly visited the bars of Buenos Aires to pick up and have sex with a sailor from a foreign ship in the port.

Three short extracts of the story were selected for the study of variation. These were:

Extract 1
Emma Zunz's reaction after the Swedish sailor has left the room where they have had sex, and her journey across the city towards the rendezvous point.

Cuando se quedó sola, Emma no abrió en seguida los ojos. En la mesa de luz estaba el dinero que había dejado el hombre: Emma se incorporó y lo rompió como antes había roto la carta. Romper dinero es una impiedad, como tirar el pan; Emma se arrepintió, apenas lo hizo. Un acto de soberbia y en aquel día . . . El temor se perdió en la tristeza de su cuerpo, en el asco. El asco y la tristeza la encadenaban, pero Emma lentamente se levantó y procedió a vestirse. En el cuarto no quedaban colores vivos; el último crepúsculo se agravaba. Emma pudo salir sin que la advirtieran; en la esquina subió a un Lacroze, que iba al oeste. Eligió, conforme a su plan, el asiento más delantero, para que no le vieran la cara. Quizá le confortó verificar, en el insípido trajín de las calles, que lo acaecido no había contaminado las cosas. Viajó por barrios decrecientes y opacos, viéndolos y olvidándolos en el acto, y se apeó en una de las bocacalles de Warnes. Paradójicamente su fatiga venía a ser una fuerza, pues la obligaba a concentrarse en los pormenores de la aventura y le ocultaba el fondo y el fin.[4]

Extract 2
Emma Zunz's intention to escape punishment and to kill Loewenthal.

(No por temor, sino por ser un instrumento de la Justicia, ella no quería ser castigada.) Luego, un solo balazo en mitad del pecho rubricaría la suerte de Loewenthal. Pero las cosas no ocurrieron así.[5]

Extract 3
The last paragraph of the story, where we learn that her version of events will be accepted as true.

La historia era increíble, en efecto, pero se impuso a todos, porque sustancialmente era cierta. Verdadero era el tono de Emma Zunz, verdadero el pudor, verdadero el odio. Verdadero también era el ultraje que había padecido; sólo eran falsas las circunstancias, la hora y uno o dos nombres propios.[6]

The rationale for the choice of these specific extracts is that they are central to the ethical and emotional narrative thread, each displaying important features expressing attitude (especially affect) by the character or narrator.[7] In Extract 1, it is Emma Zunz's physical and moral revulsion after giving herself to the sailor, but also her calculating and nervous preparation for the act of revenge. In Extract 2, we briefly see her hopes, fears and plans for the meeting and the triumph this would bring. In Extract 3, the parallelism of marked syntactic structures, in which the judgement adjective *verdadero* ('true') appears in clause-initial or sentence-initial position four times, emphasizes the narrator's assertion of the underlying truth of her story, despite the falsifications.

Variation between the two texts was analysed manually in order to ensure qualitatively satisfactory results. This is possible because the extracts were brief. However, classificatory difficulties occurred. For example, conceptual decisions as to what constitutes variation need to be taken in examples such as the following:

> *El asco y tristeza la encadenaban.*
> ['Disgust and sadness were enchaining her']
> <u>Grief</u> and <u>nausea</u> <u>were</u> chain<u>ing</u> <u>her</u> (Yates)
> <u>Sadness</u> and <u>revulsion</u> <u>lay upon</u> <u>Emma</u> <u>like</u> chains (Hurley)

The <u>underlined words</u> show the points of variation, but how should *chaining/chains* be analysed? Yates' use of the verb form *chaining* and Hurley's of the noun *chains* are clearly from the same semantic root. In this study, the root has been considered to be invariant within different functional grammatical structures. Similar questions arise elsewhere when grammatical or morphological categories are retained but the semantic realization alters, e.g. <u>concealed</u> (Yates) and <u>masked</u> (Hurley). Syntactic and structural levels also may need to be factored in. In the very first sentence, invariance at word level is easy to identify but the position of the adverb *immediately* alters to sentence-final position in Hurley and therefore is classified as varying:

> *Cuando se quedó sola, Emma no abrió <u>en seguida</u> los ojos*
> ['When she remained alone, Emma did not open <u>at once</u> the eyes']
> When she was alone, Emma did not <u>immediately</u> open her eyes (Yates)
> When she was alone, Emma did not open her eyes <u>immediately</u> (Hurley)

This is an area of theme and information structure (Halliday and Matthiessen 2004: 64–105), part of the textual function (see Chapter 1, Section 1.1), which organizes the clause 'as message' and assists in foregrounding specific elements. It is particularly relevant to Extract 3, where, as noted above, the ST has the marked form *verdadero* in clause-initial position. Here, the textual metafunction reinforces the strength of the evaluation. The translations of this extract are as follows:

> **Extract 3a** Yates translation (Borges 1962: 24)
> Actually the story *was* incredible, but it impressed everyone because substantially it was true. True was Emma Zunz' tone, true was her shame, true was her hate. True also was the outrage she had suffered: only the circumstances were false, the time, and one or two proper names.

> **Extract 3b** Hurley translation (Borges 1998b: 219)
> The story was unbelievable, yes – and yet it convinced everyone, because in substance it was true. Emma Zunz's tone of voice was real, her shame was real, her hatred was real. The outrage that had been done to her was real, as well; all that was false were the circumstances, the time, and one or two proper names.

In a generally appreciative review of Hurley's translation, Gene H. Bell-Villada (1998) comments on this specific sentence: '[w]hile Hurley's prose sounds more idiomatic, like everyday speech, Yates's, with its inversions that mirror the original yet also strike us with their strangeness, seems appropriate to the odd mental conceit being argued here'. Yates does retain the sentence-initial and clause-initial repetition of *true*, foregrounding an absolutely crucial judgement element of the story. In Hurley's translation of the extract, the second sentence (*Emma Zunz's tone of voice* . . .) and the beginning of the third (*The outrage* . . .) are normalized, SV constructions, only slightly compensated by the subsequent emphatic cleft construction *all that was false were* . . .

Both Bell-Villada's observation and this analysis suggest that Hurley's assertion that he pursued an 'anti-fluent', source-oriented, or foreignizing, style is not always borne out, certainly in comparison with Yates's work. But the study takes the interest in variation further, first by a more detailed comparison of the two extracts (see Appendix 5.1), which shows that approximately 208 lexical forms are identical in the two TTs, amounting to approximately 65 per cent of the Yates translation and 63 per cent of the Hurley translation.[8] Lexical variation between the two translations therefore comprises around one third of the total text. I shall limit myself to an examination of the most common variations, which occurred in 'content' words and in processes (verbal and nominalized forms, see Tables 5.1 and 5.2) and modal forms (mainly epithets, or adjectives, see Table 5.3).

The main trends in the tables are:

1. slightly more variation in verbal processes than in nominalizations or indeed in the modal category, where explicit inscription of attitude may be thought most likely to occur, as it links to the interpersonal function;
2. variation lies in *linguistic realization* rather than necessarily in the presence or distortion of appraisal itself. So, very similar evaluation is conveyed by both *incredible* and *unbelievable*, for ST *increíble*;

TABLE 5.1 Examples of variation in verbal processes in Yates and Hurley TTs

Borges	Yates	Hurley
se arrepintió	repented	wished she hadn't
se perdió	was lost	melted
encadenaban	chaining	chains
se agravaba	was weakening	made it drearier
salir	leave	slip out
subió a	got on	mounted
le confortó	it comforted her	she was comforted
se apeó	alighted	got off
ocultaba	concealed	masked
rubricaría . . . la suerte	seal . . . fate	put an end to . . . life
se impuso	impressed	convinced
que había sufrido	that she had suffered	that had been done to her

TABLE 5.2 Examples of variation in noun forms in Yates and Hurley TTs

Borges	Yates	Hurley
el temor	fear	foreboding
la tristeza	grief	sadness
el asco	nausea	revulsion
el asco	disgust	revulsion
su fatiga	fatigue	weariness
el trajín	rapid movement	banal bustle
la aventura	adventure	mission
el fondo	the background	its true nature
el fin	the objective	its final purpose
el odio	hatred	hate

3. Yates's attitudinal items stand out because of lexical interference from the ST (e.g. *opaque* for *opacos*) or for the use of the most obvious translation equivalent (e.g. *fear* for *temor* or *adventure* for *aventura*), compared to Hurley's more idiomatic and interpretive renderings of the same words (e.g. *gloomy, foreboding, mission*).

Of course, there are also instances, at crucial moments in the text or in central concepts in the story, where there is no variation in the realization of appraisal. For example, Emma's reaction to her experiences at the end of the story is translated by both Yates and Hurley as *shame* (ST *pudor*) and *outrage* (ST *ultraje*). On the other hand, the third point above relates to places where variation in Hurley leads to important evaluative reformulations of the original through lexical choice. Such

TABLE 5.3 Examples of variation in modal forms in Yates and Hurley TTs

Borges	Yates	Hurley
se arrepintió	repented	wished she hadn't[1]
pudo	was able to	managed to
contaminado	contaminated	polluted
decrecientes	diminishing	shrinking
opacos	opaque	gloomy
no quería	did not want to	intended not to
increíble	incredible	unbelievable
en efecto	actually	yes
verdadero	true	real
solo	only	all

1 Here, Yates translates the emotive Spanish mental process verb *se arrepintió* by the emotive mental cognate *repented* whereas Hurley uses the desiderative mental process *wished she hadn't*, also an example of modal inclination (cf. Halliday and Matthiessen 2004: 208 and 618). Hence the example appears in both Table 5.1 and 5.3.

variation may happen in any category, and Table 5.1 shows some tendency for the intensification of graduation in the selection of value-laden non-core TT forms such as *slip out* and *mounted* for common ST verbs *salir* ['leave'] and *subió* ['got on']. Yet the most striking contrasts are to be found in Table 5.2, where the shifts in what are overwhelmingly abstract nouns sometimes radically alter the perspective of the text. Yates intensifies Emma's 'affective' reaction with TT equivalents such as *grief* and *nausea* (for ST *tristeza* and *asco* – compare Hurley's *sadness* and *revulsion*), while Hurley adds a more forceful, and alliterative, explicitation of the street scene (ST *trajín*, Yates *rapid movement*, Hurley *banal bustle*) and reinterprets ST affect items as *foreboding* (for ST *temor*, cf. Yates's *fear*) and the more cognitive *mission* (for ST *aventura* – compare Yates's *adventure*). Indeed, the example of *mission* is the clearest evaluative reinterpretation in these TT extracts:

Yates (variations <u>underlined</u>)
Paradoxically her <u>fatigue was</u> turn<u>ing out to be</u> a strength, <u>since</u> it <u>obliged</u> her to concentrate on the details of **the adventure** and <u>conceal</u>ed from her <u>the background</u> and <u>the objective</u>.

Hurley (variations <u>underlined</u>)
Paradoxically, her <u>weariness</u> turn<u>ed into</u> a strength, <u>for</u> it <u>forced</u> her to concentrate on the details of **her mission** and <u>masked</u> from her <u>its true nature</u> and <u>its final purpose</u>.

Mission fits far more closely with the cold premeditation driving Emma Zunz's revenge. Hurley has added force and ethical judgement with this TT equivalent. Explicit evaluation is also to be found in both TTs in the counter-expectancy adverb *paradoxically* (ST *paradójicamente*) in first position. Other variants such as *since/for*, *oblige/force* and *conceal/mask* are minor stylistic changes and scarcely alter the text. However, the use of possessive pronouns in the Hurley text (*her mission . . . its true nature . . . its final purpose*) compared to Yates's, and the ST's, definite articles, make a much tighter cohesive framework that may alter the texture of the text and of the narrative.[9]

Most importantly, however, and irrespective of any general overall strategy or higher-level discoursal or narratological shifts, a tentative hypothesis based on the analysis of these extracts is that most of the variants seem to occur on the paradigmatic axis of language; that is, at the level of choices for different linguistic 'slots' in the text. Thus, the first two clauses of the above example could be represented as in Table 5.4.

Categorization on the paradigmatic axis generates many questions about the unit of translation employed, about the grammatical and functional categories where variation is most likely to occur and which variations are most significant, the latter accompanied by the supplementary question: In what way are they significant?

Analysis of the lists in Tables 5.1 to 5.3 has highlighted that the most dramatic shifts to evaluation and expressions of attitude occur through shifts of abstract noun forms such as *adventure/mission*. It is noticeable that cognate forms tend to be shunned by Hurley. Indeed, evidence from Hurley himself shows that this was a deliberate decision:

> Some cognates are *false* cognates; some lead to only slight distortions in meaning; only rarely are cognates really usable by a translator in a serious translation. Borges himself once told Margaret Sayers Peden over breakfast at an MLA convention in Chicago – this conversation reported to me by Petch Peden the other day on the telephone – that his translators 'killed him with cognates'. Translators must be trained *not* to use that fatal weapon.[10]

TABLE 5.4 Variation on the paradigmatic axis in Yates and Hurley TTs

Paradoxically	her	fatigue	was turning out to be[1]	a	strength,
		weariness	turned into		

since	it	obliged	her	to concentrate on	the
for		forced			

details	of	the	adventure	. . .	
		her	mission	. . .	

1 It is possible to analyse the fourth slot (for ST *venía a ser*) as two, namely the semantic lexical core of *turn out to be* (and its stylistic variant *turn into*) plus the past tense modal and morpheme (*was -ing/ -ed*).

5.2 The experiment

In this study, exploration into variation was extended by an experiment involving 15 other translations of the passages from the ST. The 15 translations were commissioned from volunteers amongst MA students at the University of Leeds, UK, in the calendar year 2007. Students were asked to read the whole story but to translate just the three extracts given below. They were allowed to consult any resources except the already published translations. The reasoning behind the latter constraint was in order to ensure as far as possible that the variations were due to the translators' own interpretations, recoding or idiolect, without influence from the published TTs.

The volunteers were given two weeks to submit their translations by email, together with a brief questionnaire about their background, translation strategy and specific problems. The respondents were a broadly homogenous group as far as their level of Spanish and translation experience was concerned. Twelve were UK nationals, two were US nationals and one was Colombian.[11] Most had a first degree in Hispanic or Ibero-American Studies or a dual-honours Modern Languages degree, though other disciplines featuring included Philosophy and English. Few had actually studied Borges and few had been to Buenos Aires, where the story was set.

It should be emphasized that this case study was designed to test variation in attitude. The subjects were not yet fully fledged experienced professional translators.[12] The focus was not on translator competence or on error analysis, but rather on micro-analysing those elements of a text, particularly those expressions of attitude, that are most likely to remain stable and those that are most susceptible to change.

The 15 translated extracts from the respondents were submitted electronically but analysed manually. Even based on short extracts of around 300 words, this still gives a significant corpus of translation for close analysis.

5.2.1 Invariance

The 15 target versions were first analysed for lexical invariance in a similar way to the Yates/Hurley translations. Table 5.5 compares invariance in the two corpora (the two published TTs vs the 15 respondents' TTs). The left-hand column reproduces Yates' TT and underlines those items that appear differently in Hurley's later TT. The right-hand column shows items which are invariant across all 15 respondent TTs. The most obvious, and scarcely surprising, finding is that the amount of invariance (i.e. word-forms that remain stable throughout all translations) has dramatically shrunk in the student translations to 58 lexical items, from 208 in the Yates/Hurley corpus. To this might be added invariance in verb tenses where the semantic core alters, such as the use of a past tense in *Emma sat up/got up* or in *she rode through/travelled through* and the preservation of sentence breaks as a unit of translation by all respondents. Based on an average rounded total of 320 TT tokens, lexical invariance stands at about 18 per cent. Classification of the right-hand

TABLE 5.5 Invariance in published TTs vs respondents' TTs

Extract 1a Published TTs, based on Yates's translation (underlined sections show Yates/Hurley variance)	Invariance in the 15 respondents' TTs
When she was alone, Emma did not <u>immediately</u> open her eyes.	. . . did not . . . . . . open her eyes.
On the <u>little</u> night-table was the money <u>that</u> the man had left: Emma sat up and tore it to <u>pieces</u> as <u>before</u> she had torn the letter.	On . . . table . . . the money . . . the man had left . . . . . . she had . . . the letter.
Tearing up money is an impiety, like throwing away bread; Emma <u>repented</u> the <u>moment after</u> she did it.	. . . money . . . . . . bread . . .
<u>A</u>n act of pride and on that day. . . <u>Her fear was lost</u> in the <u>grief</u> of her body<u>, in</u> her <u>disgust</u>.	. . . day . . .
<u>Grief</u> and <u>nausea were</u> chain<u>ing her</u>, but <u>Emma</u> slowly got up and <u>proceeded</u> to dress <u>herself</u>.	. . . and . . . slowly . . . and . . .
<u>In</u> the room <u>there were</u> no <u>longer any</u> bright colour<u>s</u>; the last light of <u>dusk was weakening</u>.	. . . room . . . colour
Emma <u>was able</u> to <u>leave</u> without <u>anyone</u> see<u>ing her; at</u> the corner she <u>got on</u> a Lacroze <u>streetcar heading</u> west.	Emma . . . . . . the corner she . . .
She <u>selected, in keeping with</u> her plan, the seat <u>farthest towards the</u> front, so that her face would no<u>t be</u> seen.	she . . . plan . . . seat, so . . . her face
Perhaps <u>it</u> comforted her to <u>verify</u> in the <u>rapid movement along</u> the streets that what had happened had not <u>contaminated</u> thing<u>s</u>.	. . . street . . .
She rode through <u>the diminishing opaque suburbs</u>, seeing them and forgetting them <u>at the same</u> instant, and <u>alighted</u> at one of the <u>side streets of</u> Warnes.	She . . . through . . .
Paradoxically her <u>fatigue was</u> turn<u>ing out to be</u> a strength, <u>since</u> it <u>obliged</u> her to concentrate on the details of <u>the adventure</u> and <u>concealed</u> from her <u>the background</u> and <u>the objective</u>.	. . . her to . . . on the

(continued)

TABLE 5.5 Invariance in published TTs vs respondents' TTs *(continued)*

Extract 2a Yates's translation	*Invariance in the 15 respondents' TTs*
(Not out of fear but because of being an instrument of Justice she did not want to be punished.)	(a . . . of justice, . . . to be punished.)
Then, one single shot in the centre of his chest would seal Loewenthal's fate. But things did not happen that way.	. . . chest . . . . . . Loewenthal . . .

Extract 3a Yates's translation	*Invariance in the 15 respondents' TTs*
Actually the story was incredible, but it impressed everyone because substantially it was true.	. . . the story . . . . . . because . . . it was . . .
True was Emma Zunz' tone, true was her shame, true was her hate.	. . . Emma Zunz . . .
True also was the outrage she had suffered: only the circumstances were false, the time, and one or two proper names.	. . . the . . .

column in Table 5.5 leads to the following breakdown of invariant grammatical items across the respondent TTs:

- nouns 18 (*eyes, table, money* [2], *man, letter, bread, day, room*★, *colour*★, *corner, plan*★, *seat, face, street, story, justice, chest*)
- articles 9 (*the* [8], *a*)
- subject or object pronouns/names 8 (*she* [3], *Emma, Loewenthal, Emma Zunz, it, her*)
- prepositions 6 (*on, of, to* [2], *on, through*)
- verbal processes 4 (*open, left, punished, was*)
- auxiliaries 4 (*did, had* [2], *be*)
- connectors 4 (*and* [2], *so, because*)
- possessive pronouns 2 (*her* [2])
- negative particle 1 (*not*)
- adverb 1 (*slowly*).

Simple sum totals of this nature must obviously be treated with caution, since their relative significance will depend on the overall numbers of each category in the target texts. So, for example, the total number of nouns in the texts will be much higher than the number of adverbs. In addition, invariance in the semantic core may conceal other, notably grammatical, changes. The three asterisked (★) nouns in the first category hide slight variants – *room* was rendered as *bedroom* by one respondent, both *colour* and *colours* were used, *plan* appeared once in the verbal process *planned*, and *did not* in the first sentence was four times rendered as *didn't*.[13]

The most interesting observation is that, with the exception of *plan* and *justice*, all the nouns in the invariant list are concrete, common, unrelated to a process or to the expression of attitude. Also, they do not generally have obvious competitor synonyms in English in the contexts in which they appear in these extracts. If to these we add the invariant articles and possessive pronouns that accompany them and the pronouns/proper names that mark clause participants, we find a total of 36 of the 58 invariant forms occur in non-process noun phrases.

Invariant items related to actual processes are few: three material process verbs (*open, left, punished*) and one relational (*was*). There are also few related to modality and attitude: four auxiliaries and the one negative particle, *not*. There is just one adverb in this list, *slowly*, the translation of *lentamente* in the sentence *Emma lentamente se levantó*. Even there, *slowly* varies in its clause position in the respondents' translations. Finally, and most drastically, no adjectives, the most explicit features of attitude, appear.

An immediate, though inevitably tentative, hypothesis is that full lexical invariance may tend to be restricted to simple, basic, experiential or denotational processes, participants and relations (note the basic nature of the connectors *and, so, because*). At the same time, variation is to be *expected* in the lexical expression of attitude in translation. Although stability is greatest in basic core realizations, full invariance in any sample may be exploded by just one maverick translator's unique choice, so the wider picture is more nuanced, a cline of probability rather than total invariance. For example:

- *olvidar* is translated by a variant of the mental process *forget* 15 times (*forgetting* [13], *forgot* [1], *forgotten* [1])
- *temor* is translated as *fear* on 14 occasions (once as *anxiety*)
- *circunstancias* is translated as *circumstances* 14 times (once as *circumstantial factors*)
- *pormenores* is translated as *details* 14 times (the other is *peculiarities*)
- the modal *quizá* is translated as *perhaps* 13 times (2 are *maybe*)
- *paradoxically* is used 11 times for *paradójicamente* (the others are *strangely* [2], *ironically* [2]).

In all these cases, there seems to be a stable core of translational equivalence centred on a common dictionary equivalent. When there exist common near-synonyms, greater lexical variation is to be expected. Hence, the time adverb *luego* is translated more evenly, with the equivalents *later* (8 times), *then* (6) and *soon* (1).

5.2.2 Linguistic variation in attitude and appraisal

In Section 5.0 we saw that Babych and Hartley (2004) suggested that variation was linked to the salience of elements in a text. In the Yates/Hurley TTs, this seems to be borne out in that the sentence which produced the greatest variation in 'content' words is also one of the most emotive, a strong expression of affect:

> *El temor se perdió en la tristeza de su cuerpo, en el asco*
> ['The fear lost itself in the sadness of her body, in the disgust']
> Her <u>fear</u> was <u>lost</u> in the <u>grief</u> of her body, in <u>her</u> <u>disgust</u> (Yates)
> <u>Foreboding</u> <u>melted</u> in<u>to</u> the <u>sadness</u> of her body, in<u>to</u> <u>the</u> <u>revulsion</u> (Hurley).[14]

Here, Emma Zunz experiences a mixture of fear, sadness and physical disgust after having sex with the sailor and as she pursues the next, decisive stage of her plan. Yates emphasizes the behavioural and emotive *grief*, uses a passive calque *was lost* and the emotive *disgust*. Hurley opts for interpretation with the cognitive and emotive *foreboding* (rather than *fear*), the idiomatic, metaphoric process *melted into* and the emotive *revulsion*. Comparison with the respondent translations of this sentence makes it possible to see how far these terms are generally susceptible to lexical variation. The respondent translations were:

> Fear was lost in the sadness and disgust of her body.
> Fear was lost in the sadness of her body, in the repugnance that she felt.
> Her fear was lost in the sorrow of her body, in the disgust.
> Her fear was lost in disgust and the physical effects of her sorrow.
> Her fear was lost in her body's sadness, in its disgust.
> Fear was lost in the sadness of her body, in the disgust.
> Fear got lost in the sorrow of her body, in the revulsion.
> Fear lost itself in the sorrow of her body, in the repulsion.
> Fear lost itself in the sadness present in her body, in disgust.
> The fear disappeared into the sadness of her body, into the disgust.
> Her fear disappeared with the sadness and disgust she felt.
> Her fear disappeared into the sadness of her body.
> Fear gave way to a sadness in her entire body.
> Fear was overcome by the sadness of her body, by disgust.
> Her anxiety dissolved into a sad ache.

If we concentrate on the translation of the central content words[15] (the affect words *temor*, *tristeza* and *asco* and the process *se perdió*), we can see that Yates' *grief* and Hurley's *foreboding* and *melted into* are not repeated. These unique items may have something to tell us about the specific translator's idiosyncrasies and conscious interpretive or unconscious idiolectal choices. Likewise, amongst the respondents' translations there is uniqueness in the selections of *gave way*, *was overcome by*, *anxiety*, *dissolved* and *sad ache*. The last three appear in one and the same TT, the last in the list. Such a concentration of unique items is unusual in the sample and marks this TT extract for its lexical creativity (cf. Kenny 2001, Munday 2009b).

Consideration of all the TT sentences above shows a predominant selection of *fear* (for *temor*), *sadness* for *tristeza*, *disgust* for *asco* and some formulation of *lost* (*was lost/got lost/lost itself*) for *se perdió*. These are relatively stable elements. Three of these equivalents appear in the Yates TT but only one in the Hurley TT. Such findings may serve to reinforce hypotheses for further testing – for example, that Yates tends to prefer core lexical and attitudinal equivalents, whereas Hurley's lexis is more idiosyncratic and interpretive, often shunning cognates and common equivalents (see Section 5.1.1 above).

Examination of the similarly emotive following clause shows that such variation patterns tend to repeat themselves:

> *El asco y la tristeza la encadenaban*
> ['The disgust and the sadness her were chaining']
> <u>Grief</u> and <u>nausea</u> <u>were</u> chaini<u>ng</u> <u>her</u> (Yates)
> <u>Sadness</u> and <u>revulsion</u> <u>lay upon</u> <u>Emma</u> <u>like</u> chain<u>s</u> (Hurley)
>
> Disgust and sadness were chained to her
> Disgust and sadness enchained her
> Disgust and sorrow had Emma in chains
> The disgust and sadness paralysed her
> Disgust and sadness were paralysing her
> They seemed to paralyse her
> Repulsion and sorrow were paralysing her
> Revulsion and sorrow paralysed her
> She was paralysed by a feeling of disgust and sorrow
> Sadness and disgust gripped her
> Sadness and disgust enveloped her
> Feelings of disgust and sadness were haunting her
> Repulsion and sorrow consumed her
> She was bound by repugnance and sadness
> Though weighed down by this sadness and loathing.

As might be expected, Hurley and 13 of the respondents (but strangely not Yates) repeat the same abstract nouns of affect that were used in the previous sentence (*sadness, disgust*, etc.). The only common element to all the TTs is the connector *and* between these two nouns. This again supports the preliminary findings of Babych and Hartley (2004) of individual consistency in the translation of salient items even if there is variation between translators. The treatment of the forceful emotive metaphor *encadenaban* ('were chaining'), retained by both Yates and Hurley, is the most interesting. Of the respondents, only three used a variant of the same metaphor (*chained, enchained, had ... in chains*), one used the related metaphor *bound by*, six opted for a metaphor with *paralyse* and five produced a totally new metaphor: *gripped, enveloped, consumed, were haunting* and *weighed down by*. On all occasions, therefore, attitude is conveyed by a physical metaphor, even if the linguistic and conceptual realizations vary. This ties in with the general finding of Chapter 2, Section 2.2.4, where there was a tendency to reduce the intensity of such provoked attitude but where the translations centred around a semantic core of the metaphoric element.

5.2.3 Attitude-rich words

One possibility that I should like to propose is that there are what I shall term 'attitude-rich' words which carry the attitudinal burden of the text through their function in describing the central axiological values of the protagonists, narrator or writer. These are important critical points. The list below contains the most obvious instances of such terms in the three extracts in question, classified according to their realization of attitude or graduation. They are supplied with their TT equivalents in the Yates, Hurley and respondents' versions:

Affect

- **se arrepintió**: *repented* (Yates), *wished she hadn't* (Hurley); *regretted* (13), *repented* (1), *felt guilty* (1)
- **el temor**: *fear* (Yates), *foreboding* (Hurley); *fear* (14), *anxiety* (1)
- **la tristeza**: *grief* (Yates), *sadness* (Hurley); *sadness* (10), *sorrow* (5), *sad ache* (1)
- **el asco**: *disgust, nausea* (Yates), *revulsion* (Hurley); *disgust* (10), *revulsion* (2), *repulsion* (1), *repugnance* (1), *loathing* (1)
- **la aventura**: *adventure* (Yates), *mission* (Hurley); *adventure* (13), *scheme* (1), *venture* (1)

Judgement/ethics

- **una impiedad**: *an impiety* (Yates), *an act of impiety* (Hurley); *a sin* (6), *an ungodly act* (3), *an act of ungodliness* (1), *ungodliness* (1), *an impiety* (1), *impious* (1), *a merciless act* (1), *a pitiless task* (1)
- **increíble**: *incredible* (Yates), *unbelievable* (Hurley); *unbelievable* (6), *incredible* (6), *astounding nature* (1), *far-fetched* (1), *implausible* (1)
- **cierta**: *true* (Yates, Hurley); *true* (12), *real* (1), *the truth* (1), *what happened* (1)
- **el pavor**: *shame* (Yates, Hurley); *shame* (9), *fear* (2), *modesty* (2), *sense of shame* (1), *chaste nature* (1)
- **el ultraje**: *outrage* (Yates, Hurley); *outrage* (9), *insult* (3), *atrocity* (2), *wrong* (1)

Appreciation

- **contaminado**: *contaminated* (Yates), *polluted* (Hurley); *contaminated* (6), *affected* (4), *tainted* (2), *influenced* (1), *ruin* (1), *spoilt* (1)
- **[barrios] decrecientes y opacos**: *diminishing, opaque* (Yates), *shrinking, gloomy* (Hurley); *dwindling* (4), *diminishing* (3), *declining* (2), *deprived* (1), *ever-decreasing* (1), *fading* (1), *increasingly distant* (1), *run-down* (1), *waned* (1); *dull* (5), *gloomy* (5), *opaque* (2), *dark* (1), *lifeless* (1), Ø (1)
- **insípido trajín**: *rapid movement* (Yates), *banal bustle* (Hurley); *insipid* (6), *dull* (2), *banal* (1), *mundane* (1), *monotonous* (1), *simmering* (1), *trite* (1), *tedious* (1), ø (1); *bustle* (3), *hustle and bustle* (3), *comings and goings* (3), *to-ing and fro-ing* (1), *goings on* (1), *commotion* (1), *little ride* (1), *rush* (1), ø (1)

Graduation (counter-expectation and intensification)

- **paradójicamente**: *paradoxically* (Yates, Hurley); *paradoxically* (11), *ironically* (2), *strangely* (2)
- **sustancialmente** *[cierto]*: *substantially* (Yates), *in substance* (Hurley); *essentially* (5), *fundamentally* (4), *in essence* (3), *almost* (1), *on the whole* (1), *substantially* (1).

Examination of the variation in the TT equivalents shows that in some cases (e.g. *temor, tristeza, asco, se arrepintió, paradójicamente, aventura, cierta, pavor, ultraje*) there is a relative consensus in the TTs (*fear, sadness, disgust, regretted, paradoxically, adventure, true, shame, outrage*). Possible reasons may again be that these are the most common dictionary equivalents and that there are no obviously strong alternative candidates. In the translation equivalents for the other items, there is considerably more variation. Lexical calques or literal translations might account for *impiety, insipid, contaminated, incredible, opaque*, and *substantially*, but none of these scores higher than 6 out of 15. There is in fact a striking variety of translations proposed for *impiedad, insípido, trajín* and *decrecientes*: eight variations of each, plus one more from Yates or Hurley. Why should this be so? Partly, no doubt, because they have no obviously satisfactory literal translation or calque in English.[16] But this cannot tell the whole story. These are evaluative words of judgement (*impiedad*) and, especially, of appreciation ('*insípido* trajín' and 'barrios *decrecientes*'). The latter perhaps constitute cases of Borges' 'displacement of adjectives' (see Hurley, Section 5.1), creative collocations, non-standard lexical primings, where the translator is forced to interpret the referent and the form of appraisal without being able to rely on a stock of ready-made translation equivalents (cf. Toury 1995: 97–8, Babych and Hartley 2004: 833). At such points where translator interpretation has to operate, there seems to be potential for variation in graduation, particularly of force. Thus, the translations of the epithet **insípido** *trajín*, an instance of negative appreciation, range from the weak **rapid** *movement* (Yates)[17] to the strong *trite* and *simmering*; barrios [neighbourhoods] **decrecientes** is rendered most frequently as the core *dwindling* or *diminishing*, most strongly as *deprived, run-down* and most weakly, perhaps, as the amplification *increasingly distant*. These mark a difference of attitudinal interpretation between neutral descriptions (e.g. *diminishing*) and strong negative appreciation bordering on judgement (*deprived, run-down*). The creativity of the ST collocation requires interpretation, a critical point where translators reveal their footnotes underlying evaluation of Borges' narration.

The greatest variation in a single word involves the category of engagement (see Chapter 1, Section 1.3.3). It is the translation of the verb *verificar* in the sentence:

> *Quizá le confortó* **verificar,** *en el insípido trajín de las calles, que lo acaecido no había contaminado las cosas*
>
> ['Perhaps it comforted her to **verify**, in the insipid bustle of the streets, that the events had not contaminated things']

A realization of the ideational not interpersonal metafunction (see Chapter 1, Section 1.2), *verificar* may be a mental process of perception (Hurley's *see*) or a near-mental behavioural process of actively looking (Yates' *verify*). The ambiguous function of this verb (or, to put it another way, its potential to fulfil either or both roles) requires interpretation from the translator and this may account for the astonishing number of 11 variants in the 15 respondent TTs: these are split between the less forceful mental processes of knowing (*be sure that* [2], *know*, *realized*, *realization*) and seeing (*note*, *see*) and the more forceful behavioural *verify* (2), *make sure that* (2), *check*, *confirm*, *confirmation*. Importantly, the choice between these process types inscribes attitude and is indicative of the translator's interpretation of the narrator's and character's own judgement. *See*, for example, would place Emma Zunz in a passive role, while *verify, check*, etc. would show that she was more actively engaged in the plot. This in some ways resembles the function of reporting verbs (e.g. *claim, assert, reject* – see the Introduction), which transmit the truth-assertion of the commentator and either contract or expand the dialogic voices of the text.

But the amount of lexical variation involved does not always directly indicate a critical point. This is illustrated by the abstract noun *aventura*. In the list above it is included as an element of affect, overwhelmingly translated by its calque, *adventure*. The definition of *adventure* justifies its inclusion in affect:

> If someone has an adventure, they become involved in an unusual, exciting and rather dangerous journey or series of events.
>
> *(Cobuild 1995: 26)*

Clearly three translators are uneasy with this potential equivalent, since it is used to describe Emma Zunz's journey to exact revenge: unusual and dangerous certainly, but hardly exciting. In its place, Hurley uses *mission* and two respondents use *scheme* and *venture*. These equivalents produce a shift of attitudinal category to judgement, particularly in Hurley's translation. *Mission* is 'an important task that people are given to do . . . a special journey . . . a strong commitment and sense of duty to do or achieve something' (Cobuild 1995: 1062). The shift from *adventure* to *mission*, from affect to judgement, results in a major renegotiation of the depiction of the whole cycle of revenge. It is without doubt a critical point in those three TTs.

5.2.4 Genre differences

The experiment was repeated in 2011 with three similar respondents who were also asked to identify and discuss the six points in a text where they encountered most difficulty and doubts. Their comments represented a kind of retrospective protocol analysis of their decisions. In addition, they also volunteered to take a translation task based on a technical text in order to begin to see how much variation related to text-type.

In the Borges text, many of the features noted above were reinforced in the TTs. Thus, *aventura* was variously interpreted as *undertaking, mission, venture* and the large amount of variation in *barrios decrecientes y opacos* persisted:

dull, run-down neighbourhoods
diminishing and lifeless neighbourhoods
fading, dull neighbourhoods

The stability of *neighbourhoods* remained, while the variation in attitudinal interpretations of the epithets meant that only *dull* was repeated. The differing attitudes are most strongly exemplified in the use of the very negative *run-down* and *lifeless* compared to *dull* and *fading*. That this is a definite problematic or critical point is shown by its selection as such by one of the three respondents. But the reason given is the collocation with *neighbourhood* rather than the interpretation of the adjective itself:

'Decreciente' can be translated as 'decreasing', 'fading' or 'waning', but I didn't feel that [these] could be used to translate a neighbourhood, so I settled on 'fading' as I thought it was perhaps the idea that as she travels through them, the neighbourhoods fade away.

By comparison, the translation of the word *ultraje* in Extract 3 was seen by one respondent to be very much a question of strength of emotion; in appraisal terms, affect:

I really struggled with this word; I wanted to convey the same emotion in the English but couldn't seem to find the right word. I considered *insult* to be perhaps more appropriate but not strong enough here.

The respondent chose *outrage* as a stronger alternative. Intensification therefore was an explicit criterion for selection. But at the same time one must not discount the value of calque (*ultraje > outrage*). Indeed, for four other key doubts the same respondent said she opted for what was literal translation or calquing of the ST lexis, both to allow the reader closer insight into the original and to reduce the possibility of misinterpretation. Thus, for Extract 2 she commented:

I struggled to get into the Borges mentality and really engage with the words; that is to say really understand what he was trying to convey here, so I just stuck to the Spanish quite closely.

At critical points literal translation may be a risk-reduction strategy.

The Field of the technical translation text was specifications for overhauling railway stock. Here, in the absence of obvious emotive or other attitudinal vocabulary, the doubts raised by the respondents mainly related to technical terminology and comprehension of the ST concept: for example, did *cajas* mean *vehicle bodies* or *casing, housing* or even *railway vehicles*? Was *soportes* to be translated as *brackets* or *supports*? This bears out the findings from the examination of online forums in Chapter 3 where professional technical translators tended to be most concerned about terminology.

When it comes to lexical variation, a brief comparison of variation in the translations of the opening two paragraphs is illuminating:

ST
El objeto de esta especificación técnica es el de fijar las condiciones de cálculo a aplicar en las cajas y soportes a instalar en las UTE-Si Rehabilitadas.
Esta especificación se basa en la Especificación de Compra: 05.U0.99.12.005, a la que anula y sustituye desde el punto de vista de condiciones de cálculo, ya que la amplía y puede ser aplicada a otros equipos que no comprende la anterior Especificación.[18]

TT1 (variation is shown by underlining)
The aim of this technical specification is to establish the terms of calculation to apply to the vehicle bodies and supports to be installed in the refurbished UTE-Sis.

This specification is based on the purchasing specification 05.U0.99.12.005, which is nullified and replaced, from the point of view of the terms of calculation, by this specification, since it is broader and can be applied to other equipment not covered by the previous specification.

TT2 (variation is shown by underlining)
The purpose of this technical specification is to set the test conditions to be applied on vehicle bodies and brackets to be installed on the Rehabilitated UTE-Si.

This specification is based on the Purchase Specification: 05.U0.99.12.005, which cancels and replaces, from the point of view of test conditions, as it extends the previous specification and may be applied to other equipment that the previous specification does not include.

TT3 (variation is shown by underlining)
The purpose of this technical specification is to state the conditions by which calculations are made that must be applied both to vehicle bodies and to the supports that are to be installed in restored UTE-Si locomotives.

This specification is based on Purchase Specification 05.UO.99.12.005, a Specification that the former overrides and replaces in terms of conditions by which calculations are made, given that it expands upon the previous Specification insofar as it can be applied to a wider range of equipment.

Underlining highlights lexical variation, while non-underlined words remain constant across the three translations. It is clear again that there is important variation

TABLE 5.6 Analysis of technical TTs on paradigmatic axis

TT1	The	aim	of this	technical specification	is	to	establish	the
TT2		purpose					set	
TT3		purpose					state	

TT1	terms of calculation	to		Ø	apply	Ø	to	the	vehicle bodies
TT2	test conditions			be	applied	Ø	on	Ø	
TT3	conditions by which calculations are made	that must	be	applied	both	to	Ø		

TT1	and	Ø	Ø	supports
TT2		Ø	Ø	brackets
TT3		to	the	supports

on the paradigmatic axis, as can be seen in the first sentence in Table 5.6 (compare Table 5.4 above for the Borges text).

Here, the structure of the sentence remains broadly the same – the variation centres on synonyms of the abstract noun *aim/purpose* and of the verb *establish/set/state*. More important is the variation of the technical terms *supports/brackets* and, particularly, of *terms of calculation/test conditions/conditions by which calculations are made*. The latter really brings home the argument of Babych and Hartley (2004, above) that salient words in a TT will tend to be intratextually consistent but liable to variation between translators. Hence, each translator goes on to repeat the same equivalent in the second sentence.

The two technical terms are critical points in such a text and are specifically identified by the translators of TT1 and TT2. That they may be related to translator experience and competence is suggested by the fact that none of the three translators found the most common and accepted terminological equivalent for *condiciones de cálculo*, which happens to be the calque *calculation conditions*. The propensity for calque as a risk-averse strategy is therefore seen to be dependent upon the translator's confidence in the acceptability of the proposed term. When it is a question of technical terms that lie outside the expertise of the translator, calques may give way to more general equivalents such as those offered in the three TTs – including the explicitation *conditions by which calculations are made*.

Analysis of the second sentence in the TTs above shows that, in addition to synonym differences at specific junctures (e.g. *nullifies*, *cancels* and *overrides* as equivalents for ST *anula*) there are also several syntactic modifications. These include the order of elements and the choice of passive or active constructions – for example, the end of the sentence which reads *not covered by the previous specification* or *that the previous specification does not include* or, with a reversal of point of view, *it can be applied to a wider range of equipment*. It is interesting to posit that translators may be willing to engage in such syntactic changes more frequently in a technical than a literary text. Clearly, though, this must remain a very tentative suggestion at this stage.

5.3 Conclusion

This chapter has explored variation in the translation of attitude, particularly of affect. Even though it restricted itself to short extracts, totalling under 300 words, the sample of two published TTs plus 18 respondent TTs (comprising the 15 of the original experiment and the three from 2011) generated a vast amount of data for micro-analysis. Based on the findings, one important initial conclusion is that there is little obvious variation in the frequency and category of attitude, but variation in its lexical realization is extremely common. In the Yates and Hurley TTs, variation lies in the linguistic realization of attitude (more interference in Yates), though there is some intensification of emotional affect (such as *grief, mission*) and interpretation. Although the technical TTs displayed greater syntactic shifting, variation most often seems to occur on the paradigmatic axis of language. That is, the critical choice seems to be mostly at the level of the individual word. In the respondent translations of the Borges text, full lexical invariance amounts to around 18 per cent of the text and is centred on simple, concrete nouns (*table, money, bread* . . .) and process participants (*she, Emma, Loewenthal* . . .). In the remaining 82 per cent of the text, where subjective attitude is most likely to be located, lexical equivalence is more or less unstable. While the obvious deduction is that variation is a norm and that it most often occurs where their attitudinal values are projected, even a sample of 18 respondents is limited in its coverage. Reliable comparators from other studies would also be needed in order to draw more solid conclusions.

APPENDIX 5.1

'Emma Zunz' extracts translated by Yates and Hurley

Extract 1a Yates's translation (variations underlined)	Extract 1b Hurley's translation (variations underlined)
When she was alone, Emma did not immediately open her eyes.	When she was alone, Emma did not open her eyes immediately.
On the little night-table was the money that the man had left: Emma sat up and tore it to pieces as before she had torn the letter.	On the night table was the money the man had left: Emma sat up and tore it to shreds, as she had torn up the letter a short time before.
Tearing up money is an impiety, like throwing away bread; Emma repented the moment after she did it.	Tearing up money is an act of impiety, like throwing away bread; the minute she did it, Emma wished she hadn't –
An act of pride and on that day. . . Her fear was lost in the grief of her body, in her disgust.	an act of pride, and on that day. . . . Foreboding melted into the sadness of her body, into the revulsion.
Grief and nausea were chaining her, but Emma slowly got up and proceeded to dress herself.	Sadness and revulsion lay upon Emma like chains, but slowly she got up and began to dress.
In the room there were no longer any bright colours; the last light of dusk was weakening.	The room had no bright colour; the last light of evening made it all the drearier.
Emma was able to leave without anyone seeing her; at the corner she got on a Lacroze streetcar heading west.	She managed to slip out without being seen. On the corner she mounted a westbound Lacroze[19]
She selected, in keeping with her plan, the seat farthest towards the front, so that her face would not be seen.	and following her plan she sat in the car's frontmost seat, so that no one would see her face.
Perhaps it comforted her to verify in the rapid movement along the streets that what had happened had not contaminated things.	Perhaps she was comforted to see, in the banal bustle of the streets, that what had happened had not polluted everything.
She rode through the diminishing opaque suburbs, seeing them and forgetting them at the same instant, and alighted at one of the side streets of Warnes.	She rode through gloomy, shrinking neighbourhoods, seeing them and forgetting them instantly, and got off at one of the stops on Warnes.[20]
Paradoxically her fatigue was turning out to be a strength, since it obliged her to concentrate on the details of the adventure and concealed from her the background and the objective.	Paradoxically, her weariness turned into a strength, for it forced her to concentrate on the details of her mission and masked from her its true nature and its final purpose.

Extract 2a Yates's translation (variations underlined)	**Extract 2 Hurley's translation (variations underlined)**
(Not out of fear but because <u>of</u> being an instrument of Justice she <u>did</u> not <u>want</u> to be punished.)	(<u>It was</u> not out of fear, but because <u>she was</u> an instrument of <u>that</u> justice, <u>that</u> she <u>herself intended</u> not to be punished.)
Then, <u>one</u> single <u>shot</u> in the centre of his chest would <u>seal</u> Loewenthal's <u>fate</u>. But things did n<u>ot</u> happen that way.	Then, <u>a</u> single bullet in the center of his chest would <u>put an end</u> to Loewenthal's <u>life</u>. But things didn<u>'</u>t happen that way.

Extract 3a Yates's translation (variations underlined)	**Extract 3b Hurley's translation (variations underlined)**
<u>Actual</u>ly the story <u>*was*</u> in<u>credible</u>, <u>but</u> it <u>impres</u>sed everyone because substan<u>tially</u> it was true.	The story was un<u>believable, yes – and yet</u> it <u>convinc</u>ed everyone, because <u>in</u> substan<u>ce</u> it was true.
<u>True</u> was Emma Zunz' tone, <u>true</u> was her shame, <u>true</u> was her hat<u>e</u>.	Emma Zunz<u>'s</u> tone <u>of voice</u> was <u>real</u>, her shame was <u>real</u>, her hat<u>red</u> was <u>real</u>.
<u>True</u> <u>also</u> was the outrage <u>she</u> had <u>suffered</u>: <u>only</u> the circumstances <u>were</u> false, the time, and one or two proper names.	The outrage <u>that</u> <u>had been done</u> <u>to her</u> was <u>real, as well</u>; <u>all that was </u>false were the circumstances, the time, and one or two proper names.

6

EVALUATION IN TRANSLATION – SOME CONCLUDING THOUGHTS

From the very beginning of this book I have emphasized my belief, following Volosinov (1973 [1929]), that evaluation is present behind every utterance. The choices made by the writer/speaker/translator/interpreter are potentially significant and indicative of both an ideological and axiological position. First, words do not exist in isolation; they have an 'intertextual freight' (Volosinov 1973 [1929]: 80, Bakhtin 1981: 283) from previous utterances that imbue them with a meaning greater than their denotative sense. Second, the choices are made from a range of competing equivalents. Preferred equivalents realize the 'meaning potential' which unfolds through the text (Halliday 1978; see Chapter 1, Section 1.2). At the same time, the candidate equivalents that are rejected reveal the 'penumbra of unselected information' (Grant 2007: 134; see Chapter 1, Section 1.1). The comparative analysis of selected and unselected information tells us much about the concept of equivalence in translation and the decision-making processes that underlie the choices. Translation is a constant evaluative process: it encompasses the checking of possible TT equivalents against the ST and against each other in a process of refinement that leads to the selection of a single equivalent.[1] Each draft of the TT constitutes a slightly different version, which reveals information that was deselected and replaced by an alternative. Where multiple TTs exist, it is a given that each will generate many different TT equivalents, indicative of some axiological choice on the part of the translator. Analysis of these different scenarios, supported by interviews with translators and studies of their discussions, has been the basis of this research.

6.1 The results of the case studies

The results of the various translation scenarios, notably the interviews and forums of technical translators in Chapter 3, show that the translators are mostly concerned with understanding and selecting the 'correct' equivalent for technical terms. This requires the input of subject-specific knowledge from an expert or, failing that, from a substitute virtual authority such as online parallel texts or corpora, which in their crudest form comprise a search using Google™ or other search engine to gauge frequency of occurrence. The focus is on informational knowledge to cover gaps in the translator's knowledge or the lack of semantic correspondence between languages. Where it is impossible to gain expert input or where the ambiguity of the ST cannot be resolved, the translator may select the most neutral TT rendering in order to control risk (see below). Sometimes these ideational meanings carry attitudinal values. The naming of politically and religiously sensitive concepts discussed in the Introduction was an extreme example. In literary texts, the treatment of regional dialects and of the names of flora and fauna unknown to the TT reader are a type of engagement that force the translator to position the reader in relation to the ST.

From the examples we have studied, overt distortion of values is not a common occurrence in translation. Even the examples of insults in the European Parliament discussed in the Introduction were retained in the simultaneous interpreting, with slight adjustment of intensity. Indeed, any overt distortion or manipulation would be highly marked and would be associated with recontextualization (Fairclough 2003, Bielsa and Bassnett 2008) or some higher-level censorship of values that are deemed to be inappropriate or threatening to the target culture. This occurred in the Chinese, Burmese and other TTs of Obama's inaugural – references to Communism and to a non-democratic or corrupt regime were deleted. In Chapter 4, other paratextual interventions come from the addition of prefaces, explanatory notes, etc., which guide the reading and may impose a tactical or even resistant reading on a text (as in the Tacitus revisions). This level of intervention is critical for the reception of the text.

The findings of lexical analysis of attitude in the empirical case studies show that critical points do seem to depend somewhat on word class. Concrete nouns are less likely to carry attitude and are often relatively stable in translation. Solid words such as *table, man, money, bread* did not vary in the multiple translations in Chapter 5. Those abstract terms with an obvious dictionary equivalent (e.g. *temor > fear*) were also relatively stable. The little variation (*foreboding* instead of *fear*) was often associated with the more experienced translator (Hurley), who tended to work from an overall strategy of rejection of Latinate forms. In the interpreting of the Obama speech in Chapter 2, there was little variation in abstract nouns that had an obvious TL equivalent. All the more so when the obvious 'dictionary' equivalent was structurally similar, so a noun and concept such as *responsibility* was consistently translated as the Spanish *responsabilidad*. To sum up, the lexical realization of attitudinal nouns seems to centre around a core translation, often a dictionary equivalent or calque translation, with an interpretive periphery of marked alternatives.

Elements that were sometimes omitted, especially in interpreting, were the evaluative epithets in noun–epithet combinations (e.g. **swift** action, **far-reaching** network) and adverbs or modal particles that act as modifiers (e.g. **badly** weakened).

In Chapter 3 this was supported by comments from one experienced translator and reviser that she often had to alert less experienced colleagues to the importance of German modal particles for the transmission of attitude. So it seems possible that, in the translator and interpreter's subconscious, there may exist an informal hierarchy of word classes: concrete nouns, abstract nouns and then evaluative epithets. The construction of chunks of the TT is again focused on what the translator or interpreter perceives to be core elements of communication in a given context. There was considerable stability in syntax, too, with most variation occurring on the paradigmatic axis, choices being made between competing lexical equivalents at specific points in a sentence. The full stop is a critical point, not for variation but for the analysis and structuring of the text, as indicated explicitly by one of the technical translators in Chapter 3.

Rather than huge instances of distortion, the case studies have highlighted more subtle variation that may be characteristic of rewriting and recontextualization. The close analysis of the Obama speech found little shift in the categorization of inscribed attitude, but much more interesting was the translation of indirect invoked attitude. Examples included culture-specific historical references such as the battles of Concord, Gettysburg, Normandy and Khe Sanh, key moments in the history of the United States that index the courage and spirit and values of the people. Context-dependent concepts such as *old* and *patchwork heritage* are similarly evocative, saturated with value within their culture. For such terms I have proposed the category of 'invoked-associative' attitude. They harbour a wealth of associations that may require explicitation in translation if the translator considers that they are not triggered in the TT audience and are essential for the successful function of the TT chunk. A related group are what I have termed 'attitudinally rich epithets', words such as *decrecientes* and *opacos* in the Borges text in Chapter 5. These showed huge variation in the respondent TTs and attracted a wide range of interpretation from neutral descriptive appreciation (*shrinking*) to strongly negative appreciation that verges on judgement (*deprived, run-down*).

Crucially, sources of graduation are subject to considerable shifting. Non-core words, especially verbs (e.g. *wield, harness*), part of provoked attitude, sometimes lost their intensity in translation. More explicit markers of force and focus, such as adverbs and modal particles, were omitted far more frequently than expected. In the Obama speech TTs, intensification was lessened in around 35 per cent of cases and not increased in any. Also interesting is the possibility that graduation may be related to mode and stage of translation. Thus, reduction of graduation in interpreting could be explained by time and processing constraints that force concentration on ideational content. Examination of draft translations and online forum comments suggest that the same may occur in the initial stages of written translation but that graduation is increased at the revision stage, associated in literary translation certainly with an overriding concern for stylistic adjustment to produce a more natural TT. An illustration in Chapter 3, Section 3.2 is the initial overlooking of the intensifying adverb *barely*, a key counter-expectancy indicator of attitude and intensification. The same happens in Bellos' translation of Perec (Chapter 4,

Section 4.3), where the later self-revision shows a trend to increased intensification. Examples in other texts, such as the German *anspruchsvoll* (Chapter 3, Section 3.1), are often modified in TTs to increase graduation and thereby remove ambiguity.

6.2 Reading positions

Martin and White (2005: 206; see Chapter 1, Section 1.6) describe three possible reader responses to a text: compliant, resistant and tactical. What is the most likely reading by a translator? Compliant, by reproducing the ideology of the source (and its writer–reader relationship); resistant, by opposing it; or, perhaps the most likely, tactical, by consciously or unconsciously both reproducing and reworking, with an unavoidable repositioning of the audience in relation to the writer/speaker? Competent translators operate on a more strategic level, as attested by the correspondence of the literary translators in Chapter 4. Yet, despite their attempts to ensure coherence, a shifting reading position is almost inevitable because of the translator's position at the 'interstices' of intersubjective communication (Bakhtin 1981, Grant 2007), where meaning is negotiated at both the lexicogrammatical and higher levels. Translators, like writers, are constantly tinkering with wordings, attempting to edge ever closer to an optimal solution under the constraints of time and linguistic differences and competing stylistic and strategic priorities. The interplay of various factors is so complex that it is impossible to identify a single basis for attitudinal expressions. Nevertheless, I would suggest that these translator-reading positions may be adopted with reference to the overall evaluative prosody of the text – thus, the context-dependent evaluative examples of *old* and *patchwork heritage* from the Obama speech depended on the positive resonance of the surrounding text for their attitudinal value. In order to reproduce such prosody the translator sometimes feels obliged to explicate the value (e.g. 'multi-ethnic heritage') in the interests of the target audience. But this move from invokedness to inscription makes the attitude more explicit, which then controls engagement and reduces the openness of response and the heteroglossia of a text.

In some instances the translator may not believe in the ideas and values expressed in the ST and may not share the values of the TT readers.[2] In his description of the 'stance triangle', focused on dialogic face-to-face communication, Du Bois (2007: 173) makes the crucial point that evaluation includes responsibility for and ownership of that act as well as an assertion of a system of value. 'Responsibility for the stance act is serious business, with potentially profound consequences' because it gives a value to the object in a socio-cultural system and 'reshapes' that value system by the evaluative act. The ethical responsibility is weightiest in political, religious and other sensitive texts that can directly lead to decisions affecting the lives of others, such as the Iraq war dossier analysed in the Introduction. When translators or interpreters are involved, they also have an ethical responsibility, both in their interpretation of the evaluation of the source act and in any additional attitudinal value they might introduce into the TT.

The translator always reports or represents the evaluation of the ST author or speaker, although, for the average TT reader, the translator's words are the unmediated words and values of the ST. In theoretical terms, the translator or interpreter 'avers' (cf. Sinclair 1986, Hunston 2000: 178). That is, the translator's words speak directly for the ST author, which also involves the translator in performing the speech act. The more high-stake and controversial the speech act, the more risk is entailed for the translator, at least at certain points in the text (Pym 2010). But in his/her own mind the translator must also 'attribute' the words to the author in a kind of pseudo-reported speech. So, as the translator writes or interpreter speaks, he/she is obliged to reproduce the ideas of the ST author as their own, but in that very act there is a conscious knowing that the words are someone else's, that the ideas conveyed in the TL are second-hand. For translation, this attribution remains within the mind of the translator; for interpreting, the audience is aware of the acoustic and visual presence of the ST speaker.

The interpreter's use of the first person pronoun is explicit averral in what we call 'translator voice' (p. 77), a mimicking of what Martin and White (2005) call 'writer voice' (see Chapter 1, Section 1.5).[3] Those situations in which the bilateral interpreter uses the third person to refer to the speaker (*she said that . . .*) show attribution and would correspond to Martin and White's reporter/commentator voice. The Peruvian Canal N interpreter of the Obama inaugural speech was unusual in switching between reporter and translator voice in simultaneous interpreting as an emergency strategy in order to achieve some kind of coherence when her interpreting abilities came under stress. However, such a strategy would not be permissible in a more formal conference. As Macken-Horarik says (2003a: 295), only certain voices are approved in a given setting. In simultaneous interpreting the expectation is for the interpreter to adopt the translator voice. In most written translation, that translator voice is constrained by the ST and by the ethical (and contractual) obligation to render 'accurately'. This may explain the reactions of different translators when they encounter critical points. Conscious of their obligations, and of the power of the ST, most translators prefer to reduce evaluation to 'hedge their bets' and opt for a standardized translation 'that can't be wrong'. Exceptions are some in-house translators, who are able to discuss the options with their bosses and who are thus willing to be more creative, and literary translators, who are free from the oversight of the ST author because he/she is dead. In Chapter 4, the Tacitus case study showed how a classical text can become a battleground for the construal of race and for the political merits of competing translations.

6.3 For the future

These findings tell us much about the usefulness of appraisal theory for the analysis of translation. As in other systemic functional linguistic studies, the detailed taxonomy of lexicogrammatical realizations is certainly helpful in understanding how a text construes value. However, it seems that major shifts in key attitudinal markers are not likely to occur except perhaps in certain genres, such as appellative texts, where the TL conventions are strongest. This was not seen in the texts we studied, but was apparent in the analysis of the translation of advertisements into Chinese in Zhang and Qian (2009; see Chapter 1, Section 1.3.2).

The textual analysis of the Obama inaugural showed the potential for appraisal theory to help in the analysis of shifts in translation and at the same time it began to uncover how translation might alert appraisal theory to new evaluative points where meaning is negotiated. These include word class, invoked-associative attitude, graduation shifts and translator voice discussed above. This can now be replicated on other speeches and would benefit from being extended to include other languages, particularly those in which the realization of the interpersonal meaning is very different (e.g. the pronoun conventions of some Asian languages) or between cultures where different value systems operate. Repeating the analysis for other modes, such as bilateral interpreting where greater onus is on the interpreter to select and organize the TT material, may well also be fruitful.

Analysis of translator drafts and correspondence and online forums has also been very promising in examining what Angelone (2010: 18) calls 'a problem nexus . . . an observable interruption in the natural flow of translation' related to 'uncertainty . . . a cognitive state of indecision'. It gives us access to some real-time translation decisions, traced through the process of revision or through conscious verbalization. It will now be interesting to pursue this research with other experimental methods, such as think-aloud protocols. The study of variation in multiple translations (Chapter 5) is well worth continuing. An immediate line of inquiry is what effect the commissioning of more translations will have and whether it will be possible to identify a core of invariance. Of more interest will be to chart invariance and to test out those critical points that have already been identified. More strictly controlled and triangulated experimental techniques should be able to investigate the effects of translator experience, competence, disposition, etc. on their selections. Text genre is another important factor to test out more thoroughly, as is the possibility that certain configurations of evaluative devices may characterize translated language. Finally, this book has focused on the translator's value system and subjectivity. It will be important to balance this with an investigation of reader response. How far do the choices made impact on readers and how are the different axiological choices in the TT read off by the TT audience? These are many unanswered questions. It is my hope that this book will have contributed by highlighting the importance of interpersonal meaning in translation and by opening up stimulating avenues for future investigation.

NOTES

Introduction

1 Sam Hileman to Carlos Fuentes, 26 May 1966, Princeton University Library, Manuscripts Division, Department of Rare Books and Special Collections, Carlos Fuentes Papers, Correspondence, Series 4A, Box 108, Folder 13.

2 Sam Hileman to Carlos Fuentes, 16 November 1965, Carlos Fuentes Papers, Correspondence, Box 108, Folder 13.

3 Published by the Bible Society of Malay, Kuala Lumpur, 1996, a revision of the *Today's Malay Bible* 1987.

4 The *Today's Malay* Version is published by the Bible Society of Malaysia, Kuala Lumpur.

5 Published by the Konferensi Waligerja Indonesia (Indonesian Bishops Conference), 2004.

6 Saeed Ahmed, 'Bibles seized as Malaysian minorities fear fundamentalism', *CNN* 29 October 2009, http://edition.cnn.com/2009/WORLD/asiapcf/10/29/malaysia.bibles.seized/

7 For a follow-up rebuttal, see Ng Kam Wang 'Consistent, sensitive translations', *The Sun Daily*, 17 March 2009, http://www.sun2surf.com/article.cfm?id=31185

8 'Malaysian churches attacked', *Aljazeera*, 8 January 2010, http://english.aljazeera.net/news/asia-pacific/2010/01/20101871816435228.html

9 Speech viewable, with interpreting, at http://www.europarl.europa.eu/wps-europarl-internet/frd/vod/player?language=en&menusearchfrom=bymep&pageby=unit&idmep=4525&discussionId=0&page=0&category=0&format=wmv&askedDiscussionNumber=13

10 See, for example, 'Tirade against "damp rag" EU president shocks MEPs', 24 February 2010, http://news.bbc.co.uk/1/hi/8535121.stm

11 *Tiene usted el carisma de un trapo y una apariencia de un contable de un banco* ['you have the charisma of a cloth and an appearance of an accountant of a bank'].

12 'Iraq's weapons of mass destruction: the assessment of the British government', http://www.fco.gov.uk/resources/en/pdf/pdf3/fco_iraqdossier

13 The website 'Iraq Dossier', run by freelance journalist Chris Ames, has devoted itself to detailing the modifications made to the dossier and suggesting the underlying reasons. Ames provides a detailed table of such changes, http://iraqdossier.com/sexing/table.pdf

14 This is related to Halliday's probability type of modality (Halliday and Matthiessen 2004: 150; see this volume, Chapter 1.2). Elsewhere this is known as epistemic modality (Palmer [1989] 2001) and evidentiality (Chafe and Nichols 1986; see this volume, Chapter 1, Section 1.5).

15 'Iraq's weapons of mass destruction', p. 5.
16 'The Hutton Inquiry: Investigation into the circumstances surrounding the death of Dr David Kelly', http://www.the-hutton-inquiry.org.uk/index.htm
17 'Review of intelligence on weapons of mass destruction', 14 July 2004, http://image.guardian.co.uk/sys-files/Politics/documents/2004/07/14/butler.pdf
18 Martin Howard's testimony, *The Hutton Inquiry*, 11 August 2003, pm, section 131, lines 7–18, http://www.the-hutton-inquiry.org.uk/content/transcripts/hearing-trans03.htm. These and other examples, including Jones' testimony, are discussed by Ames, 'The language of the dossier', http://iraqdossier.com/sexing/thelanguage
19 'Iraq's weapons of mass destruction', p. 5.
20 Transcript of Jones' testimony, *The Hutton Inquiry*, 3 September 2003, am, section 93, line 21–section 94, line 4, http://www.the-hutton-inquiry.org.uk/content/transcripts/hearing-trans28.htm
21 'Iraq's weapons of mass destruction', p. 5.
22 Ibid.
23 'Translation' is used here and elsewhere throughout the book as a superordinate term that covers the different modalities of translation and interpreting. 'Interpreting' will be used in specific contexts related to that modality.

1 Evaluation and translation

1 Compare Lemke (1992: 85): 'Every text-meaning is made in a social universe where alternative or contrary meanings have been or readily could be made.'
2 Founded in 1926, the Prague School of Linguists included Vilém Mathesius (1882–1945), Jan Firbas (1921–2000) and, most famously, Roman Jakobson (1896–1982).
3 See Halliday and Matthiessen (2004: 43).
4 As will become evident in Sections 1.3.1.4 and 1.3.3, usuality is closely related to counter-expectancy and graduation.
5 Probability is sometimes known as epistemic modality or evidentiality, especially when concerned with the certainty or truth value of a proposition (see Introduction, note 15 and this chapter, Section 1.5). Obligation is elsewhere called deontic modality (Palmer [1989] 2001).
6 See also Ward (2004: 282–4), who discusses the various relationships triggered by *we* and notes that the relationship may shift throughout an utterance.
7 Hatim and Mason (1997: 144) draw on the work of Paul Simpson (1993) for their definition of ideology: 'the taken-for-granted assumptions, beliefs and value-systems which are shared collectively by social groups'. See Munday (2008: 43–8) and Fawcett and Munday (2009) for further discussion of ideology in translation studies.
8 See Hatim (2004, 2009), and also the concept of salience discussed in Chapter 5.
9 More drastically, Bennett (2007) has claimed that English has also imposed itself on academic writing in Portuguese, decimating the conventional patterns discourse.
10 However, Englebretson (2007: 17) sees 'stance' as being superordinate, divided into 'evaluation' (value judgements, assessments and attitudes), 'affect' (personal feelings) and 'epistemicity' (commitment).
11 Martin and White's (2005) is the most detailed analysis, but amongst the many other sources are also Martin (2000), Macken-Horarik and Martin (2003), White (2002, 2005), Bednarek (2006, 2008) and Bednarek and Martin (2010).
12 See also Martin (2003: 171).
13 These two key issues underlie the definition of the appraisal system given by Martin and White (2005: 164) as 'the global potential of the language for making evaluative meanings, e.g. for activating positive/negative viewpoints, graduating force/focus, negotiating intersubjective stance'.
14 See also Martin (2004b: 278).
15 www.apartmentservice.com/search/France/Paris/property1551, accessed 27 April 2009.

16 See also Martin (2004b: 274) and the brief comment in Halliday and Matthiessen (2004: 319).
17 Thompson (1998) refers to this as 'resonance'.
18 http://german.about.com/library/blwortjahr02ff.htm
19 http://www.un.int/france/documents_francais/030214_cs_france_irak.htm
20 Transcription from the simultaneous interpretation, available at http://www.pbs.org/ newshour/bb/middle_east/iraq/france_2-14.html
21 *Terrorist* vs *freedom-fighter* is another stereotypical example.
22 In addition, White and Thomson (2008) replace Martin and White's (2005) term 'invite' with 'evoke' and remove the sub-classifications of 'flag', for non-core lexis, and 'afford', for ideational material.
23 It also recalls Bakhtin and Volosinov's 'intertextual freight of words', discussed in Section 1.0.
24 In his discussion, White sees links with work on metadiscourse (e.g. Crismore 1989); indeed, reciprocally Hyland (2005: 37) aligns with stance, evaluation and engagement, giving a definition of 'metadiscourse' as 'the cover term for the self-reflective expressions used to negotiate interactional meanings in a text, assisting the writer (or speaker) to express a viewpoint or engage with readers as members of a particular community'. The lexical realizations considered in metadiscourse studies (e.g. Ifantidou 2005, Hyland 2005) include discourse connectives (*but, therefore, so*), adverbs, modals, speech-act verbs, mental-state verbs, personal pronouns, text developers (*namely, in other words, first*), as well as forms of 'hedging' (Hyland 1998).
25 The term 'key' was used in Martin and White (2005: 164).
26 'Voice' is thus a description of the patterns of evaluation in a particular genre or text. This use is distinct from the concept of textual voice and authorial presence in translation studies (e.g. Hermans 1996, Schiavi 1996, Mossop 2007, Munday 2009c).
27 Halliday and Matthiessen (2004: 150) discuss this under the modality of probability (see Section 1.2 above).
28 In a seminal early paper Lemke (1992: 85) thus calls for 'a more sophisticated theoretical [analytical] framework [than] the naive view … that texts are simply the products of authors or speakers, who address themselves in an immediate context of situation … to other participants, all within the context of a shared context of culture.'
29 Compare Macken-Horarik's terms 'partial', 'resisted' and 'reconstrued' readings (Macken-Horarik 2003b: 317).
30 Highlights are added.
31 Here, 'encoding' and 'decoding' are not restricted to the linguistic concepts that underpin the notion of ST–TT equivalence in Eugene Nida's modelling of the translation process (Nida and Taber 1969: 33).
32 Later *A Thousand Nights and a Night*, available at http://www.burtoniana.org/ books/1885-Arabian%20Nights/index.htm

2 The interpretation of political speech

1 At the time of writing, a video recording of the broadcast speech, from C-Span.org, is available at http://www.youtube.com/watch?v=VjnygQ02aW4. The official White House transcript is available at http://www.whitehouse.gov/blog/inaugural-address/, which also shows a more informal video recording.
2 See a video clip of this moment at http://news.bbc.co.uk/1/hi/world/asia-pacific/ 7842076.stm
3 Numbers refer to lines in the ST transcript, reproduced in Appendix 2.1.
4 Lwin (2009) points out that this section about deceit was also censored in Burma.
5 One exception being 'Obama lauded in Asia for inspiring hope, cooperation', *The Earth Times*, 21 January 2009, http://www.earthtimes.org/articles/show/251728,obama-lauded-in-asia-for-inspiring-hope-cooperation--summary.html#ixzz0hrmBU01V
6 'When it comes to human rights and religious freedom, China remains on the wrong side of history', http://edition.cnn.com/ALLPOLITICS/1998/06/11/clinton.china/

7   http://www.chinadaily.com.cn/world/2009-01/21/content_7415436.htm

8   http://www.danwei.org/featured_video/cctv_interrupts_live_broadcast.php

9   For example, http://www.liveleak.com/view?i=79a_1232547964

10 'Barack Obama's inauguration: China cuts references to communism from speech', http://www.telegraph.co.uk/news/worldnews/northamerica/usa/barackobama/4303068/Barack-Obama-inauguration-China-cuts-references-to-communism-from-speech.html; 'China edits Obama's inaugural speech', http://www.hollywoodreporter.com/hr/content_display/television/news/e3i1631bdc8fee89cc769c25e442aad9c7c; 'Chinese censors snipped 'communism' from Obama address', *Time Online*, 21 January 2009, http://www.timesonline.co.uk/tol/news/world/us_and_americas/article5560869.ece

11 'China gives first response to Google threat', http://news.bbc.co.uk/1/hi/world/asia-pacific/8458462.stm

12 A full transcription is given in Appendix 2.1.

13 Transcriptions of the Spanish TTs are to be found online at http://www.leeds.ac.uk/arts/people/20059/spanish_portuguese_and_latin_american_studies/person/998/jeremy_munday

14 Favreau calls this the 'download' (Alter 2010: 271).

15 As always, however, this will depend very much on the sociohistorical context of use. In 1982, what Argentina termed *la Guerra de las Malvinas* (the War of the Malvinas) was, for the British government of the time, *the Falklands conflict*. By the time of the twenty-fifth anniversary in 2007, *conflict* had more or less been displaced in English by *the Falklands War*.

16 *El País* (Madrid), 21 January 2009, http://www.elpais.com/articulo/internacional/Discurso/inaugural/presidente/Barack/Obama/espanol/elpepuint/20090120elpepuint_16/Tes translated by María Luisa Rodríguez. This was posted on http://www.whitehouse.gov and is referred to in this chapter as TT4.

17 *Our Enduring Spirit* is even the title of a prominent illustrated book of the speech (Obama 2009).

18 *Nuestra capacidad se mantiene* (TT1), *nuestra capacidad no ha sido disminuida* (TT2) and *nuestra capacidad mantiene su fuerza* (TT3).

19 *Sus problemas.*

20 *Se aguantaron . . . las dificultades.*

21 *Generosidad . . . generosidad.*

22 *Espíritu.*

23 *Amabilidad . . . altruismo, Cinco Dias*, 21 January 2009, http://www.cincodias.com/articulo/economia/Discurso-inaugural-presidente-Barack-Obama-espanol/20090120cdscdseco_20/cdseco/

24 *Amabilidad . . . desinterés*, http://www.spanish-english-translation-costa-rica.com/

25 *Bondad . . . abnegación*, EFE (the major Spanish-language news agency, ww.efe.com), 20 January 2009, available on many media websites, including http://www.diariolasamericas.com/noticia/70603/pda

26 *Comenzaremos de manera responsable, dejando a Irak en manos de su pueblo.*

27 *Vamos a empezar a dejar la responsabilidad de su gestión a Irak y a su pueblo.*

28 See, for example, the definition in the *Collins Cobuild English Dictionary* (1995: 594): 'In American English, if you face someone down, you oppose them or beat them by being **confident** and looking at them **boldly**' (emphasis added).

29 *Menundukkan fasisme dan komunisme.*

30 Based on log likelihood scores for collocates located within three words to the right of the lemma *wield*, using the Leeds internet corpus. http://corpus.leeds.ac.uk/cgi-bin/cqp.pl?q=wield&c=INTERNET-EN&contextsize=60c&sort1=word&sort2=right&terminate=100&searchtype=colloc&llstat=on&cleft=0&cright=3&cfilter=

31 'Work very hard doing unpleasant or tiring tasks', *Collins Cobuild Dictionary*, p. 1762.

32 'Many people work together there in poor conditions for low pay', ibid., p. 1688.

33 'a blow with a whip, especially a blow on someone's back as a punishment', ibid., p. 934.

34 *Por nosotros ellos trabajaron en fábricas, conquistaron el Oeste; . . . se aguantaron . . . las dificultades.*

35 *Por nosotros lucharon en talleres y fábricas, colonizaron el Oeste; sufrieron el azote del látigo y labraron la dura tierra.*

36 Compare the many examples in Baker (2006) for how the dynamics of narrative representation may be altered in translation.

37 *Por nosotros, trabajaron sin descanso en fábricas déspotas y se instalaron en occidente,* http://www.spanish-english-translation-costa-rica.com/

38 Interpreted as 'worn out' (*desgastados*, TT1) and 'big' (*grandes*, TT2, TT3).

39 Interpreted as 'bitterness' (*amargura*, TT1, TT3) and 'bitter drink' (*trago amargo*, TT2).

40 http://news.cctv.com/world/20090121/100117.shtml

41 Here, Chinese examples are supplied by Binhua Wang and Japanese examples by Kiyoshi Kawahara and Yukie Ono (email correspondence).

42 A metaphorical use, since the literal meaning is of material that is sewn together in small pieces of different colours to form a quilt or similar item.

43 http://corpus.leeds.ac.uk/cgi-bin/cqp.pl?q=patchwork&c=INTERNET-EN&contextsize=60c&sort1=word&sort2=right&terminate=100&searchtype=colloc&llstat=on&cleft=0&cright=1&cfilter=

44 The full concordance is available at http://corpus.leeds.ac.uk/cgi-bin/cqp.pl?q=patchwork+of&c=INTERNET-EN&searchtype=conc&contextsize=60c&sort1=word&sort2=right&terminate=100&llstat=on&cleft=0&cright=1&cfilter=

45 http://www.adamsmith.org/cissues/pharmacy-distribution.htm, 'More automatic dispensing – Adam Smith Institute'.

46 http://www.garella.com/rich/camret.htm, 'Rich Garella: Returning to Cambodia'.

47 http://www.time.com/time/europe/magazine/article/0,13005,901030217-420981,00.html , 'TIME Europe Magazine: Retail Politics – Feb. 17, 2003'

48 For example, 'Sweep away post-holiday inbox clutter in hotmail', http://blogs.msdn.com/b/robmar/archive/2011/07/07/sweep-away-post-holiday-clutter-with-hotmail.aspx

49 *Nosotros sabemos ... que es una fortaleza ... el hecho de que somos un país de cristianos y musulmanes, de ateos* ('we know ... that it is a strength ... the fact that we are a country of Christians and Muslims, of atheists').

50 *Cinco Dias*, 21 January 2009, see note 23.

51 http://www.spanish-english-translation-costa-rica.com/

52 EFE, 20 January 2009, see note 25.

53 The French translation for France 24 used 'our heritage in patchwork' (*notre heritage en patchwork*), http://www.france24.com/fr/20090120-etats-unis-discours-investiture-obama-washington-president- Other translations by prominent outlets used 'heritage in diversity' (*héritage de diversités*), Radio France Internationale, http://www.rfi.fr/actufr/articles/109/article_77584.asp and 'our multiple heritage' (*notre héritage multiple*), Agence France Presse, http://www.google.com/hostednews/afp/article/ALeqM5g1qB116u7PSucU4M8gAir2KUgvFA. The Italian *La Repubblica* also used borrowing, ' our heritage in patchwork' (*il nostro retaggio a patchwork*), http://www.repubblica.it/2009/01/sezioni/esteri/obama-insediamento/testo-discorso-italiano/testo-discorso-italiano.html

54 A full list of metaphors in the Obama speech is given in the online appendix (see Note 13).

55 *44 estadounidenses ... han ... juramentado para ser presidentes. Las palabras se han dicho en **momentos** ... de prosperidad y en **aguas** de paz. Pero de tanto en tanto, el juramento se produce en medio de **nubarrones** y de **tormentas.***

56 *44 estadounidenses ... han ya prestado ... el juramento presidencial. Las palabras han sido pronunciadas durante ... **tiempos** de prosperidad y de paz ... Sin embargo, de vez en cuando ... se presta el juramento ... entre **nubarrones** y **tormentas.***

57 *44 ... americanos han ... tomado el juramento como presidentes. Durante prosperidad se han hablado ciertas palabras. Sin embargo, de cuando en cuando el juramento se toma en medio de ... **dificultades** y **tormentas**.*

58 *Crecientes oleadas, Cinco Días,* see note 23.

59 *Aguas pacíficas y tranquilas.*

60 *Tranquilas aguas,* http://www.spanish-english-translation-costa-rica.com/

61 *Aguas tranquilas,* EFE, see note 25.

62 *Fieras tormentas, Cinco Días,* see note 23.

63 *Furiosas tormentas,* EFE, see note 25.

64 *Lo han hecho durante mareas de prosperidad y en aguas pacíficas y tranquilas. Sin embargo, en ocasiones, este juramento se ha prestado en medio de nubes y tormentas* (TT4: 6–8).
65 See note 40 above.
66 Posted online by Deaf Link Inc., http://www.youtube.com/watch?v=ZbljtRYeObU
67 Charteris-Black (2005: 45) also notes that it is a 'potent source domain for metaphor' in the speeches of Winston Churchill, Martin-Luther King. Margaret Thatcher, Bill Clinton and Tony Blair.
68 *Cinco Días*, see note 23.
69 http://www.spanish-english-translation-costa-rica.com/
70 http://www.merriam-webster.com/netdict/stand%20pat
71 Translated by the literal *estrangulado* in TT1 and TT3, and by the diluted explicative metaphor *enredado* ('entangled') in TT2.
72 Compare written TT4's *el amargo sabor* ('the bitter taste').
73 Where the abstract is presented as concrete (Charteris-Black 2004: 21).
74 This is also the solution adopted by many of the written TTs.
75 A notable example of tactical reading is to be found in Japan, where textbooks of Obama's speeches are sold as an English-learning resource and have become bestsellers (Kubota 2009).
76 This photo may be viewed at http://www.angelfire.com/realm/police-scanner/kehoe. html in a story that discusses the subsequent problems suffered by Kehoe as a result of the publicity.
77 *Es el coraje de un bombero para entrar en una escalera llena de humo.*
78 *Es el coraje de un bombero que se enfrenta a una escalera llena de humo.*
79 *Es el espíritu que muchas veces tienen los bomberos cuando ayudan.*
80 For a full list, see the online appendix.
81 Chilton (2004: 59) considers the Self to be the 'origin of the epistemic *true* and the deontic *right*' (e.g. *I must, I shall*). This is certainly the case if by this we mean that the Self has the power to express the degree of truth value and moral compulsion, but it should not of course be understood that politicians will never admit nor express an untruth.
82 A search for the lemma BESTOW in the Leeds internet corpus shows overwhelmingly the most common structure to be *bestow something on/upon somebody*.
83 In one further example, Obama effaces himself into the third person: 'a man whose father less than 60 years ago might not have been served in a local restaurant can now stand before you' (150–1). See also p. 78.
84 See the online appendix for a full list.
85 See Fairclough's analysis of the discourse of British Prime Minister Margaret Thatcher (Fairclough [1989] 2001: 148–9) and the discourse of New Labour (Fairclough 2000: 164).
86 A full list of uses is given in the online appendix.
87 The *Washington Post* reported Federal agency estimates that up to 1.8 million people attended in the capital, which would make it a record attendance for an inauguration. Michael E. Ruane and Aaron C. Douglas, 'D.C.'s inauguration headcount: 1.8 million', *Washington Post*, 20 January 2009, http://www.washingtonpost.com/wp-dyn/content/article/2009/01/21/AR2009012103884.html?sid=ST2009012102519
88 See Livingstone (2004) for the challenges and opportunities such dispersion presents to research.
89 This line was written by Obama himself and he 'intentionally refused to strip it of its colloquial quality' (Alter 2010: 107).
90 An 'addressee' is a person who is 'known' to be a participant in the speech context, 'ratified' (acknowledged by the speaker) and 'addressed' directly (Bell 1984, 2002).
91 Known and ratified but not directly addressed (Bell ibid.).
92 'Rimettiamoci al lavoro insieme per ricostruire una grande America', http://www. repubblica.it/2009/01/sezioni/esteri/obama-insediamento/testo-discorso-italiano/testo-discorso-italiano.html, 20 January 2009.
93 See note 23.
94 http://www.nikkei.co.jp/senkyo/us2008/news/20090120e3k2001720.html

95 Email correspondence from Kiyoshi Kawahara and Yukie Ono, 2 September 2011.

96 See the online appendix for a full list of examples for the present and future frames.

97 Furthermore, for the American audience targeted by the ASL interpretation, these names are finger-spelled (as is common practice) with no explicitation.

98 **Comete unos errores al juramentar** ... *y lo haré en lo mejor de mis habilidades.* **Ahora sí inicia el discurso** ... *Queridos conciudadanos,* **dice Barack Obama**, *me paro hoy aquí* ...

99 Here we use the term 'translator voice' as a general term to describe the text that is uttered as a translator/interpreter and to avoid confusion with the term 'interpreter voice', used by Martin and White (2005: 185) as a counterpart for 'correspondent voice' in history texts.

100 *La pregunta tampoco es si el mercado es una fuerza ... sabemos que ... el poder de ... el deseo de generar dinero es claro, pero esta crisis nos ha hecho ver que el país no puede prosperar si favorece sólo a los prósperos ... También habla sobre aquellos sectores que quedan a los lados de la prosperidad esta es el camino más seguro para el bien común, dice Barack Obama, hace referencia a la crisis económica, a la avaricia y en estos momentos rechazamos ... rechazamos tener que escoger entre nuestras ideas y la seguridad nacional.*

101 *Éste es el mensaje que dirige Barack Obama al mundo entero, él quiere la paz y así lo quiere el pueblo estadounidense, eso lo dice en su discurso inaugural.*

102 'Mi papá hace 60 años pudo no haber sido atendido en un restaurante local, dice Barack Obama, pero ahora sí y él está justamente representando este gran cambio en la historia estadounidense al asumir como el presidente número 44 de los Estados Unidos.'

103 Transcription made by the author from the White House video recording at www. whitehouse.gov/biog/inaugural-address.

3 The view from technical translators

1 Linguee (www.linguee.com) is a tool that combines dictionary and a large database of online translated texts to allow searches for individual words and their translation equivalents.

2 http://www.linguee.com/english-german/search?sourceoverride=none&source=auto &query=Leistung

3 http://www.wellness-hotels-hungary.com/de/hotel/budapest_hotel.php?id=111& name=_Hotel_Szarvaskut_

4 http://www.wellness-hotels-hungary.com/en/hotel/budapest_hotel.php?id= 111&name=_Hotel_Szarvaskut_

5 Contrary to my expectations, a Google search reveals 1,600 instances of this collocation, a sample of which proved to be positive in the 'meticulous attention to detail' sense.

6 http://www.linguee.com/english-german/search?sourceoverride=none&source=auto &query=anspruchsvoll+

7 German: www.rheinmetall.de/index.php?lang=2&fid=1193

8 English: www.rheinmetall.de/index.php?lang=3&fid=1198

9 German: www.wintershall.com/pi-06-12.html?&L=1

10 English: www.wintershall.com/pi-06-12.html?&L=11

11 http://www.tab-beim-bundestag.de/de/publikationen/berichte/ab112.html

12 http://www.tab-beim-bundestag.de/en/publications/reports/ab112.html

13 http://eur-lex.europa.eu/LexUriServ/LexUriServ.do?uri=CELEX:32000R0050: EN:HTML

14 www.proz.com/kudoz

15 This is a bone of contention, but not one that I shall comment further on here.

16 http://itlaw.wikia.com/wiki/Bleeding_edge_technology, amongst others.

17 http://translation.babylon.com/english/Bleeding-edge/

18 http://www.urbandictionary.com/define.php?term=new-fangled

19 http://corpus.leeds.ac.uk/cgi-bin/cqp.pl?q=newfangled&c=INTERNET-EN&contex tsize=60c&sort1=word&sort2=right&terminate=100&searchtype=colloc&llstat=on&c left=0&cright=1&cfilter=

20 http://www.proz.com/kudoz/spanish_to_english/tourism_travel/4350977-proyecta_hacia_la_vanguardia.html

21 Indeed, the proposer of this solution explains: '*Vanguardia* implies one of the first to do new things and offer new methods and technologies in their field.'

22 http://eurogeo5.org/alojamientos_i.php

23 http://www.proz.com/kudoz/english_to_arabic/other/4352365-superstitious.html?keyword_kudoz=superstitious

24 http://www.proz.com/kudoz/danish_to_english/law%3A_contracts/4352110-ubillig.html

25 http://www.sense-online.nl/

26 An annual subscription for 2011 was €65 (around £60).

27 See the discussion on semantic prosody or association in Chapter 1, Section 1.3.1.4 and the concept of invoke/associate evaluation in Chapter 2, Section 2.2.5.

4 The literary translator and reviser

1 Labov's well-known concept of 'the observer's paradox' (Labov 1972a: 209).

2 Penguin Classics Archive (AC/040), University of Bristol, Folder DM 1107/L241.

3 Handford wrote on unused, lined University of London examination paper, which gave wide margins and room at the top and bottom of the pages.

4 E.V. Rieu to Professor Humphrey Kitto, 4 November 1944, DM1938/1-2.

5 A.S.B. Glover to Mattingly, 3 January 1949, DM1107/LS.

6 Stephen Mattingly to Sir Allen Lane, 18 September 1967, DM1107/LS.

7 Indeed, the terms 'The Translator' and 'The Reviser' were specifically designated in the legal agreement of 9 November 1968, DM1107/LS.

8 Attached as schedule to legal agreement of 9 November 1968, signed by Penguin, Handford and the Mattinglys.

9 Further points of interest should be noted: some ten years before, Rives had already published a translation, with introduction and commentary, of *Germania* with Oxford University Press (Tacitus 1999). While it might seem that revision of the Penguin volume would present a conundrum – namely, how does a translator revise in such a way as not to self-plagiarize a translation under copyright to another publisher? Is variation likely to be greater in view of this pressure? – in fact Rives (personal communication) says that he deliberately avoided returning to his Oxford translation.

10 A corrected edition of *Agricola*, by Ogilvie and Winterbottom, and a new version of *Germania*, by Winterbottom.

11 'Brief reviews', *Greece & Rome* 18: 52 (January 1949): 44–6, http://www.jstor.org/stable/641805

12 Robert Crowe, Penguin Archive Project Classics researcher, email correspondence, 10 March 2010.

13 However, this was not the case with Bellos translation of Perec (see Section 4.3).

14 Dieter Pevsner to Michael Rubinstein, 3 January 1968, DM1107/L5.

15 Michael Rubinstein to Dieter Pevsner, 10 January 1968, DM1107/L5.

16 Stanley Handford to Christine Collins (editor at Penguin), 13 July 1970. The final version of this part of the preface, with semi-colon installed, reads, 'When this translation first appeared it was accepted as one of the best translations available of these two books; but in the course of time certain opinions have been revised, both about translations in general and about the approach to Tacitus' work' (Handford in Tacitus 1970: 7).

17 Corpus searches show *gaping nostrils* to be used in sarcasm, in vicious racist stereotyping and of animals. For instance, the nineteenth-century 'scientific racist' depictions of Irish Americans as 'apelike creatures with large mouths, thick lips, protruding lower jaws, jagged teeth, short noses with gaping nostrils, sloping heads, receding chins and dangling arms' (Dente Ross 2003: 133).

18 Handford (in Tacitus 1970: 160) substitutes *Indian* with *colonial*.

19 'The Nobel Prize in Literature 2010'. Nobelprize.org. 8 Sep 2011, www.nobelprize.org/nobel_prizes/literature/laureates/2010/

20 This section is based on material in the Mario Vargas Llosa papers at Princeton University, Library, Manuscripts Division, Department of Rare Books and Special Collections.

21 Gregory Rabassa to Mario Vargas Llosa, 1 July 1967, Series 3A Correspondence, Box 18.4.

22 Gregory Rabassa to Mario Vargas Llosa, 21 September 1967, Box 18.4.

23 'Es que sólo quería que usted averigüe que una cosa sea una planta o un animal'; Gregory Rabassa to Mario Vargas Llosa, 22 November 1967, Box 18.4.

24 Gregory Rabassa to Mario Vargas Llosa, 29 January 1968, Box 18.4.

25 Gregory Rabassa to Mario Vargas Llosa, 22 November 1967 and 2 March 1968, Box 18.4. The UK translation, by Darwin Flakoll and Claribel Alegría, was entitled *Cyclone* (London: Peter Owen, 1967). Rabassa's own translation appeared as *Strong Wind* (New York: Delacorte, 1968), Box 18.4.

26 'Si usted quiere eliminar cuanto posible lo folklórico y exótico, en algunos casos sería posible eliminar la palabra exacta y usar la genérica, monkey simplemente en vez de frailecillo monkey, por ejemplo'; Gregory Rabassa to Mario Vargas Llosa, 21 January 1968, Box 18.4.

27 'Mis preguntas siempre son las mismas, cierta expresión rara que no encuentro en el diccionario (aunque ahora tengo el Collins) … Naturalmente muchos peruanismos que no se encuentran en otros léxicos …'; Gregory Rabassa to Mario Vargas Llosa, 28 February 1972, Box 18.4.

28 Such as *cholo*, which Rabassa describes as being a mix of 'halfbreed' and 'peasant'; Rabassa's letter to Vargas Llosa, 9 January 1968, Box 18.4.

29 Ronald Christ to Mario Vargas Llosa, 17 January 1977, Box 6.11.

30 Ronald Christ to Mario Vargas Llosa, 4 January 1976, Box 6.11, highlight in original.

31 Mario Vargas Llosa Papers, Series 4, Box 11.

32 The 21st edition of the *Diccionario de la lengua Española* of the Real Academia, now online, gives seven senses for *criollo*; http://buscon.rae.es/draeI/SrvltConsulta?TIPO_BUS=3&LEMA=criollo

33 In English *creole* refers to the language, a person of mixed African/European race, a person descended from the Europeans who colonized the West Indies and southern United States, and the cultures of those communities (Oxford English Dictionary online).

34 See the *Collins Spanish Dictionary* (9th edition, 2009) and the *Oxford Spanish Dictionary* (3rd edition, 2003).

35 P. 181 of Helen Lane's draft translation.

36 On this point, see the comments by translator Gregory Rabassa on his collaboration with Vargas Llosa at an earlier stage in the author's career: 'Mario looked over my work as I went along and would offer suggestions. Most were appreciated, especially where it had been some jungle peculiarity I had missed. At times, however, he would latch on to what he thought was a mistake and offer a correction. His limited English had simply kept him unaware of the fact that my word was nothing but a synonym for the one he was suggesting' (Rabassa 2005: 78).

37 Mario Vargas Llosa Papers, Sub-Series 2E, Box 33, Folder 4.

38 In each case, the option that appears in the published TT is indicated in **bold**.

39 As is stated on his website, 'Richard Booth's bookshop', http://www.richardbooth.demon.co.uk/

40 Compare the analysis of point of view in translation in Levenston and Sonnenschein (1986), Munday (2008) and Saldanha (2011), amongst others.

41 The meaning here is more 'to rummage'. This is sense B in the *Collins Spanish Dictionary* (9th edition, 2009), equivalent to sense 2 of *hurgar* in the Real Academia's *Diccionario de la Lengua Espanola*, 21st edition, online (www.rae.es).

42 Only one hit in Spanish using a Google™ search.

43 27,500 hits in Google™.

44 At the time of the translation, Bellos (b. 1945) was Professor of French at the University of Manchester. Since 1997, he has worked at Princeton. He was made Chevalier de l'Ordre des Palmes Académiques in 1988 and won the Prix Goncourt de la Biographie in 1994 for his biography of Perec. In 2005, he was the first winner of the Man Booker International Translator's Award for his translations, from French, of the Albanian novelist Ismail Kadare.

45 See Federici (2009) for an analysis of Calvino's own translations of Queneau.

46 See Bernard Magné (1993) 'Transformations of constraint', *Review of Contemporary Fiction*, 22 March 1993. Outstanding examples are Perec's own lipograms *La Disparition* (1969, translated by Gilbert Adair as *A Void* [1994]), marked by the absence of the letter *e*, and *Les Revenentes* (1972, translated by Ian Monk, or 'E.N. Monk', as *The Exeter Text: Jewels, Secrets, Sex* and published in the collection *Three* [Godine, 1996]), in which the only vowel used is *e*.

47 In his biography of Perec, *Georges Perec: A life in words* (London: Harvill, and New York: Godine, 1993), Bellos reports that Perec 'had given Helmlé many clues about the "various constraints" used and had annotated a copy of the novel with the sources of most German-language quotations (though said "doesn't matter" at the head of some chapters)' (Bellos 1993: 709).

48 At least 203 in total, according to Bellos (1987: 189).

49 'Notes on the translation and typescript of George Perec's Great Novel Compendium', p. 3, Translation archive, David Bellos papers, 'Perec La vie mode d'emploi', LIT/TA/DB/1, Box 2, University of East Anglia, Norwich, UK.

50 Ibid.

51 That there was no earlier draft is confirmed by Bellos himself (personal communication).

52 In his 'Translator's note' (Perec 2008: 581), Bellos records that he used, 'occasionally somewhat modified', translations from published sources, and he names the 21 translators.

53 14 January 2011.

54 It should be noted that there is some overlap of categories, with 11 changes having been allocated to more than one category.

55 LIT/TA/DB/1, Box 2.

56 Galley proofs p. 102.

57 Handwritten list of points (undated) entitled 'La Vie Mode d'emploi – Traduction Bellos', sent by Jacques Beaumatin through his son Eric, LIT/TA/DB/1, Box 2; letter from Bellos to Jacques Beaumatin, 22 January 1988, thanking him for reading and responding to some of the points; these form the basis of Bellos' typed list, 'Life A User's Manual: Corrections to be made to current state of text: 19 February 1988', Box 1.

58 My translation. 'Sac long, ouvert par le milieu et dont les extrémités forment deux poches', Paul Robert, A. Rey and J Rey-Debove, *Le Petit Robert* (Paris: Robert, 1984): 177.

59 http://www.google.co.uk/imgres?imgurl=http://www.deliciousmagazine.co.uk/images/articles/241/241_2.jpg&imgrefurl=http://www.deliciousmagazine.co.uk/articles/a-guide-to-christmas-techniques&usg=__FO_igDxZ5Y-RCMzeKtXYpiFBMVo=&h=364&w=560&sz=55&hl=en&start=7&um=1&itbs=1&tbnid=5c-GK4L-BNPkyM:&tbnh=86&tbnw=133&prev=/images%3Fq%3Djambon%2Bpersille%26um%3D1%26hl%3Den%26rlz%3D1T4DKUK_en-GBGB310GB310%26tbs%3Disch:1n-GBGB310GB310%26tbs%3Disch:1

5 Translation variation and its link to attitude

1 Peter Bush's brief analysis (Bush 2000: 434–5) of five translations of this sentence (by Anthony Bonner, James Irby, Anthony Kerrigan, Norman Thomas di Giovanni, and Hurley, all frontline literary translators) shows that only di Giovanni varies in the translation of the adjective, preferring the non-Latinate *encompassing*.

2   Such variation is ironic when related to a Borges text, when one thinks of his legendary 'Pierre Menard, author of the Quixote' (1939) story. The fictional Menard sets out to relive the process of writing Cervantes' novel. He ends up reproducing it word for word, but, having arrived there by a new route, recontextualizes the project through his twentieth-century French biography (Waisman 2005: 85–6). As Hurley puts it in his translation of the story, 'The Cervantes text and the Menard text are verbally identical, but the second is almost infinitely richer' (Borges 1998a: 94).

3   Wheelock is author of *The Mythfinder: A Study of Motif and Symbol in the Short Stories of Jorge Luis Borges* (Austin: University of Texas Press, 1969).

4   Literal translation: 'When she remained alone, Emma did not open immediately the eyes. On the light table was the money that had left the man: Emma sat up and tore it like before she had torn the letter. Tearing money is an impiety, like throwing away bread; Emma regretted, as soon as she did it. An act of arrogance and on that day … Fear lost itself in the sadness of her body, in disgust. Disgust and sadness were chaining her, but Emma slowly got up and proceeded to dress. In the room did not remain vivid colours; the last twilight was getting worse. Emma was able to leave without them notifying her; at the corner she got on a Lacroze, which was going west. She chose, following her plan, the seat right at the front, so that they should not see her face. Perhaps it comforted her to verify, in the insipid bustle of the streets, that what had happened had not contaminated things. She travelled through decreasing and opaque neighbourhoods, seeing them and forgetting them on the spot, and she alighted at one of the side streets of Warnes. Paradoxically her fatigue came to be a strength, since it obliged her to concentrate on the details of the adventure and concealed from her its backdrop and purpose.'

5   '(Not out of fear, but because she was an instrument of Justice, she did not want to be punished.) Then, a single bullet-shot in the middle of the chest would seal the fate of Loewenthal. But things did not occur like that.'

6   'The story was incredible, indeed but it imposed itself on all, because substantially it was correct. True was the tone of Emma Zunz, true the shame, true the hatred. True also was the outrage that she had suffered; only were false the circumstances the time and one or two proper names.'

7   The story is told in the third person, with an omniscient narrator. However, on occasions the reader is given almost direct access to Emma Zunz's thoughts and words, in a type of free indirect thought (Fowler 1996, Simpson 1993), e.g. 'Romper el dinero era una impiedad', 'Un acto de soberbia, y en aquel día …'

8   Word-count totals for the extracts in the ST and the two published TTs produces the following results: ST 289 tokens; Yates TT 317 tokens; Hurley TT 326 tokens. 'Tokens' here means the total number of word-forms that comprise the text. But such figures are crude, not least because, as is well known, the figures can be skewed by punctuation conventions such as hyphens. For example, should *night-table* in Yates be treated as one word-form or as two, as in Hurley's *night table*? The increase in the number of tokens in the TTs can be explained partly because of the obligatory addition of pronouns in English (e.g. *eligió/she selected*) and particles in phrasal verbs (e.g. *tirar/ throw away*).

9   In Hallidayan linguistics, cohesion is part of the textual function and not directly related to the appraisal theory framework discussed in Chapter 1, Section 1.2. This does not, however, mean that it does not contribute in some form to the coherence of the narrative point of view (see Munday 2008: 26–7). The focus here on interpersonal appraisal precludes more detailed treatment of cohesion.

10   Andrew Hurley to Michael Mount, 15 September 1994, p. 5, 'The Borges project and sabbatical', Folder 2 of 2. Andrew Hurley papers, Harry Ransom Center, University of Texas at Austin, Special Collections.

11   Although this respondent had near-native competence in English, the possibility of her translation skewing the results was carefully considered. However, only one of the lexical choices in her TT (*waned* for *decrecientes* in Extract 1) was unique to the group (an

interesting finding in itself), so her translation did not otherwise seriously affect the results in Table 5.5.

12 This restricts comparability with studies such as Malmkjaer's (2003, 2004) on the translations of Hans-Christian Andersen. Malmkjaer counts over 100 extant English translations or versions, though these have been produced in differing historical circumstances and with each translator being aware of the existence of prior versions. Mention should also be made of the parallel Norwegian–English–German corpus at the University of Oslo, where 12 translations of a short story had been commissioned from practising literary translators in Norway (Johansson 2003). To date, this corpus remains a generally underused resource. See the information on the Oslo Multilingual Corpus at www.hf.uio.no/ilos/english/services/omc/

13 On this point, Olohan (2004: 153–60) looks at contractions in translations by Peter Bush and Dorothy Blair as an idiosyncratic style marker but suggests that the influence of the ST genre may be greater than translator variation.

14 Variance is again highlighted by underlining.

15 In these TTs there are of course also shifts in grammatical words (articles, prepositions, etc., for example Yates' use of the possessive pronoun *her*, which increases surface cohesion) and word order (e.g. those five respondent TTs which place the translation of *asco* in the sentence-final, focal position). These may influence the textual metafunction and the spatio-temporal point of view (see Munday 2008) but they fall beyond the focus on the main realizations of attitude.

16 *Insípido* might be considered a slight exception, since six respondents chose the calque *insipid*. Yet its possible inadequacy is highlighted by the large number of alternatives: nine respondents were not happy with *insipid*, even in the absence of an obvious alternative.

17 This may even be a case of omission if *rapid movement* is understood as an equivalent of *trajín* alone.

18 'The objective of this technical specification is that of fixing the conditions of calculation to apply in the bodies and supports to install in the Rehabilitated UTE-Sis.

This specification bases itself on the Purchase Specification: 05.U0.99.12.005, which it annuls and replaces from the point of view of conditions of calculation, since it extends it and may be applied to other equipment which does not cover the previous Specification [S].'

19 *A westbound Lacroze:* The Lacroze Tramway Line served the northwestern area of Buenos Aires at the time; today the city has an extensive subway system.

20 *Warnes:* A street in central Buenos Aires near the commercial district of Villa Crespo, where the [Loewenthal] mill is apparently located.

6 Evaluation in translation – some concluding thoughts

1 Compare Pym's (2003: 489) definition of translation competence as 'the ability to generate a series of more than one viable target text ... [and] ... the ability to select only one viable TT from this series quickly and with justifiable confidence'.

2 In the discussion of history textbooks, Coffin (2002: 512, 521) also notes that it cannot be assumed that value-judgement is shared between author and reader (see also Fairclough 2003: 57).

3 Martin (2003) identifies 'syndromes of choice' associated with different combinations of appraisal resources, and it may be possible to identify those that occur in translation or in the work of specific translators. It is possible to draw a parallel with Toury's laws of translation (Toury 1995). See Mossop (2007) for a detailed discussion of the many possible voice selections in translation.

BIBLIOGRAPHY

Abbamonte, Lucia and Flavia Cavaliere (2006) 'Lost in translation: the Italian rendering of UNICEF "The State of the World's Children 2004" Report', in Susan Šarcevic and Mauricio Gotti (eds) *Insights into Specialized Translation*, Bern: Peter Lang, 235–60.

Agar, Michael (1991) 'The biculture in bilingual', *Language in Society* 20: 167–81.

Agar, Michael (1994) 'The intercultural frame', *International Journal of Intercultural Relations* 18.2: 221–37.

Aikhenveld, Alexandra (2004) *Evidentiality*, Oxford: Oxford University Press.

Alarcón, Daniel (2009) 'Lost in translation', *Granta*, 19 January 2009, available online at www.granta.com/Online-Only/Lost-in-Translation

Alter, Jonathan (2010) *The Promise: President Obama, Year One*, New York: Simon and Schuster.

Álvarez, Román and Mª-África Vidal Claramonte (eds) (1996) *Translation and Power*, Clevedon: Multilingual Matters.

Angelone, Erik (2010) 'Triangulating uncertainty management in translation through a metacognitive lens', in Godfrey Shreve and Erik Angelone (eds) *Translation and Cognition*, Amsterdam and Philadelphia: John Benjamins, 17–40.

Ardekani, Mohammed Ali Mokhtari (2002) 'The translation of reporting verbs in English and Persian', *Babel* 48.2: 125–34.

Babych, Bogdan and Anthony Hartley (2004) 'Modelling legitimate translation variation for automatic evaluation of MT quality', *Proceedings of LREC 2004*, 833-6, available online at http://www.mt-archive.info/LREC-2004-Babych-2.pdf

Baker, Mona ([1992] 2011) *In Other Words: A Textbook on Translation*, 2nd edition, Abingdon and New York: Routledge.

Baker, Mona (2006) *Translation and Conflict: A Narrative Account*, Abingdon and New York: Routledge.

Bakhtin, Mikhail M. ([1953] 1986) 'The problem of speech genres', in Caryl Emerson and Michael Holquist (eds) *Speech Genres and Other Late Essays*, translated by Vern W. McGee, Austin, TX: University of Texas Press, 60–102.

Bakhtin, Mikhail M. (1981) *The Dialogic Imagination: Four Essays*, edited by Michael Holquist, translated by Caryl Emerson and Michael Holquist, Austin, TX: University of Texas Press.

BBC Monitoring (2009) 'World media on Obama inauguration', 20 January 2009, available online at news.bbc.co.uk/1/hi/world/americas/obama_inauguration/7842752.stm

Beaton, Morven (2007) 'Interpreted ideologies in institutional discourse: the case of the European Parliament', *The Translator* 13.2: 271–96.

Bednarek, Monica (2006) *Evaluation in Media Discourse: Analysis of a Newspaper Corpus*, London and New York: Continuum.

Bednarek, Monika (ed.) (2008) *Evaluation in Text Types*, Special issue of *Functions of Language* 15.1: 1–7.

Bednarek, Monica and Jim Martin (eds) (2010) *New Discourse on Language: Functional perspectives on Multimodality, Identity and Affiliation*, London: Continuum.

Bell, Allan (1984) 'Language style as audience design', *Language and Society* 13: 145–204.

Bell, Allan (2002) 'Back in style: reworking audience design', in Penelope Eckert and John Rickford (eds) *Style and Sociolinguistic Variation*, Cambridge: Cambridge University Press, 139–69.

Bell, Roger (1991) *Translation and Translating: Theory and Practice*, Harlow: Longman.

Bellos, David (1987) 'Literary quotations in Perec's "La Vie mode d'emploi"', *French Studies* 41.2: 181–94.

Bellos, David (1993) *Georges Perec: A Life in Words*, London: Harvill/New York: Godine.

Bell-Villada, Gene H. (1998) 'Collected fictions: review', *Commonweal*, 18 December 1998, available online at www.encyclopedia.com/doc/1G1-53857605.html

Benveniste, Emile ([1958] 1971) 'Subjectivity in language', in *Problems in General Linguistics*, Coral Gables, FL: University of Miami Press, 223–30.

Biber, Douglas and Edward Finegan (1988) 'Adverbial stance types in English', *Discourse Processes* 11.1: 1–34.

Biber, Douglas and Edward Finegan (1989) 'Styles of stance in English: Lexical and grammatical marking of evidentiality and affect', *Text* 9.1: 93–124.

Biel, Lucja (2007) 'Translation of multilingual EU law as a sub-genre of legal translation', *Court Interpreting and Legal Translation in the Enlarged Europe 2006*, Warsaw: Translegis, 144–63.

Bielsa, Esperança and Susan Bassnett (eds) (2008) *Translation in Global News*, Abingdon and New York: Routledge.

Billiani, Francesca (ed.) (2007) *Translation and Censorship*, Manchester: St Jerome.

Bolívar, Adriana (2001) 'The negotiation of evaluation in written text', in Mike Scott and Geoff Thompson (eds) *Patterns of Text: In Honour of Michael Hoey*, Amsterdam and Philadelphia: John Benjamins, 129–58.

Borges, Jorge Luis (1962) *Labyrinths: Selected Stories and Other Writings*, translated by Donald Yates and James E. Irby, New York: New Directions.

Borges, Jorge Luis (1998a) *Collected Fictions*, translated by Andrew Hurley, New York and London: Penguin.

Borges, Jorge Luis (1998b) 'Emma Zunz', in Jorge Luis Borges (1998a) *Collected Fictions*, translated by Andrew Hurley, New York and London: Penguin, 215–19.

Brewster, Murray (2009) 'Some Afghans getting lost in translation and sent to jail: former adviser', *The Canadian Press*, 1 November 2009, available online at www.canadaeast.com/rss/article/842993

Bristow, Michael (2009) 'Obama speech censored in China', BBC News, 21 January 2009, available at http://news.bbc.co.uk/1/hi/7841580.stm

Bush, Peter (2000) 'Latin American fiction in Spanish', in Peter France (ed.) *The Oxford Guide to Literature in English Translation*, Oxford and New York: Oxford University Press, 433–37.

Calzada Pérez, María (ed.) (2003) *Apropos of Ideology: Translation Studies on Ideology – Ideologies in Translation Studies*, Manchester: St Jerome.

Calzada Pérez, María (2007) *Transitivity in Translating: The Interdependence of Texture and Context*, Oxford: Peter Lang.

Chafe, Wallace (1986) 'Evidentiality in English conversation and academic writing', in Wallace Chafe and Johanna Nichols (eds) *Evidentiality: The Linguistic Coding of Epistemology*, Norwood, NJ: Ablex, 261–72.

Chafe, Wallace and Johanna Nichols (eds) (1986) *Evidentiality: The Linguistic Coding of Epistemology*, Norwood, NJ: Ablex.

Chakrabongse, Prince Chula (1960) *Lords of Life: The Paternal Monarchy of Bangkok, 1782–1932*. New York: Taplinger Publishing.

Charteris-Black, Jonathan (2004) *Corpus Approaches to Critical Metaphor Analysis*, Houndmills: Palgrave Macmillan.

Charteris-Black, Jonathan (2005) *Politicians and Rhetoric: The Persuasive Power of Metaphor*, Houndmills: Palgrave Macmillan.

Charteris-Black, Jonathan (2007) *The Communication of Leadership: The Design of Leadership Style*, Abingdon and New York: Routledge.

Chiaro, Delia (2009) 'Issues in audiovisual translation', in Jeremy Munday (ed.) *The Routledge Companion to Translation Studies*, Abingdon and New York: Routledge, 141–65.

Chilton, Paul (2004) *Analysing Political Discourse: Theory and Practice*, Abingdon and New York: Routledge.

Coffin, Caroline (2002) 'The voices of history: Theorizing the interpersonal semantics of historical discourses', *Text* 22.4: 503–28.

Coffin, Caroline (2006) *Historical Discourse: The Language of Time, Cause and Evaluation*, London: Continuum.

Cohn, Deborah (2006) 'A tale of two translation programs: politics, the market, and Rockefeller funding for Latin American Literature in the United States during the 1960s and 1970s', *Latin American Research Review* 41.2: 139–64.

Collins Cobuild Dictionary (1995) London: HarperCollins.

Conrad, Susan and Douglas Biber (2000) 'Adverbial marking of stance in speech and writing', in Susan Hunston and Geoff Thompson (eds) *Evaluation in Text: Authorial Stance and the Construction of Discourse*, Oxford: Oxford University Press, 56–73.

Crismore, Avon (1989) *Talking with Readers: Metadiscourse as Rhetorical Act*, New York: Peter Lang.

Cunico, Sonia and Jeremy Munday (eds) (2007) *Translation as Ideology*, Special issue of *The Translator* 13.2.

Dahlgren, Peter (2005) 'The internet, public spheres and political communication: dispersion and deliberation', *Political Communication* 22: 147–62.

Dente Ross, Susan (2003) 'Images of Irish Americans: invisible, inebriated or irascible', in Paul Martin Lester and Susan Dente Ross (eds) *Images that Injure: Pictorial Stereotypes in the Media*, Westport, CT: Praeger, 133–38.

Dougherty, Robert (2009) 'Obama Inaugural Address Delivered', Yahoo Associated Content, 20 January 2009, available online at www.associatedcontent.com/article/1404344/obama_inaugural_address_delivered.html?cat=49

Du Bois, John W. (2007) 'The stance triangle', in Robert Englebretson (ed.) *Stancetaking in Discourse: Subjectivity, Evaluation, Interaction*, Amsterdam and Philadelphia: John Benjamins, 139–82.

Eco, Umberto (1984) *The Role of the Reader: Explorations in the Semiotics of Texts*, Bloomington: Indiana University Press.

Englebretson, Robert (ed.) (2007) *Stancetaking in Discourse: Subjectivity, Evaluation, Interaction*, Amsterdam and Philadelphia: John Benjamins.

Esposito, Scott (2010) 'Editing Perec', interview with Susan Barba, wordswithoutborders.org/dispatches/article/editing-georges-perec/

European Commission and Directorate-General for Translation (2011) *Study on Law-Making in the EU Multilingual Environment*, Brussels, ec.europa.eu/dgs/translation/publications/studies/index_en.htm

Fairclough, Norman ([1989] 2001) *Language and Power*, London: Longman.

Fairclough, Norman (1992) *Discourse and Social Change*, Cambridge: Polity Press.

Fairclough, Norman (2000) *New Labour, New Language?*, London and New York: Routledge.

Fairclough, Norman (2003) *Analysing Discourse: Textual Analysis for Social Research*, London and New York: Routledge.

Fawcett, Peter and Jeremy Munday (2009) 'Ideology', in Mona Baker and Gabriela Saldanha (eds) *The Routledge Encyclopedia in Translation Studies*, Abingdon and New York: Routledge, 139–41.

Federici, Federico (2009) *Translation as Stylistic Evolution: Italo Calvino, Creative Translator of Raymond Queneau*, Amsterdam and Atlanta: Rodopi.

Finegan, Edward (1995) 'Subjectivity and subjectivisation: an introduction', in Dieter Stein and Susan Wright (eds) *Subjectivity and Subjectivisation: Linguistic Perspectives*, Cambridge: Cambridge University Press, 1–15.

Firth, John R. (1957) *Papers in Linguistics 1934–1951*, London: Oxford University Press.

Fish, Stanley (2009) 'Yes, I can', *New York Times*, 7 June 2009, available online at http://opinionator.blogs.nytimes.com/2009/06/07/yes-i-can/

Forey, Gail and Geoff Thompson (2009) 'Introduction', in Geoff Thompson and Gail Forey (eds) *Text-Type and Texture: In Honour of Flo Davies*, London and Oakville: Equinox, 1–7.

Fowler, Roger (1996) *Linguistic Criticism*, 2nd edition, Oxford: Oxford University Press.

Fuller, Gillian (1998) 'Cultivating science: negotiating discourse in the popular texts of Stephen Jay Gould', in J.R. Martin and Robert Veel (eds) *Reading Science: Critical and Functional Perspectives on Discourses of Science*, London: Routledge, 35–62.

Gentzler, Edwin (2006) *Translation and Identity in the Americas*, Abingdon and New York: Routledge.

Goddard, Phil (2010) 'The power of Proz. Interview with Henry Dotterer', *ITI Bulletin* January–February 2010: 20–21.

Grant, Colin B. (2007) *Uncertainty and Communication: New Theoretical Investigations*, Basingstoke: Palgrave Macmillan.

Gutt, Ernst-August (2000) *Translation and Relevance: Cognition and Context*, Oxford: Blackwell; Manchester: St Jerome.

Habermas, Jürgen (1984) *The Theory of Communicative Action*, London: Heinemann.

Hall, Stuart ([1980] 1999) 'Encoding, Decoding', in Simon During (ed.) *The Cultural Studies Reader*, 2nd edition, London and New York: Routledge, 507–17. Originally published in Stuart Hall (1980) *Cultural, Media, Language*, London: Hutchinson.

Halliday, Michael A. K. (1978) *Language as Social Semiotic: The Social Interpretation of Language and Meaning*, London: Arnold.

Halliday, Michael A. K. (1994) *An Introduction to Functional Grammar*, 2nd edition London: Arnold.

Halliday, Michael and Ruqaiya Hasan (1989) *Language, Context and Text: Aspects of Language in a Social-semiotic Perspective*, 2nd edition, Oxford: Oxford University Press.

Halliday, Michael A. K. and Christopher Matthiessen (2004) *An Introduction to Functional Grammar*, 3rd edition, London: Arnold.

Hardman, Martha James (1986) 'Data-source marking in Jaqi languages', in Wallace Chafe and Johanna Nichols (eds) *Evidentiality: The Linguistic Coding of Epistemology*, Norwood, NJ: Ablex, 113–36.

Hatim, Basil (2004) 'The translation of style: linguistic markedness and textual evaluativeness', *Journal of Applied Linguistics* 1.3: 229–46.

Hatim, Basil (2005) 'Intercultural communication and identity: an exercise in applied semiotics', *Intercultural Communication Studies* 14.4: 33–56.

Hatim, Basil (2009) 'Translating text in context', in Jeremy Munday (ed.) *The Routledge Companion to Translation Studies*, Abingdon and New York: Routledge, 36–53.

Hatim, Basil and Ian Mason (1990) *Discourse and the Translator*, Harlow and London: Longman.

Hatim, Basil and Ian Mason (1997) *The Translator as Communicator*, London and New York: Routledge.

Hermans, Theo (1996) 'The translator's voice in translated narrative', *Target* 8.1: 23–48.

Hermans, Theo (2007) *The Conference of the Tongues*, Manchester: St Jerome.

Hoey, Michael (1983) *On the Surface of Discourse*, London and Boston: Allen & Unwin.

Hoey, Michael (2005) *Lexical Priming: A New Theory of Words and Language*, London and New York: Routledge.

Hood, Susan (2006) 'The persuasive power of prosodies: radiating values in academic writing', *Journal of English for Academic Purposes* 5.1: 37–49.

House, Juliane (1981) *A Model for Translation Quality Assessment*, Tübingen: Gunter Narr.

House, Juliane (1997) *Translation Quality Assessment: A Model Revisited*, Tübingen: Gunter Narr.

House, Juliane (2001) 'How do we know when a translation is good?', in Erich Steiner and Colin Yallop (eds) *Exploring Translation and Multilingual Text Production: Beyond Content*, Berlin: Walter de Gruyter, 127–60.

House, Juliane (2008) 'Beyond intervention: universals in translation?', *Trans-Kom* 1.1: 6–19.

House, Juliane (2011) 'Using translation and parallel text corpora to investigate the influence of global English on textual norms in other languages', in Alet Kruger, Kim Wallmach and Jeremy Munday (eds) *Corpus-Based Translation Studies*, London and New York: Continuum, 187–208.

Howe, Nicholas (1988) 'Metaphor in contemporary American political discourse', *Metaphor and Symbolic Activity* 3.2: 87–104.

Hunston, Susan (1994) 'Evaluation and organization in a sample of written academic discourse', in Malcolm Coulthard (ed.) *Advances in Written Text Analysis*, London: Routledge, 191–218.

Hunston, Susan (2000) 'Evaluation and the planes of discourse: Status and value in persuasive texts', in Susan Hunston and Geoff Thompson (eds) *Evaluation in Text: Authorial Stance and the Construction of Discourse*, Oxford: Oxford University Press, 176–207.

Hunston, Susan (2004) 'Counting the uncountable: problems of identifying evaluation in a text and in a corpus', in Alan Partington, John Morley and Louann Haarman (eds) *Corpora and Discourse*, Bern: Peter Lang, 157–88.

Hunston, Susan (2007) 'Using a corpus to investigate stance quantitatively and qualitatively', in Robert Engelbretson (ed.) *Stancetaking in Discourse: Subjectivity, Evaluation, Interaction*, Amsterdam and Philadelphia: Benjamins, 27–48.

Hunston, Susan (2008) 'The evaluation of status in multi-modal texts', *Functions of Language* 15.1: 64–83.

Hunston, Susan and Geoff Thompson (2000) (eds) *Evaluation in Text: Authorial Stance and the Construction of Discourse*, Oxford: Oxford University Press.

Hurley, Andrew (1998) 'A note on the translation', in Jorge Luis Borges, *Collected Fictions*, translated by Andrew Hurley, New York and London: Penguin, 517–21.

Hurley, Andrew (1999) 'What I lost when I translated Jorge Luis Borges', *Cadernos de Tradução* 4: 289–303.

Hyland, Ken (1998) *Hedging in Scientific Research Articles*, Philadelphia and Amsterdam: John Benjamins.

Hyland, Ken (2005) *Metadiscourse: Exploring interaction in Writing*, London: Continuum.

Hyland, Ken and Polly Tse (2004) 'Metadiscourse in academic writing: a reappraisal', *Applied Linguistics* 25.2: 156–77.

Iedema, Rick, Susan Feez and Peter R. R. White (1994) *Media Literacy*, Sydney, Disadvantaged Schools Program, NSW Department of School Education.

Ifantidou, Elly (2005) 'The semantics and pragmatics of metadiscourse', *Journal of Pragmatics* 37.9: 1325–53.

Iglesias Fernández, Emilia (2010) 'Verbal and non-verbal concomitants of rapport in health care encounters: Implications for interpreters', *Journal of Specialized Translation*, 14, available online at www.jostrans.org/issue14/art_iglesias.php

Isaac, Benjamin (2004) *The Invention of Racism in Classical Antiquity*, Princeton: Princeton University Press.

Jaffe, Alexandra (2009) (ed.) *Stance: Sociolinguistic Perspectives*, Oxford: Oxford University Press.

Johansson, Stig (2003) 'Reflections on corpora and their uses in cross-linguistic research', in Federico Zanettin, Silvia Bernadini and Dominic Stewart (eds) *Corpora in Translator Education*, Manchester: St Jerome, 135–44.

Kaltenbacher, Martin (2006) 'Exploring culture related linguistic differences in tourist board websites: The emotive and the factual', in Geoff Thompson and Susan Hunston (eds) *System and Corpus: Exploring Connections*, London: Equinox, 269–92.

Kang, Ji-Hae (2007) 'Recontextualization of news discourse: a case study of translation of news discourse on North Korea', *The Translator* 13.2: 219–42.

Kenny, Dorothy (2001) *Lexis and Creativity in Translation: A Corpus-Based Study*, Manchester: St Jerome.

Kim, Sangkeun (2004) *Strange Names of God: The Missionary Translation of the Divine Name and the Chinese Responses to Matteo Ricci's 'Shangti' in late Ming China, 1583–1644*, Frankfurt: Peter Lang.

Klaudy, Kinga (2008) 'Explicitation', in Mona Baker and Gabriela Saldanha (eds) *The Routledge Encyclopedia of Translation Studies*, Abingdon and New York: Routledge, 80–85.

Kubota, Yoko (2009) 'Japan learns English from Obama speech textbook', Reuters, 20 January 2009, available online at www.reuters.com/article/2009/01/20/us-usa-obama-textbook-idUSTRE50J7BJ20090120

Labov, William (1972a) *Sociolinguistic Patterns,* Oxford: Blackwell.

Labov, William (1972b) 'The transformation of experience in narrative syntax', in William Labov *Language in the Inner City: Studies in the Black English Vernacular*, Philadelphia: Pennsylvania University Press, 354–96.

Labov, Wiliiam (1984) 'Intensity', in Deborah Schiffrin (ed.) *Meaning, Form, and Use in Context: Linguistic Applications*, Washington, DC: Georgetown University Press, 43–70.

Lakoff, George and Mark Johnson (1980) *Metaphors We Live By*, Chicago: University of Chicago Press.

Leech, Geoffrey and Michael Short (1981) *Style in Fiction: A Linguistic Introduction to English Fictional Prose*, London and New York: Longman.

Lefevere, André (1992) *Translation, Rewriting and the Manipulation of Literary Fame*, London and New York: Routledge.

Lemke, Jay L. (1989) 'Semantics and social values', in James D. Benson, William S. Greaves, Peter H. Fries and Christian Matthiessen (eds) *Systems, Structures and Discourse: Selected Papers from the Fifteenth International Systemic Congress*, 37–50. Reprinted in *Word* 40: 1–2.

Lemke, Jay L. (1992) 'Interpersonal meaning in discourse: value orientations', in Martin Davies and Louise Ravelli (eds) *Advances in Systemic Linguistics: Recent Theory and Practice*, London: Pinter, 82–104.

Lemke, Jay (1995) *Textual Politics: Discourse and Social Dynamics*, London and New York: Routledge.

Lemke, Jay L. (1998) 'Resources for attitudinal meaning: evaluative orientations in text semantics', *Functions of Language* 5.1: 33–56.

Levenston, E. A. and Gabriela Sonnenschein (1986) 'The translation of point-of-view in fictional narrative', in Juliane House and Shoshona Blum-Kulka (eds) *Interlingual and Intercultural Communication: Discourse and Cognition in Translation and Second Language Acquisition Studies*, Tübingen: Narr, 49–59.

Liberman, Mark (2009a) 'Inaugural pronouns', *Language Log*, 8 June 2009, http://languagelog. ldc.upenn.edu/nll/?p=1489

Liberman, Mark (2009b) 'Royal baloney', *Language Log*, 9 June 2009, http://languagelog.ldc. upenn.edu/nll/?p=1490

Livingstone, Sonia (2004) 'The challenge of changing audiences: or, what is the researcher to do in the age of the internet?', *European Journal of Communication* 191: 75-86, available online at http://eprints.lse.ac.uk/412/1/Challenge_of_changing_audiences_-_spoken_version.pdf

Louw, Bill (1993) 'Irony in the text or insincerity in the writer? The diagnostic potential of semantic prosodies', in Mona Baker, Gill Francis and Elena Tognini-Bonelli (eds) *Text and Technology*, Amsterdam and Philadelphia: John Benjamins, 157–76.

Luhmann, Niklaus (1996) *Social Systems*, translated by John Bednarz Jr with Dirk Baecker, Stanford: Stanford University Press.

Lwin, Min (2009) 'Obama speech censored in Burma', *The Irrawaddy*, 26 January 2009, available online at www.irrawaddy.org/article.php?art_id=14994

Lyons, John (1977) *Semantics*, Cambridge: Cambridge University Press.

Lyons, John (1982) 'Deixis and subjectivity: loquor, ergo sum?', in Robert J. Jarvella and Wolfgang Klein (eds) *Speech, Place and Action: Studies in Deixis and Related Topics*, Chichester, NY: Wiley, 101–24.

Lyons, John (1995) *Linguistic Semantics: An Introduction*, Cambridge: Cambridge University Press.

Macken-Horarik, Mary (2003a) 'APPRAISAL and the special instructiveness of narrative', *Text* 23.2: 285–312.

Macken-Horarik, Mary (2003b) 'Envoi: intractable issues in appraisal analysis?', *Text* 23.2: 313–19.

Macken-Horarik, Mary and James R. Martin (eds) (2003) 'Introduction' *Text* 23.2: 171–81.

Magné, Bernard (1993a) 'De l'exhibitionnisme dans la traduction. À propos d'une traduction anglaise de *La vie mode d'emploi* de Georges Perec', *META* 38.3: 397–402.

Magné, Bernard (1993b) 'Transformations of constraint', *Review of Contemporary Fiction* 13.1: 111–24.

Maher, Brigid (2010) 'Attitude and intervention: *A Clockwork Orange* and *Arancia meccanica*', *New Voices in Translation Studies* 6: 36–51.

Maier, Carol (2007) 'The translator as an intervenient being', in Jeremy Munday (ed.) *Translation as Intervention*, Abingdon and New York: Routledge, 1–17.

Makihara, Mili and Bambi Schieffelin (eds) (2007) *Consequences of Contact: Language Ideologies and Sociocultural Transformations in Pacific Societies*, Oxford: Oxford University Press.

Malmkjaer, Kirsten (2003) 'What happened to God and the angels: an exercise in translational stylistics'. *Target* 15.1: 37–58.

Malmkjaer, Kirsten (2004) 'Translational stylistics: Dulcken's translations of Hans Christian Andersen', *Language and Literature* 13.1: 13–24.

Malrieu, Jean P. (1999) *Evaluative Semantics: Cognition, Language and Ideology*, London: Routledge.

Martin, J.R. (1992) *English Text: System and Structure*. Amsterdam and Philadelphia: John Benjamins.

Martin, James R. (1999) 'Modelling context: a crooked path of progress in contextual linguistics', in Mohsen Ghadessy (ed.) *Text and Context in Functional Linguistics*, Amsterdam and Philadelphia: John Benjamins, 25–62.

Martin, James R. (2000) 'Beyond exchange: appraisal systems in English', in Susan Hunston and Geoffrey Thompson (eds) *Evaluation in Text*, Oxford: Oxford University Press, 142–75.

Martin, James R. (2003) 'Introduction', in *Negotiating Heteroglossia: Social Perspectives on Evaluation*, Special issue of *Text* 23.2: 171–81.

Martin, James R. (2004a) 'Mourning: how we get aligned', *Discourse and Society* 15.2–3: 321–44.

Martin, James R. (2004b) 'Sense and sensibility: texturing evaluation', in Joseph Foley (ed.) *Language, Education and Discourse: Functional Approaches*, London: Continuum, 270–304.

Martin, James R. and Guenter Plum (1997) 'Construing experiences: some story genres', *Journal of Narrative and Life History* 7.1–4: 299–308.

Martin, James R. and Peter R. R. White (2005) *The Language of Evaluation: Appraisal in English*, London: Palgrave.

Mason, Ian (1994 [2010]) 'Discourse, ideology and translation', in Robert de Beaugrande, Abdullah Shunnaq and Mohamed Helmy Heliel (eds) *Language, Discourse and Translation in the West and Middle East*, Amsterdam and Philadelphia: John Benjamins, 23–34. Reprinted, with new postscript, in Mona Baker (ed.) (2010) *Critical Readings in Translation Studies*, Abingdon and New York: Routledge, 83–95.

Mason, Ian (2004) 'Text parameters in translation: transitivity and institutional cultures', in Lawrence Venuti (ed.) *The Translation Studies Reader*, 2nd edition, London and New York: Routledge, 470–81.

Mason, Ian and Adriana Serban (2003) 'Deixis as an interactive feature in literary translations from Romanian into English', *Target* 15.2: 269–94.

Maynard, Senko K. (1993) *Discourse Modality: Subjectivity, Emotion and Voice in the Japanese Language*, Amsterdam: John Benjamins.

McCabe, Anne (2004) 'Mood and modality in Spanish and English history textbooks: the construction of authority', *Text* 24.1: 1–29.

Miller, Donna R. (2004a) ' "... to meet our common challenge": engagement strategies of alignment and alienation in current US international discourse', in Maurizio Gotti and Christopher N. Candlin (eds) *Intercultural Discourse in Domain-Specific English*, *Textus* 17.1: 39–62.

Miller, Donna (2004b) 'Truth, justice and the American way: the Appraisal system of Judgement in the US House debate on the impeachment of the President, 1998', in Paul Bayley (ed.) (2004) *Cross-Cultural Perspectives on Parliamentary Discourse*, Amsterdam and Philadelphia: John Benjamins, 272–300.

Morley, David (1980) 'Texts, readers, subjects', in Stuart Hall, Dorothy Hobson, Andrew Lowe and Paul Willis (eds) *Culture, Media, Language: Working Papers in Cultural Studies: 1972–79*, London: Hutchinson, 163–73.

Morley, David (1992) *Television, Audiences and Cultural Studies*, London and New York: Routledge.

Mossop, Brian (2007) 'The translator's intervention through voice selection', in Jeremy Munday (ed.) *Translation as Intervention*, London: Continuum, 18–37.

Munday, Jeremy (2002) 'Systems in translation: a systemic model for descriptive translation studies', in Theo Hermans (ed.) *Cross Cultural Transgression: Research Models in Translation Studies II*, Manchester: St Jerome, 76–92.

Munday, Jeremy (ed.) (2007) *Translation as Intervention*, London: Continuum.

Munday, Jeremy (2008) *Style and Ideology in Translation: Latin American Writing in English*, New York and London: Routledge.

Munday, Jeremy (2009a) 'The concept of the interpersonal in translation', *SYNAPS* 23: 15–30.

Munday, Jeremy (2009b) 'The creative voice of the translator of Latin American literature', *Romance Studies* 27.4: 246–58.

Munday, Jeremy (ed.) (2009c) *The Routledge Companion to Translation Studies*, Abingdon and New York: Routledge.

Nida, Eugene and Charles Taber (1969) *The Theory and Practice of Translation*, Leiden: E.J. Brill.

Obama, Barack (2009) *Our Enduring Spirit: President Barack Obama's First Words to the American People*, illustrated by Greg Ruth, New York: HarperCollins.

Ochs, Elinor (ed.) (1989) *The Pragmatics of Affect*, special issue of *Text* 9.1.

Ochs, Elinor and Bambi B. Schieffelin (1989) 'Language has a heart', *Text* 9.1: 7–25.

Olohan, Maeve (2004) *Introducing Corpora in Translation Studies*, Manchester: St Jerome.

Palmer, Frank R. ([1989] 2001) *Mood and Modality*, Cambridge: Cambridge University Press.

Peden, Margaret Sayers (2002) 'A conversation on translation with Margaret Sayers Peden', in Daniel Balderston and Marcy E. Schwartz (eds) *Voice-overs: Translation and Latin American Literature*, Albany: State University of New York Press, 71–83.

Pennebaker, James W. (2009) 'What is "I" saying?', *LanguageLog*, 9 August 2009, available online at http://languagelog.ldc.upenn.edu/nll/?p=1651

Perec, Georges (1978) *La vie mode d'emploi*, Paris: Hachette.

Perec, Georges ([1987] 2003) *Life, a User's Manual*, translated by David Bellos, London: Collins-Harvill.

Perec, Georges (2008) *Life: A User's Manual*, revised edition, Boston: David R. Godine.

Pilkington, Ed (2009) 'Obama inauguration: words of history crafted by 27-year-old in Starbucks', *Guardian*, 20 January 2009, available online at www.guardian.co.uk/world/2009/jan/20/barack-obama-inauguration-us-speech

Pöchhacker, Franz (2004) *Introducing Interpreting Studies*, London and New York: Routledge.

Pym, Anthony (2003) 'Redefining translation competence in the electronic age: in defence of a minimalist approach', *META* 48.4: 481–97.

Pym, Anthony (2010) *Test and Risk in Translation*, Version 2.0, available online at http:// usuaris.tinet.cat/apym/on-line/translation/risk_analysis.pdf

Qian, Hong (2007) 'Investigating "unfaithful" translation via the appraisal theory: a case study of translations of public notices', paper presented at FIT 5th Asian Translators' Forum, Bogor, Indonesia, 11–12 April 2007.

Rabassa, Gregory (1975) 'A conversation with the translator', *Review* 75 (Spring): 17–21.

Rabassa, Gregory (2005) *If This Be Treason: Translation and Its Dyscontents*, New York: New Directions.

Razak, Dzulkifli Abdul (2009) 'Inconsistent, insensitive translations of "Allah" ', *Sun Daily*, 11 March 2009.

Reiss, Katharina ([1971] 2000) *Möglichkeiten und Grenzen der Übersetzungskritik*, Munich: M. Hueber, translated (2000) by Errol F. Rhodes as *Translation Criticism: Potential and Limitations*, Manchester: St Jerome and American Bible Society.

Robert, Paul, AlainRey and Josette Rey-Debove (eds) (1984) *Le Petit Robert*, Montréal: Canada.

Rostagno, Irene (1997) *Searching for Recognition: The Promotion of Latin American Literature in the United States*, Westport, CT: Greenwood.

Rothery, Joan and Maree Stenglin (1997) 'Entertaining and instructing: exploring experience through story', in Frances Christie and James R. Martin (eds) *Genre and Institutions: Social Processes in the Workplace and School*, London: Cassell, 231–63.

Rothery, Joan and Maree Stenglin (2000) 'Interpreting literature: the role of appraisal', in Len Unsworth (ed.) *Researching Language in Schools and Communities: Functional Linguistic Perspectives*, London: Cassell, 222–44.

Ruane, Michael E. and Aaron C. Douglas (2009) 'D.C.'s inauguration headcount: 1.8 million', *Washington Post*, 20 January 2009, available online at http://www.washingtonpost.com/wp-dyn/content/article/2009/01/21/AR2009012103884.html?sid=ST2009012102519

Saldanha, Gabriela (2011) 'Style of translation: the use of source language words in translations by Margaret Jull Costa and Peter Bush', in Alet Kruger, Kim Wallmach and Jeremy Munday (eds) *Corpus-Based Translation Studies*, London: Continuum, 237–58.

Sánchez, Dolores (2007) 'The truth about sexual difference: scientific discourse and cultural transfer', *The Translator* 13.2: 171–94.

Sarangi, Srikant (2003) 'Editorial: evaluating evaluative language', *Text* 23.2: 165–70.

Schäffner, Christina (ed.) (1999) *Translation and Norms*, Clevedon: Multilingual Matters.

Schäffner, Christina (2008) ' "The Prime Minister said . . .": voices in translated political texts', *SYNAPS* 22: 3–25.

Schiavi, Giuliana (1996) 'There is always a teller in a tale', *Target* 8.1: 1–21.

Simpson, Paul (1993) *Language, Ideology and Point of View*, London and New York: Routledge.

Sinclair, John (1986) 'Fictional worlds', in Malcolm Coulthard (ed.) *Talking about Text*, University of Birmingham: English Language Research, 43–60.

Sinclair, John (1991) *Corpus, Concordance, Collocation*, Oxford: Oxford University Press.

Smalley, William Allen (1994) *Linguistic Diversity and National Unity: Language Ecology in Thailand*, Chicago and London: University of Chicago Press.

Soesilo, Daud (n.d.) *The Revised Malay Bible*, Bible Society of Malaysia, available online at www.bible.org.my/updates/body.php?id=58

STANCE (Interactional practices and linguistic resources of stance taking in spoken English) (2006) 'Bibliography of stance', University of Oulu, Finland, www.oulu.fi/hutk/english/stance/references.html

Stein, Dieter and Susan Wright (eds) (1995) *Subjectivity and Subjectivisation: Linguistic Perspectives*, Cambridge: Cambridge University Press.

Steiner, Erich and Colin Yallop (eds) (2001) *Exploring Translation and Multilingual Text Production: Beyond Content*, Berlin and New York: Mouton de Gruyter.

Stewart, Dominic (2009) *Semantic Prosody*, Abingdon and New York: Routledge.

Stubbs, Michael (1996) *Text and Corpus Analysis*, Oxford: Blackwell.

Tacitus, Cornelius (1948) *On Britain and Germany*, translated and with an introduction by Harold Mattingly, Harmondsworth: Penguin.

Tacitus, Cornelius (1970) *Agricola and Germania*, translated by Harold Mattingly, revised by Stanley Handford with an introduction by Harold Mattingly, Harmondsworth: Penguin.

Tacitus, Cornelius (1999) *Germania*, translated by James Rives, Oxford: Oxford University Press.

Tacitus, Cornelius (2009) *The Agricola and the Germania*, translated by Harold Mattingly, revised and with an introduction by James Rives, Harmondsworth: Penguin.

Teich, Elke (2003) *Cross-Linguistic Variation in System and Text: A Methodology for the Investigation of Translations and Comparable Texts*, Berlin and New York: Mouton de Gruyter.

Thompson, Geoff (1998) 'Resonance in text', in Antonia Sánchez-Macarro and Ronald Carter (eds) *Linguistic Choice across Genres: Variation in Spoken and Written English*, Philadelphia and Amsterdam: John Benjamins, 29–46.

Thompson, Geoff (2005) 'But me some buts: a multidimensional view of conjunction', *Text* 25.6: 763–91.

Thompson, Geoff and Susan Hunston (2000) 'Evaluation: an introduction', in Susan Hunston and Geoff Thompson (eds) *Evaluation in Text: Authorial Stance and the Construction of Discourse*, Oxford: Oxford University Press, 1–27.

Thompson, Geoff and Jianglin Zhou (2000) 'Evaluation and organization in text: the structuring role of evaluative disjuncts', in Susan Hunston and Geoff Thompson (eds) *Evaluation in Text: Authorial Stance and the Construction of Discourse*, Oxford: Oxford University Press, 121–41.

Thompson, Geoff and Ye Yiyun (1991) 'Evaluation in reporting verbs used in academic papers', *Applied Linguistics* 12.4: 365–82.

Thomson, Elizabeth A. and Peter R.R. White (eds) (2008) *Communicating Conflict: Multilingual Case Studies of the News Media*, London: Continuum.

Toury, Gideon (1995) *Descriptive Translation Studies and Beyond*, Amsterdam and Philadelphia: John Benjamins.

Tymoczko, Maria and Edwin Gentzler (eds) (2002) *Translation and Power*, Amherst: University of Massachusetts Press.

van Dijk, Teun A. (2008) *Discourse and Power*, Houndmills: Palgrave Macmillan.

Vargas Llosa, Mario (1991) 'El paraíso de los libros', *El País*, 30 June 1991, available online at www.elpais.com/articulo/opinion/REINO_UNIDO/paraiso/libros/elpepiopi/19910630elpepiopi_12/Tes

Vargas Llosa, Mario (1993) *Un pez en el agua: memorias*, Barcelona: Seix Barral.

Vargas Llosa, Mario (1994a) *A Fish in the Water: A Memoir*, London: Faber and Faber.

Vargas Llosa, Mario (1994b) 'The paradise of books', translated by George Davis, text of speech delivered for the Georgetown University Library's Two Millionth Volume Celebration, 4 May 1994.

Verscheuren, Jef (1999) *Understanding Pragmatics*, London, New York: Arnold.

Vinay, Jean-Paul and Jean Darbelnet ([1958] 1995) *Comparative Stylistics of French and English: A Methodology for Translation*, translated and edited by Juan C. Sager and Marie-Jo Hamel, Amsterdam and Philadelphia: John Benjamins.

Volosinov, Valentin ([1929] 1973) *Marxism and the Philosophy of Language*, translated by Ladislav Matejka and Irwin Titunik, New York: Seminar Press.

Waisman, Sergio (2005) *Borges and Translation: The Irreverence of the Periphery*, Cranbury, NJ: Associated University Presses.

Wales, Katie (1996) *Personal Pronouns in Present-Day English*, Cambridge: Cambridge University Press.

Ward, Maurice (2004) 'We have the power – or do we?: pronouns of power in a union context', in Lynne Young and Claire Harrison (eds) *Systemic Functional Linguistics and Critical Discourse Analysis: Studies in Social Change*, London: Continuum, 280–95.

White, Peter R. R. (2000) 'Dialogue and inter-subjectivity: reinterpreting the semantics of modality and hedging', in Michael Coulthard, Janet Cotterill and Frances Rock (eds) *Working with Dialog*, Tübingen: Niemeyer, 67–80.

White, Peter R. R. (2002) 'Appraisal – the language of evaluation and stance', in Jef Verschueren, Jan-Ola Östman, Jan Blommaert and C. Bulcaen (eds) *The Handbook of Pragmatics*, Amsterdam and Philadelphia: John Benjamins, 1–27. Online.

White, Peter R. R. (2003a) 'Appraisal and the resources of intersubjective stance', unpublished manuscript, available online at www.grammatics.com/appraisal

White, Peter R. R. (2003b) 'Beyond modality and hedging: a dialogic view of the language of intersubjective stance', *Text* 23.2: 259–84.

White, Peter R. R. (2004) 'Subjectivity, evaluation and point of view in media discourse', in Caroline Coffin, Ann Hewings and Kieran O'Halloran (eds) *Applying English Grammar: Functional and Corpus Approaches*, London: Arnold, 229–46.

White, Peter R. R. (2005) 'The Appraisal website', available online at www.grammatics.com/appraisal/index.html

White, Peter R. R., (2006) 'Evaluative semantics and ideological positioning in journalistic discourse: a new framework for analysis', in Inger Lassen, Jeanne Strunck and Torben Vestergaard (eds) *Mediating Ideology in Text and Image*, Amsterdam and Philadelphia: John Benjamins, 37–67.

White, Peter R. R. and Elizabeth Thomson (2008) 'Analysing journalistic discourse', in Elizabeth Thomson and Peter R. R. White (eds) *Communicating Conflict: Multilingual Case Studies of the News Media*, London: Continuum, 1–23.

Widdowson, Henry G. (2004) *Text, Context, Pretext: Critical Issues in Discourse Analysis*, Oxford: Wiley-Blackwell.

Yates, Donald A. (2002) 'In the labyrinth of language: leaves from a translator's notebook', *Apuntes* (publication of the Spanish group of the New York Circle of Translators) 10.2: 14–17, available online at www.apuntesonline.org/Prim02.pdf

Zhang, Meifang ([2002] 2011) 'The language of appraisal and the translator's attitudinal positioning', in J.Y. Zhang (ed.) *Functional Linguistics and Translation Studies* (语言的评价意义与译者的价值取向,《功能语言学与翻译研究》(张敬源主编), Beijing: Foreign Language Teaching and Research Press: 180–90.

Zhang, Meifang and Hong Qian (2009) 'Investigating "unfaithful" translations via the Appraisal Theory: a case study of the translation of six advertisements', Paper delivered at the 3rd IATIS Conference, Melbourne.

INDEX